The Complete
Passover Cookbook

Dates of Passover

Passover begins on the fifteenth day of the Jewish month of Nisan, generally corresponding to March-April.

Year	First Day
1981 (5741)	Sunday, April 19
1982 (5742)	Thursday, April 8
1983 (5743)	Tuesday, March 29
1984 (5744)	Tuesday, April 17
1985 (5745)	Saturday, April 6
1986 (5746)	Thursday, April 24
1987 (5747)	Tuesday, April 14
1988 (5748)	Saturday, April 2
1989 (5749)	Thursday, April 20
1990 (5750)	Tuesday, April 10
1991 (5751)	Saturday, March 30
1992 (5752)	Saturday, April 18
1993 (5753)	Tuesday, April 6
1994 (5754)	Sunday, March 27
1995 (5755)	Saturday, April 15
1996 (5756)	Thursday, April 4
1997 (5757)	Tuesday, April 22
1998 (5758)	Saturday, April 11
1999 (5759)	Thursday, April 1
2000 (5760)	Thursday, April 20
2001 (5761)	Sunday, April 8
2002 (5762)	Thursday, March 28
2003 (5763)	Thursday, April 17
2004 (5764)	Tuesday, April 6
2005 (5765)	Sunday, April 24

The festival of Passover begins the evening preceding the "first day" dates given above. On this night the first Seder is conducted.

THE COMPLETE
PASSOVER
COOKBOOK

by
Frances R. AvRutick

JD JONATHAN DAVID PUBLISHERS, INC.
MIDDLE VILLAGE, NEW YORK 11379

THE COMPLETE
PASSOVER COOKBOOK

Copyright © 1981
by
Frances R. AvRutick

Jonathan David Publishers, Inc.
68-22 Eliot Avenue
Middle Village, New York 11379

10   9   8   7   6   5   4   3

Second Printing 1982

Library of Congress Cataloging in Publication Data

AvRutick, Frances R
    The complete Passover cookbook.

    Includes index.
    1. Cookery, Jewish.   2. Passover cookery.
I. Title.
TX724.A97   641.5′676   80-39633
ISBN 0-8246-0262-5

Printed in the United States of America

To my beloved husband
Rabbi Abraham N. AvRutick
with affection

Acknowledgments

I owe a debt of gratitude to:

My husband, Rabbi Abraham N. AvRutick, for his inspiring encouragement, patience, and guidance; for his invaluable assistance, and for the neglect he suffered during the time I spent working on this book.

My beloved daughters—Rena, Judith, and Naomi—from whom I learned much. They were a driving force, and they gave me more than moral support.

My brother-in-law Louis AvRutick, who originally prodded me into writing this book.

Members of my family, members of my congregation, and a multitude of friends in the United States, Israel, Canada, and South Africa who graciously shared with me recipes from their Passover collection.

A dear friend, Meyer "Mickey" Heller, for his wholehearted and generous assistance in having the typing of my manuscript completed.

Beverly Bednarz, who so conscientiously completed the typing of the manuscript.

My publisher, Alfred J. Kolatch, and editor, David Kolatch, for their suggestions and direction.

I wish to pay tribute to the blessed memory of Ann Barth, who uncomplainingly typed and retyped my illegible notes into readable copy.

Contents

Preface

Take the obvious,
Add a cupful of brains,
A generous pinch of imagination,
A bucketful of courage and daring,
Stir well and bring to a boil.

—Bernard Baruch

Like most traditional Jews, I was brought up in a home where chicken, eggs, potatoes, and matzo were the mainstay of Passover cooking. Anxious to bring a fresh approach to Passover cuisine, years ago I started to gather, innovate, and experiment with Passover recipes. I always loved to cook, and it wasn't long before I discovered that year-'round favorites could successfully be adapted for Passover use.

As a benefit of having prepared the recipe section for various holiday pamphlets published by the Women's Branch of the Union of Orthodox Jewish Congregations of America, I was invited to prepare a Passover recipe booklet for the national organization. That booklet, "A Pesach Sampler," including recipes from appetizer to *afikomon*, was introduced to the public in January of 1976. By April of the same year the first edition had completely sold out.

The overwhelming success of this publication encouraged me to work on a fuller and more comprehensive book of Passover recipes. I recognized the need for a *complete* Passover cookbook.

It is my hope that *The Complete Passover Cookbook* will help make Passover meal preparation a challenge and fulfilling experience rather than a chore. It is designed to motivate you, the cook, to improvise and thereby create new dishes that will enhance your Passover repertoire.

The Passover recipes selected for inclusion range from the classic to the original. Always, the recipes reflect contemporary demands.

Today, with the evergrowing number of kosher for Passover products available, Passover dietary regulations should not discourage inventiveness. All one needs is "a generous pinch of imagination" and "a bucketful of courage."

With this in mind, I call attention to the fact that the recipes in this book offer general guidelines. They are not prescriptions that must be followed to the letter, and with very few exceptions they are not bound by inflexible rules. Individual preferences may dictate making adjustments.

In seasoning, use your own best instincts, since Mother Nature rarely produces foods that are uniform in their properties. Exactly the same amount of seasoning, shortening, and other ingredients may not necessarily be required each time you cook a dish; for example, the amount of sugar used may have to be adjusted to the tartness of a fruit. Taste-check in order to determine the quantities needed. After preparing the dish, check again for seasoning. There is no substitute for tasting. Unless you taste, you cannot ascertain whether the dish is seasoned to your liking. "Season to taste" means "taste to season."

According to the dictionary, all fats are shortenings. The shortening may be solid (butter, margarine, chicken fat, etc.), or it may be liquid (oil). Generally, specific types of oil or fat have not been suggested in the recipes. The choice depends upon your own preference. However, where a particular kind of shortening will yield a better result, it has been recommended.

Not all recipes require a preheated oven. Many casseroles, meats, and vegetables may be started in a cold oven with the temperature regulator set for the recommended cooking temperature. Temperatures in ovens vary, hence there may be a variation in the length of cooking time required.

Cooking is one activity a person must "indulge in" to prepare meals. Each cook is an individual, and she or he must prepare meals for individual palates, tastes, and diets. Cooks are indispensable. Owen Meredith once put it so succinctly when he wrote:

We may live without poetry, music and art;
We may live without conscience and live without heart;
We may live without friends; we may live without books;
But civilized man cannot live without cooks.

Frances R. AvRutick

Introduction

"Keep the Passover unto the Lord thy God; for the Lord thy God brought thee forth out of Egypt" (Deuteronomy 16:1).

Passover is one of the holidays most closely associated with food. When thinking of Passover food, there are two key words to remember: *matzo* and *chometz.*

Matzo is unleavened bread. The departure of the Jews from Egyptian slavery came about so hastily that our ancestors had no time to prepare their bread in the usual manner. Because the dough was baked in haste, it did not leaven (rise).

Chometz, "leaven," literally means "souring" or "fermentation." The Bible says, "Ye shall put away all leaven out of your house" (Exodus 12:15). All *chometz* dishes and utensils are replaced with dishes and utensils that are kosher for Passover.

Special dietary laws are observed during Passover. We are forbidden to eat any food which has been leavened or contains leavening ingredients. Hence, observing the laws of *kashrut* on Passover is somewhat different from observing *kashrut* throughout the year. The basic rule is: no amount of *chometz,* however infinitesimal, may be eaten on Passover or may so much as touch a Passover utensil.

Grain or cereal products, as well as derivatives of these foods, such as grain alcohol, grain vinegar, or coffee substitutes made from cereals, are not used. Legumes such as peas, beans, corn,

1

and rice are not used. (Sephardic communities permit the use of rice.)

Passover cooking is dependent on these dietary laws. There was a time when preparing varied and interesting meals for Passover posed a challenge to the homemaker. Today all sorts of fresh and canned foods never before available for Passover are for sale, making meal preparation simpler and the meals themselves more varied and exciting.

Year-'round favorite recipes that do not contain prohibited foods may, of course, be used on Passover. In cases where a specific ingredient in a favorite recipe is not kosher for Passover, it is sometimes possible to make that recipe acceptable by substituting another ingredient—for example, flour may be replaced by matzo meal, potato starch, or matzo cake meal.

Some Jews follow a custom called *no gebroks*, eating no food containing a mixture of matzo or matzo meal and a liquid, except on the last day of Passover. This custom arose from an apprehension that the matzo may not have been baked sufficiently, and should such matzo come in contact with a liquid, it may result in leavening or fermentation, which is forbidden on Passover. Potato starch or ground nuts have proven to be an excellent substitute for matzo meal in many recipes.

Foods purchased must all be kosher for Passover. As a general rule, all processed foods and drinks require certification by competent rabbinic authority. In some states, such as New York, it is a violation of law to label a product "kosher" if it in fact is not.

The legend "kosher l'Pesach" or "kosher for Passover" should be printed on the container by the manufacturer; a label pasted on is insufficient. There are products that need no special Passover endorsement *if they already have a kosher insignia*, such as aluminum foil, plastic bags, detergents, cleansers, etc.

BUYER BE WARY

All ingredients—wines, cheeses, gelatin, margarine, flavorings, etc.—called for in the recipes in this book are available in kosher for Passover form. In purchasing a product, never rely on past experience. Be ever mindful of the fact that though a product may be kosher for year-'round use, it may not necessarily be kosher for Passover.

DISHES AND UTENSILS

Ideally, sets of dishes, pots, pans, and utensils reserved only for Passover should be used for the duration of the holiday. If both dairy and meat products are used on Passover, two sets of Passover dishes and utensils are necessary. *Pareve* ("neutral") equipment is also desirable for every home.

However, if it is not possible to purchase an entire set of cookware exclusively for Passover use, note that there are certain utensils, pots, pans, and glassware which may be *kashered*, that is, made acceptable for Passover use by purging, glowing, or soaking. (Note also that there are many utensils which cannot be *kashered*.) The laws of *kashering* are many and varied. Consult a rabbi to determine whether an item may be *kashered* and the proper procedure to be followed.

Ranges and Ovens

Every part of the oven or stove must be thoroughly scraped and cleansed. This includes the inside of the oven, the grates and drip pans, and the range on top of the stove. The oven and burners on the range must then be turned on and heated to a glow. A tin sheet or heavy aluminum foil must be placed over those parts of the stove that have not been kashered—after they have been thoroughly cleaned.

Sinks

Sinks should be scrubbed and washed and new drainboards or sink liners placed inside.

Refrigerator

Refrigerators should be defrosted, scoured, and cleaned, including the metal shelves. Shelves may be covered with shelf paper, wax paper, or foil; perforate the lining so cold air can circulate.

Surfaces

All table surfaces, shelves, and kitchen and pantry surfaces that are used during the year should be thoroughly cleaned and covered during the entire week of Passover. Shelves on which Passover dishes or pots are to be placed should be relined.

Linens

Starched tablecloths may not be used. New plastic tablecloths are permissible.

Note: Just as dishes, utensils, etc., are set aside for Passover use from year to year, so too may drainboards, sink liners, dish pans and dish drainers, asbestos oven covers, plastic counter covers, etc.

HOW TO SET A PASSOVER TABLE

Passover is the only holiday we celebrate with a home service, the Seder.

The Seder table is the focal point of the Passover celebration, and upon it all the symbols of Passover are displayed.

At the head of the table, where a place has been set for the person conducting the Seder, the following essentials are placed: three whole matzos and the *k'arah* ("dish"). The three whole matzos are placed in a specially sectioned matzo cover or on a Seder dish covered with a large napkin. There is a custom of separating the three matzos, and they may be placed between three napkins if a sectional cover is not used. The three matzos symbolize the three historic religious divisions of the Jewish people: *Kohen* (priest), *Levi* (assistant to the priest), and *Yisrael* (lay-Israelite).

The **k'arah** is a large dish upon which the symbolic Seder foods are arranged. Customs differ as to how the foods are arranged on the dish. Decorative dishes with markings or indentations for the various foods are available.

The symbolic foods and the most common arrangement of these foods on the *k'arah* is as follows:

1. Zeroa
2. Beitza
3. Moror
4. Charoses
5. Karpas
6. Chazereth

Zeroa, a roasted shankbone or the roasted wing or neck of a fowl, represents the ancient sacrifice of the Paschal Lamb. To prepare the *zeroa,* broil over a flame a *kashered* lamb shank or wing or neck of a fowl until it is browned and tender. It is placed in the upper right hand corner of the *k'arah.*

Beitza is a plain or roasted hard-cooked egg, which symbolizes the offereing brought in the Temple on festivals. To prepare the *beitza,* simply hard-cook an egg. Many people customarily roast the egg after cooking by browning the unshelled boiled egg slightly over an open fire. The *beitza* is placed in the upper left hand corner of the dish, opposite the *zeroa.*

Moror, the bitter herbs, are symbolic of the bitter life the Jews led while enslaved in Egypt. Fresh horseradish root or romaine lettuce is used. To prepare the fresh horseradish, scrape the root clean, then grate or slice it. The horseradish is unflavored and unseasoned. To prepare romaine lettuce, select the leaves from the head of lettuce, then wash and clean them well. In either case, after placing a portion of the *moror* in the center of the *k'arah,* have an adequate amount prepared for another dish; this dish is passed around the table during the Seder service so each participant may have an ample serving when the appropriate blessing is recited. The *moror* is dipped into the *charoses* before being eaten.

Charoses, symbolic of the mortar used in making bricks for Pharaoh, is a sweet condiment of finely chopped nuts and apples seasoned with cinnamon and wine.

There are many recipes for *charoses*. The most common one consists of combining 2 peeled and cored apples, grated or chopped fine, with ½ cup of ground walnuts or almonds, ½ to 1 teaspoon cinnamon, and a dash of ginger. Two to 3 tablespoons of wine are then added as a binder. The consistency should be thick. This recipe will serve 8 to 10.

Sephardic Charoses consists of 4 medium-sized peeled and cored apples, 1 pound of pitted dates, ¼ cup vinegar, 2 cups of coarsely ground pecans or almonds, and ½ cup sweet red wine. In a medium-sized saucepan, combine the apples and the dates; add cold water to cover the fruit. Cook over medium heat until the apples are tender and almost all the water is evaporated. Put the apples and the dates through a grinder or blender. Transfer the mixture to a medium-sized bowl. Add the ground nuts, vinegar, and wine. If the mixture is too thick, add a little more wine or vinegar. Serves 12 to 15.

Israeli Charoses contains some matzo meal. To prepare, finely chop or put into a blender and blend at medium speed 1 peeled and cored apple, 3 sliced bananas, 10 pitted dates, ½ cup of nuts, the juice and grated rind of ½ lemon, and the juice and grated rind of ½ orange. Transfer the mixture to a bowl; add ½ cup dry red wine and 1 teaspoon of cinnamon. The mixture will be rather loose. Add enough matzo meal to achieve the desired consistency. Add sugar or honey as needed. This recipe will serve 10 to 12.

The *charoses* is placed on the lower right hand corner of the Seder dish. In addition, a small bowl of *charoses* is often passed around the table at the appropriate time during the Seder, so that each Seder participant can dip the *moror* into the *charoses*. The *moror* is dipped into the *charoses* to lessen its sharpness.

Karpas is a vegetable—customarily parsley, radish, onion, celery, or a peeled cooked potato. Family tradition dictates the choice of vegetable used. *Karpas* is dipped into salt water or vinegar and is eaten before the meal begins.

Karpas has double symbolism: it reminds us of spring, the season of hope and growth, and of the ancient custom of serving an appetizer before a meal. Eating a vegetable at the beginning of the Seder serves to arouse the curiosity of the children present and stimulates them to ask, *"Mah nishtanah ha-laila hazeh,* Why is this night different?" The salt water or vinegar into which the *karpas* is dipped symbolizes the tears and sweat which poured forth from the Jewish people while they were enslaved in Egypt.

The *karpas* is placed on the lower left hand corner of the *k'arah,* to the left of the *charoses.*

Chazereth is another form of bitter herbs. Some use it to make the Hillel sandwich (which is commonly made with *moror*), but it is basically a Seder plate symbol. The *chazereth*—usually radish or watercress—is placed on the Seder dish just below the *moror,* fourth row center.

In addition to the ceremonial foods displayed on the *k'arah,* small bowls of salt water or vinegar should be readied and placed on the table. Before the *karpas* is eaten, it is dipped into one of these solutions. To prepare the salt water, dissolve 1 tablespoon of salt in ½ cup of water.

Wine cups are provided for each Seder participant. One cup of wine is drunk at four different times during the Seder. They symbolize the Almighty's four expressions of redemption mentioned in the Bible. Coasters or saucers are placed under each wine cup to hold the drops of wine poured off while reciting the Ten Plagues. Some Jews customarily spill off some of the wine by dipping a finger or a spoon into the wine cup; others tip some wine out of the cup each time a plague is mentioned.

The Cup of Elijah, a special large wine cup, is set on the table for the prophet Elijah, who is the hoped-for guest, the legendary harbinger of peace and freedom.

A *Haggadah* is placed at each place setting. The *Haggadah* tells the story of the Exodus from Egypt and contains the complete Seder ceromonies in their prescribed order.

An *afikomon bag,* or a napkin in which to wrap the *afikomon,* should be readied. A wine decanter, as well as a dish of matzo for the meal, should be set on the table.

If the Seder gathering is to be large, it may be prudent to have several small dishes of *moror, charoses, karpas,* and salt water placed conveniently around the table, along with wine decanters and dishes of matzo to be eaten during the meal.

The leader of the Seder is provided with one or more pillows, to his left, so that he may recline against them during certain portions of the Seder service. This symbolizes the comfort enjoyed by free men referred to in the fourth of the Four Questions recited by the youngest child at the Seder. The arrangement of the pillows is known as *hessebet*.

Candlesticks with candles are placed on the table. These will be lighted and the benediction over them recited to usher in the festival of Passover.

THE SEDER MEAL

There are numerous customs connected with the Seder meal. Many Jews customarily begin the Seder meal by eating hard-cooked eggs dipped in salt water.Because the egg is a food of mourners, it is eaten at the Seder as a reminder of the destruction of the Holy Temple, where Jews offered the Paschal Lamb as a sacrifice.

Family custom dictates how the eggs are served. Sometimes a dish of whole or halved hard-cooked eggs plus a bowl or pitcher of salt water are passed around the table. A small dish is provided so that each person can help him or herself. Others serve a whole sliced hard-coooked egg in a dish containing a small amount of salt water, while still others chop the hard-cooked eggs, adding a sufficient amount of salted water to make a thick soup. The mixture is chilled thoroughly before serving. One to 1½ dozen eggs serves 8 people generously.

There is a custom amongst many not to serve knaidlach (matzo balls) or farfel with soup, based on their observance of *no gebroks*

Family custom also dictates the manner in which the meat or poultry is prepared for the Seder meal. Many Jews do not serve barbecued, broiled, or roasted meat or poultry at the Seder. In Temple times the Paschal Lamb was roasted, and since the destruction of the Temple, it has been customary to avoid duplicating the ceremonial practices of those times. However, some Jews believe that the manner in which meat or poultry is roasted today is not comparable to the method used during the time of the Temple. In any case, there is no controversy over the permissibility of serving barbecued, roasted, or broiled meats or poultry during the luncheon meals on the first two days of Passover.

There is a custom of not serving salads dressed with vinegar as part of the Seder meal. This is based on a desire to restrict the dipping of vegetables to the two occasions mentioned in the *Haggadah:* the *karpas* in salt water, and the *moror* in *charoses.*

Custom varies as to what is to be done with the wine in the goblet of Elijah. In some households, at the conclusion of the Seder the wine is poured back into the decanter. In other households, after the fourth cup of wine has been partially consumed, the wine is distributed among the Seder participants. Some keep the cup of wine for *Kiddush* the next day.

Seder menus vary. Most people serve traditional family favorites at the Seder meal, but along with the traditional specialties it is nice to include some new recipes.

The following suggested Seder menus bridge the gap between the traditional and the modern. There is the traditional gefilte fish or chopped liver. Garnish the customary clear chicken soup with Royale Custard, or set Soup Swans afloat.

The Compote Seder Cake or the Lemon Pudding is a festive finale that combines fruit and cake as the dessert. A spiced tea is a refreshing beverage with which to end the meal.

FIRST NIGHT

Wine   Matzos

Hors d'Oeuvres

Karpas in Salt Water   Bitter Herbs and Charoses

Hillel Sandwich

Appetizers

Hard-Boiled Egg in Salt Water

Gefilte Fish on Lettuce

Horseradish

Soup

Chicken Soup with Swan Afloat

Main Course

Roast Chicken With Mushroom Stuffing

or

Southern Oven-fried Chicken

Liver and Potato Kugel   Candied Carrots

Dessert

Compote Seder Cake

Beverage

Tea

SECOND NIGHT

Wine   Matzos

Hors d'Oeuvres

Karpas in Salt Water   Bitter Herbs and Charoses

Hillel Sandwich

Appetizers

Hard-Boiled Egg in Salt Water
Individual Chopped Liver Chicken Mold
Tomatoes and Lettuce

Soup

Chicken Soup With Royale Custard

Main Course

Roast Turkey
or
Gedempte Chicken

Squash Kugel   Carrot-Sweet Potato Tzimmes

Dessert

Lemon Pudding

Beverage

Tea

1

Salads and Appetizers

Times have changed. Salads are no longer necessarily served before or after a specific course in the menu. They may be served as the first course to stimulate the appetite for what is to come, along with the main course as a complement, or immediately after the main course to help the digestion and cleanse the palate. Sweetness can turn a salad into a dessert that will make an exciting finale to a meal. Serve the salads in this chapter at the point in the meal where you feel they will be most enjoyed.

The appetizer, derived from the word "appetite," is frequently referred to in Yiddish as a *forshpeis*, which literally means "before food." The *forshpeis*, which may be hot or cold, is served as a starter for a meal. It is designed to whet the appetite. In this chapter you will find some lovely appetizers, including Gehakteh Leber (a liver pâté) and Chicken Fricassee in Vegetable Gravy. But do refer to Chapter Four (Meat Specialties), Chapter Five (Fish Specialties), and Chapter Eleven (Foods With a Foreign Flavor) for other possibilities. Served in smaller portions, the recipes in those chapters will make wonderful *forshpeis*.

Israeli Carrot Salad

1 pound carrots
1 cup orange juice

⟶

Juice of ½ lemon
Sugar to taste
Salt to taste
Dash of ginger (optional)

Peel the carrots and grate them on the medium openings of a grater into a medium-sized bowl. In a glass measure, combine the orange juice with the lemon juice. Pour over the carrots. Supplement the natural sweetness of the carrots with the granulated sugar; add salt to taste. Add a dash of ground ginger. Refrigerate for several hours; stir once or twice. Serves 4 to 6.

Cole Slaw

To serve this salad attractively, select a large head of cabbage. Slice off the top half and carefully cut out the center section, leaving a cabbage bowl. Prepare the cabbage as described below and heap it into the cabbage bowl.

Salad:

1 medium-sized cabbage
1 to 2 carrots
1 green pepper, stemmed and seeded

Dressing:

¼ cup oil
¼ cup vinegar
¼ cup sugar
Dash of minced garlic or garlic powder (optional)
1 cup mayonnaise
1 teaspoon salt
Dash of pepper

Shred the cabbage, carrots, and the pepper into a large mixing bowl. Blend the dressing ingredients in a screw-top jar or in a large bowl. Pour the dressing over the cabbage. Toss the salad and taste for seasoning. Serves 6 or more.

Red Sea Slaw

This faintly sweet-sour salad is sparked with red apples.

>1 teaspoon salt
>10 cups (about 2 pounds) shredded cabbage
>3 cups boiling water
>⅓ cup lemon juice
>¼ cup oil
>3 tablespoons sugar
>¼ teaspoon black pepper
>1½ cups unpeeled diced apple
>½ cup minced onion

Sprinkle the salt over the cabbage in a large bowl; add the boiling water. Let stand for 10 minutes. Drain thoroughly. In a small bowl combine the lemon juice, oil, sugar, and pepper. Add to the cabbage along with the diced apple and minced onion. Toss until well mixed. Chill for at least ½ hour before serving. Garnish with sliced apples. Makes 8 to 10 servings.

Vegetable Spread

Horseradish adds a zip to this spread.

>4 medium-sized carrots, scraped
>½ green pepper, seeded
>3 stalks celery
>2 tablespoons chopped nut meats
>1 tablespoon prepared horseradish
>3 tablespoons mayonnaise
>1 teaspoon lemon juice
>Salt to taste

Grind together or chop very fine the carrots, green pepper, celery, and nuts. Stir in the horseradish, mayonnaise, lemon juice, and salt to taste. If the vegetables are to be used as a spread, drain the vegetables thoroughly after grinding or chopping. If a thinner (dip) consistency is desired, do not drain the vegetables and increase both the horseradish and mayonnaise to taste. Makes 2 to 3 cups.

Fruited Egg Salad

Here is a very unusual way of serving hard-cooked eggs. For sheer effect, no egg salad can match this colorful, picturesque dish.

"Apples":

Use small eggs for "crab apples" and larger eggs for "standard apples." Hard-cook the eggs. Carefully shell 1 egg at a time. While still quite warm, press both ends of each egg gently with the thumb and forefinger and hold it under cold water for about 30 seconds to form a permanent impression. The impression should be deep at the large end.

To color the eggs red, submerge them in a deep dish of beet juice until reddened. With a slotted spoon, remove the eggs. (An alternate method of coloring the "apples" is to gently massage them with paprika.) Insert an apple stem and a parsley sprig into the center of the large end of each egg.

"Pears":

Hard-cook eggs which are decidedly narrower at 1 end. Carefully shell the eggs and hold the narrow end of each between the thumb and forefinger of the right hand, shaping the egg like a pear, while making an indentation in the bottom of the wider end with the forefinger of the left hand. Cool under cold water to retain shape.

To color the "pears," in a small saucepan cook a few outer yellow onion skins in water for a few minutes. When the water is colored, cool the water and soak the eggs until they are the desired hue. Remove and dry the eggs. Insert a real pear stem and a sprig of parsley, preferably Italian parsley, in the center of the top, narrow end of each colored egg. If pear stems are not available, make an opening with a toothpick in order to insert the parsley.

"Bananas":

Hard-cook eggs which appear to be equally narrow at both ends. Carefully shell the eggs while still hot, then roll them between the palms of the hands to form a banana shape. Cool under cold water. Color in the same manner as the "pears." Insert a whole clove into the top and the bottom of each egg

To Serve:

Arrange the "apples," "pears," and "bananas" on a bed of greens and surround them with cherry tomatoes.

Vegetarian Chopped Liver

The best way to wash mushrooms is to rinse them quickly under cold running water. If the mushrooms are to be sautéed, pat them dry with paper towels. Mushrooms that are to be cooked in sauces, stews, or soups need only be drained after rinsing.

Serve this liver dish on lettuce leaves and garnish with tomato wedges and a slice of pared large black radish.

> 1 cup sliced mushrooms
> 1 cup chopped onions
> 3 tablespoons margarine
> 3 hard-cooked eggs
> ¼ pound shelled walnuts
> 1 teaspoon salt
> ¼ teaspoon white pepper

In a large skillet, sauté the mushrooms and the onions in the margarine until the onions are golden brown. Pass the mushrooms, onions, hard-cooked eggs, and walnuts through a grinder or chop very fine in a chopping bowl. Season with the salt and pepper. Refrigerate to chill thoroughly. Serves 6.

Onion and Egg Appetizer

> 1 pound onions
> 3 to 4 tablespoons margarine or oil
> 2 hard-cooked eggs
> Salt to taste

Finely dice the onions; sauté in the margarine or oil in a medium-sized skillet over medium heat until transparent and golden, not browned. Finally chop the hard-cooked eggs, then mix with the sautéed onions. Season with salt. Serve on a bed of lettuce. Serves 4 to 5.

Potato, Egg, and Onion Appetizer

3 to 4 potatoes
4 hard-cooked eggs
3 tablespoons very soft margarine or
chicken fat
Salt and freshly ground black pepper to
taste
1 onion, grated (size of your choice)
¼ cup chopped green pepper (optional)

Boil the potatoes in their jackets until tender. Cool the potatoes and peel. Chop the potatoes together with the eggs until very well chopped. Add the remaining ingredients and mix well. Chill thoroughly. Serve with a fresh vegetable salad. Makes 8 servings.

Putlejela

This delicious eggplant appetizer of Roumanian origin may be served as a matzo spread.

1 medium-sized eggplant (approximately 1 pound)
1 teaspoon lemon juice
1 teaspoon salt
⅛ teaspoon black pepper
¼ cup minced onion
¼ cup minced green pepper (optional)
1 tablespoon oil

Broil the eggplant over a direct flame, or bake in a pan lined with aluminum foil in a 450-degree F. oven, turning once or twice to bake evenly on all sides, until the eggplant is soft and the skin separates from the eggplant. Remove the skin; chop the eggplant pulp in a chopping bowl until very fine. Add the lemon juice and blend well. Mix in the salt and pepper, minced onion, and minced green pepper. Taste and adjust the seasoning; chill. Before serving, add the oil and stir until well mixed. Serve on salad greens. Garnish with tomato wedges. Serves 3 to 4.

Chopped Eggplant Salad

There are many ways to prepare an eggplant salad. Each has its own distinctive flavor. This hearty chopped eggplant salad is fortified with hard-cooked eggs, making it suitable to serve as a main dish, as well as an appetizer.

> 1 small eggplant, baked until the skin
> separates from the eggplant
> 6 hard-cooked eggs, sliced
> 1 tablespoon lemon juice
> 1 clove garlic, finely crushed through a
> garlic press, or ¼ teaspoon garlic
> powder
> Salt and black pepper to taste
> 1 tablespoon mayonnaise
> Oil

Place the eggplant pulp with the sliced hard-cooked eggs in a chopping bowl. Chop until the eggplant and eggs are very fine. Add the lemon juice, garlic, salt, pepper, and mayonnaise. Mix well. Stir in the oil, a bit at a time, stirring until the mixture is smooth. Adjust the seasoning as necessary. Serves 6.

Russian Eggplant Salad

The only way to appreciate this intriguingly different eggplant salad is to taste it!

> 1 medium-sized eggplant
> 2 hard-cooked eggs, sliced
> 2 Passover Rolls, cut into slices (see Index
> for recipe)
> Juice of 1 lemon

⟶

2 tablespoons sugar
1 to 2 tablespoons oil
  Salt and black pepper to taste
½ green pepper, chopped (optional)
1 small onion, grated (optional)

Wipe the eggplant with a damp cloth. Place it on a rack in a baking pan. Bake at 450 degrees F. to 475 degrees F. for 1 hour, turning once or twice, until the skin turns very dark and has begun to separate from the eggplant. Remove the peel and put the eggplant pulp in a chopping bowl. Chop the eggplant with the hard-cooked eggs and roll slices. Add the lemon juice, sugar, oil, salt and pepper, green pepper, and onion. Stir to blend thoroughly. Taste and adjust the seasoning. Serve cold as a salad. Serves 4 to 6.

Munchins

Crispy potato strips are good for munching. They are excellent to serve as hors d'oeuvres when highly seasoned with garlic or onion powder.

Leftover baked potato shells
Butter or margarine
Seasoning as desired, i.e.,salt, onion
powder, garlic powder, etc.

Cut the shells into ½-inch strips. Brush butter or margarine on both sides of the strips. Season to taste. Place the strips on a cookie sheet in a preheated 450-degree F. oven and bake until browned on both sides. Serve hot or warm.

Note: Leftover shells can be stored in the freezer.

Variation:

When scooping out baked potato from the shell, leave about ¼ inch of potato next to the skin. Brush the inside of the potato shell with melted butter. Sprinkle with grated cheese and bake at 375 degrees F. for about 35 minutes, until crisp and brown. Use approximately ¼ tablespoon of melted butter and ½ teaspoon of grated cheese for each potato half.

Vegetable Fricassee

The vegetable sauce, when thickened with potato starch, makes a luscious gravy for many prepared dishes.

Vegetable Balls:

> ¼ pound mushrooms
> 1 green pepper, seeded and cut into chunks
> 1 large carrot, peeled and diced
> 1 onion, peeled and quartered
> 2 stalks celery, diced
> 1 clove garlic (optional)
> 3 tablespoons margarine
> 4 eggs
> Matzo meal (approximately 2 cups)

Finally chop the vegetables in a food processor or blender. Melt the margarine in a Dutch oven or large saucepan over medium heat. Add the chopped vegetables; sauté until soft, 5 to 10 minutes, but do not brown. Transfer the vegetables to a large mixing bowl. Cool. Stir in the eggs. Add sufficient matzo meal to make a mixture thick enough to shape, approximately 2 cups. With wet hands shape heaping tablespoonfuls of the mixture into balls. Place on a piece of wax paper, cover; set aside while preparing the sauce.

Vegetable Sauce:

> ½ pound mushrooms, divided
> 3 tablespoons margarine
> 4 cups water, divided
> 1 onion, peeled and diced
> 2 stalks celery, diced
> 1 green pepper, seeded and diced
> 1 carrot, peeled and diced
> 1 clove garlic (optional)
> 1 to 2 sprigs fresh parsley

→

   1 large tomato, peeled
   Salt and freshly ground black pepper to
   taste

Thinly slice half the mushrooms. Sauté them in the margarine in
the same Dutch oven or saucepan for about 5 minutes. Place 2
cups of the water into a blender cup. Add the vegetables and
process until the vegetables are finely chopped. Pour the mixture into the pot; add the remaining 2 cups of water. Season with
salt and freshly ground pepper. Bring to a boil, lower the heat,
and simmer for ½ hour. Add the vegetable balls. Simmer covered
for an additional 30 minutes. Serve hot. Serves 6 to 8.

Variation:
   Simmer the vegetable balls in tomato sauce.

Chopped Herring

   Using a jar of prepared herring eliminates the need to soak,
skin, and bone the whole herrings usually used in preparing this
zesty dish.

   1 jar (12 ounces) herring snacks in wine
      sauce
   1 matzo
   1 small onion, finely diced
   1 medium-sized apple, peeled, cored and
      quartered
   2 hard-cooked eggs
   1 tablespoon sugar

Drain the wine sauce from the jar of herring into a small bowl.
Crush the matzo into it to absorb the liquid. Chop the herring,
the onions from the jar, the finely diced fresh onion, and the
apple until very fine. Add the soaked matzo and hard-cooked
eggs. Continue to chop until thoroughly blended. Season with
the sugar. Yields a little more than 1 pound.

Seafood Salad

Serve as an appetizer or spoon into lettuce cups for a main dish salad.

> 2 pounds haddock fillets
> 1 medium-sized onion, sliced
> 1 stalk celery, sliced
> 2 sprigs parsley
> ⅛ teaspoon white pepper
> 1 teaspoon salt
> 1½ cups boiling water
> ½ tablespoon paprika
> ¼ cup French Dressing (see Index for recipe)
> Lettuce
> Mayonnaise
> 3 hard-cooked eggs, cut into wedges

In a medium-sized saucepan, place the fish, onion, celery, parsley, pepper, and salt. Add the boiling water and simmer until the fish is tender but not broken, about 8 to 10 minutes. Drain the fish well, removing the vegetables; flake the fish in a bowl. Sprinkle the fish with paprika and moisten with French dressing; chill thoroughly. Serve with mayonnaise on a bed of lettuce. Garnish with the egg wedges. Serves 6 to 8.

Mock Seafood Salad

Your guests will never guess that there is no seafood in this salad.

> 2 large or 5 to 6 small raw parsnips
> 3 tablespoons lemon juice or French Dressing (see Index for recipe)
> 1 cup sliced celery
> ½ cup chopped walnuts
> 2 to 3 hard-cooked eggs, chopped
> Grated onion (optional)

⟶

Salt and white pepper to taste
Mayonnaise

Wash and scrape the parsnips; shred them coarsely into a large bowl. Toss the shredded parsnips with the lemon juice or French dressing. Add the sliced celery, chopped walnuts, chopped hard-cooked eggs, grated onion, and salt and pepper to taste. Add mayonnaise to moisten. Serves 6 to 8.

Sea Dip

Enjoy this combination of fish and cheese. Serve with your favorite raw vegetable sticks—carrot, celery, green pepper, cucumber, etc.—for dipping or as a spread for matzo strips.

1 pound cooked gefilte fish
½ pound cream cheese, at room
    temperature
1 teaspoon lemon juice
2 teaspoons prepared white horseradish
2 to 3 tablespoons fish broth
    Salt and freshly ground black pepper to
    taste

In a medium-sized bowl, mash the gefilte fish with the cream cheese. Add the lemon juice, horseradish, and fish broth. Stir to blend thoroughly. Season to taste with the salt and pepper. Blend well. Chill in the refrigerator for a few hours. Yields 1½ pounds of dip.

Ikra

This elegant Roumanian recipe for poor-man's caviar can be prepared with the fish roe you may have from the fish purchased to make gefilte fish.

1 cup fresh roe
1 to 2 teaspoons salt
1 tablespoon oil
1 teaspoon lemon juice

———▶

>Dash of white pepper
>Lemon wedges
>1 Spanish onion, finely diced
>1 egg yolk, cooked and sieved
>1 hard-cooked egg white, finely chopped

Place the roe in a colander set in a large bowl. Hold under cold running water, letting the washed tiny beads of roe fall through the colander openings into the bowl. Pour off the water in the bowl as it accumulates. Continue washing the roe in this manner until all the small blood vessels are removed. Strain the roe, using a very fine strainer to remove all the excess water. Transfer the roe to a bowl. Salt the roe well and refrigerate overnight. The next day, mix in the oil and lemon juice. Taste and adjust the seasoning, adding salt if necessary. Add a dash of white pepper

Serve as you would caviar. Set the bowl on a bed of cracked ice surrounded by lemon wedges, dishes of minced onion, sieved egg yolk, and a dish of the finely chopped egg white. Yields 1 cup; serves 8.

Gehakteh Leber
(Liver Pâté)

Adjust the amount of onions and eggs in this pâté to suit your taste. Those who like the pungency of onion may substitute a freshly chopped onion for one of the sauteed onions. Beef or calves' liver may be substituted for the chicken liver.

To serve the pâté attractively, line a chicken (or other shape) mold with dampened cheesecloth, pack solidly with the liver, then turn out onto a platter. Carefully remove the cheesecloth and garnish the mold, making chicken features with bits of vegetables; make the beak with a piece of almond.

>2 large onions, chopped (or more, to taste)
>3 tablespoons oil
>1 pound chicken livers
>4 hard-cooked eggs
>1 teaspoon salt
>¼ teaspoon freshly ground black pepper
>1 to 2 tablespoons mayonnaise

In a large skillet, sauté the onions in the oil until golden. Broil the livers. Using the finest blade of a grinder, grind the liver with the onions and eggs twice. Add the salt and pepper. Add 1 or 2 tablespoons of mayonnaise and mix well. Taste and adjust the seasoning. Serve chilled.

Variation:

For individual portions, place a chicken-form cookie cutter on a lettuce leaf. Spoon the liver mixture carefully into the cutter. When the cutter is filled, carefully lift it up, leaving the chicken mold on the dish.

Sautéed Chicken Livers

For a richer gravy, substitute chicken broth for the water.

> **2 large onions, thinly sliced**
> **3 stalks celery, thinly sliced**
> **¼ cup oil**
> **1 pound mushrooms, sliced**
> **1 pound chicken livers, broiled**
> **1 tablespoon potato starch**
> **1 cup water**
> **Salt and black pepper to taste**
> **1 teaspoon paprika**

In a 2-quart saucepan, sauté the sliced onions and celery in the oil until golden. Add the sliced mushrooms. Cut the broiled chicken livers into bite-sized pieces; add to the pan. Sauté together 5 to 10 minutes. Dissolve potato starch in the water; add this to the liver mixture, stirring all the while. Add the salt and pepper and the paprika. Continue to cook, stirring until thickened. For more gravy, add additional water. Serve in puff shells. Serves 6.

Liver Hors d'Oeuvres

Serve these hors d'oeuvres along with a glass of tomato juice garnished with a lemon wedge.

2 large potatoes
1 egg
2 tablespoons matzo meal
½ teaspoon salt
⅛ teaspoon black pepper
2 tablespoons minced onion
2 tablespoons fat
¼ pound broiled liver, ground
½ teaspoon salt
Grease for the pan

Boil the potatoes in their jackets. Cool, peel, and mash well in a small bowl. Beat in the egg, matzo meal, and the salt and pepper. Shape walnut-sized pieces of potato dough into a ball. Arrange them in a well-greased 7 x 9-inch baking pan. Using the thumb, indent the center of each potato ball to form a hollow. Bake at 375 degrees F. for 18 to 20 minutes, until lightly browned.

Brown the onion in the fat in a small skillet over medium heat. Add to the ground liver; season with the salt; mix well. Fill the hollows of the baked potato balls with portions of the liver mixture. Serve hot. Makes 6 to 8.

P'tcha

(Calves'-foot Jelly)

P'tcha, fisnogen, and cholodyetz are all one and the same: a brawn, most often served as an aspic. There is no one basic recipe. Ingredients and seasonings vary. Some recipes have a piquant and tart taste due to the lemon juice used; others are enriched with additional egg yolks; still others are quite aromatic due to the fresh garlic. Change the character of this version of p'tcha by adjusting the number of garlic cloves used.

1 calf or steer's foot, cut into pieces
1 large onion, sliced
3 to 4 garlic cloves
Salt and white pepper to taste
3 hard-cooked eggs, sliced

Place the cleaned foot in a medium-sized saucepan with the sliced onion, 1 clove of garlic, sliced, and a small amount of salt (½ teaspoon). Cover with cold water. Bring to a boil; cover the pot and let simmer for 3 to 3½ hours, until the meat falls off the bones. Strain the stock into a shallow 8 or 9-inch square pan. Remove the bones; chop the meat into small pieces and add to the stock. Mince the remaining garlic cloves; add to the stock; season with additional salt and pepper. Arrange the egg slices over the stock. Chill. When firm, cut into serving pieces. Serves 6 to 8.

Variation:

Grind the meat from the bones rather than cutting it into small pieces. Garlic powder may be substituted for the fresh garlic cloves.

Chicken Cholodyetz

(Chicken Brawn)

Giblets from 2 or 3 chickens
2 medium-sized onions, diced
Salt and white pepper
1 clove garlic
Cold water
1 to 2 cloves garlic, minced, or garlic
powder to taste (optional)
2 hard-cooked eggs (optional)

Chop or cut up the chicken giblets and place them in a medium-sized saucepan with the 2 diced onions. Season well with salt and pepper. Add the clove of garlic and cold water to cover. Bring to a boil, remove the scum, reduce the heat, and cook until the stock is reduced by about half. Taste and adjust the seasoning. Minced garlic or garlic powder may be added for additional garlic flavor. Pour the mixture into a shallow 8 or 9-inch pan. Garnish with sliced hard-cooked eggs if desired; chill until firm. Serves 6 to 8 as an appetizer.

Variation:

A small cut-up Cornish hen or broiler-fryer may be cooked

together with the giblets. With a slotted spoon, remove the cooked chicken from the broth. Cut the chicken into slices or cubes. Discard the skin and bones. Return the cut-up chicken to the brawn. Pour into the pan to chill.

Chicken Fricassee in Vegetable Gravy

This fricassee is unusual in that the giblets are cooked in a robust vegetable gravy. Although usually served as an appetizer, an adequate portion of this fricassee served on a bed of farfel will be enthusiastically received as a main dish.

To increase the number of servings, or to change the character of the fricassee, prepare your favorite meatball recipe using one pound of chopped meat. Add the meatballs to the cooking giblets at the same time the vegetable purée is added. Be prepared to serve seconds.

> 2 large onions, divided
> 3 stalks celery, divided
> 4 tablespoons oil or margarine, divided
> Giblets from 3 to 4 chickens
> 6 chicken wings
> 2 large sweet potatoes or yams, peeled
> 3 to 4 carrots, peeled
> 1 large parsnip, peeled
> Water
> Salt to taste
> Freshly ground black pepper to taste
> 1 teaspoon paprika

Finely slice 1 onion and 1 stalk of celery. In a deep saucepan over medium heat, sauté the sliced onion and celery in 2 tablespoons of oil or margarine until golden. Cut up the chicken giblets and add to the onion and celery sauté; add the chicken wings. Cover and let simmer over low heat while preparing the vegetable gravy. Stir occasionally.

Finely slice the remaining onion and 2 stalks of celery. Slice the sweet potatoes or yams, carrots, and parsnip. In a separate deep saucepan, heat the remaining oil or margarine; add the sliced vegetables and sauté until tender. If necessary, add a few tablespoons of water. Season with salt and pepper. When the vegeta-bles are tender, purée the vegetables with a blender or food mill.

Pour the puréed vegetables over the giblets. Add boiling water to cover. Taste and adjust the seasoning; add the teaspoon of paprika. Stir and cook covered over low heat for 1 hour or until the giblets are tender. Serves 6 to 8.

2

Soups and Soup Garnishes

Through the years each nation has developed its own special soup. The French have the pot-au-feu, the Italians the minestrone, the Spanish gazpacho, while Russia and Poland share borsht as their national soup.

Soups may be classified as being one of three types: thin and clear, such as chicken broth; thin and light, such as a cream soup or vegetable broth; or heavy and thick, a hearty soup that can be a meal-in-itself, such as the Russian meat borsht.

Soup should always be cooked in a good-sized pot. Whenever possible, the cooked soup should be refrigerated until the fat solidifies and can be removed easily. In serving soup, one cardinal rule should be observed: serve hot soups hot and cold soups cold.

Add a new dimension to the soups you serve. Make them more appetizing and appealing by enhancing them with attractive garnishes. This section is evidence that there is a wide variety of soups and garnishes to consider.

Russel

(Beet Sour)

There are endless varieties of borsht. Recipes vary from a clear all-beet borsht to a meal-in-one Russian meat borsht. Borsht may be prepared from fresh beets or from russel, fermented beet juice. The preparation of russel must commence about three weeks before Passover.

**3 to 6 pounds beet roots
Boiled water, cooled to lukewarm**

Wash and scrape the raw beets thoroughly. The amount of beets depends upon how many quarts of russel you wish to prepare (5 pounds of beets should yield at least 2 to 2½ quarts of russel, plus the beets).

Cut the beets into large pieces. Place them in a 6-quart crock or large glass jug. Fill the crock or jug with the water. The water should rise at least 2 inches above the beets. Place the cover or lid somewhat askew on the crock or jug, leaving a small opening. Then cover the entire top with a clean cloth to protect the contents from dust. Let the crock or jug stand in a warm place to ferment. In a few days a white scum will have formed on the top. Remove this completely and stir the mixture. Let stand once again. Remove the scum periodically. By Passover the russel will be ready to use. When it's ready, it should be clear and have a deep red color. Refrigerate until ready to use.

Meatless Russel Borsht

Use one cup of strained russel (recipe above) for each portion of borsht being prepared. If the russel seems too sour, dilute it with a little water. It is difficult to recommend the exact amount of seasoning to be used to arrive at the proper balance of sweet and sour. There are variables: the sourness of the beet juice and personal preference. You may have to add some lemon juice along with the sugar, salt, and pepper. Adjust to taste.

**4 cups russel
2 medium-sized onions
    Salt and black pepper to taste
    Lemon juice and sugar to taste
4 medium-sized boiled potatoes**

Pour the russel into a medium-sized saucepan. With a fork, prick the whole onions in a few places around the sides; add to the pan.

Bring to a boil, then simmer for 15 to 20 minutes, until the onions are tender. With a slotted spoon remove the onions. Add the salt, pepper, lemon juice if necessary, and sugar to taste. Chill to serve. Garnish each soup serving with a hot boiled potato. Serves 4.

Variation:

Serve garnished with a tablespoon of sour cream and a few slices of cucumber or slices of hard-cooked egg.

Russel Borsht With Meat

> 4 cups russel (see recipe)
> 2 cups coarsely grated fresh beets or 2
>   cups russel beets, chopped (see recipe)
> 4 cups water
> 1 or 2 medium-sized onions
> 2 to 3 pounds flanken or brisket
>   Marrow bones
> 1 teaspoon salt
> ¼ teaspoon freshly ground black pepper
>   Sugar
>   Lemon juice
> 2 or 3 eggs
>   Pared boiled potatoes (optional)

Combine the russel, beets, and the water in a large soup pot. Add the onions, meat, marrow bones, salt, and pepper. Bring to a boil, turn the heat down, then simmer covered for 2 to 3 hours, until the meat is tender. Skim clear when necessary.

With a slotted spoon, remove the meat; keep it hot. Season the broth with sugar and lemon juice to taste (the borsht should be somewhat sweet-sour). Remove from the heat. To thicken the broth, beat the eggs slightly in a small mixing bowl. Then slowly whisk in a cup of the hot borsht. When thoroughly blended, return this mixture to the pot; mix well to prevent curdling.

Serve the borsht in individual soup bowls. Garnish each serving with a hot boiled potato. Serve the meat, sliced, as a main dish. Serves 6 to 8.

Fleishig Russian Borsht
(Russian Meat Borsht)

Russian meat borsht may be considered a two-course dinner dish. The meat and the vegetables are cooked together, then they are separated. The first course consists of the hearty and robust soup, the second of the meat.

The flavor of fresh garlic or fresh onion is not duplicated with garlic powder or onion powder. There are occasions, however, where garlic powder or onion powder will suffice as the agent to add that extra bit of seasoning. So, to add zest to this borsht, sprinkle a dash or two of garlic powder on each serving.

> **3 pounds brisket or flanken**
> **Marrow bones**
> **3 quarts water, divided**
> **1½ teaspoons salt**
> **4 large beet roots**
> **1 onion, chopped**
> **4 fresh tomatoes, peeled and sliced, or 1**
> **can (16 ounces) tomatoes**
> **1 small cabbage, coarsely shredded**
> **½ teaspoon salt**
> **½ teaspoon black pepper**
> **½ cup lemon juice**
> **4 tablespoons sugar**

Place the brisket and the marrow bones in a large soup pot; cover with 2 quarts of the water and season with the 1½ teaspoons of salt. Bring to a boil, removing the scum as it rises. Simmer for 1 hour.

In a separate smaller soup pot, cook the beet roots in the remaining quart of water until tender. Remove the beet roots from their cooking water and grate. Add the grated beet roots to the soup stock together with the beet root cooking water. Add the chopped onion, tomatoes, cabbage, the ½ teaspoon of salt, and the pepper. Cover and simmer slowly for 1½ hours. Add the lemon juice and sugar. Continue to simmer for an additional 15 minutes; adjust the seasoning as necessary. Serves 8.

Knoble Borsht

Fresh garlic imparts a pervasive fragrance to this borsht.

> 3 quarts water
> 2 pounds flanken or brisket
> Beef bones
> 8 beets, grated
> 2 onions, diced
> 2 cloves garlic, minced
> 1 tablespoon salt
> 3 tablespoons brown sugar
> Sour salt or lemon juice to taste
> 2 eggs, beaten (optional)

In a deep saucepan, combine the water, meat, and bones. Bring to a boil. Skim. Add the beets, onions, garlic, and salt. Cover and cook over medium heat for 2 hours. Add the brown sugar and sour salt or lemon juice. Cook 30 minutes longer. Taste and adjust the seasoning.

If using the eggs, beat them in a small bowl. Gradually add a little hot soup, beating steadily to prevent curdling. Add the egg liquid to the saucepan, beating it in very well. Serve in individual soup bowls. Garnish with pieces of meat. Serves 8.

Schav Borsht

Schav is soup made from sorrel, a sour grass, and in its preparation it is just as important to strike the right balance of sweet-sour as it is when making a beet borsht. This balance may be achieved by using sugar in combination with lemon juice or sour salt. Spinach can be substituted for the sorrel, or use two packages of frozen chopped spinach in place of one pound fresh spinach.

Schav is traditionally a Shavuot (Feast of Weeks or Pentecost) dish, but it is a fine Passover soup as well.

> 1 pound sorrel
> 1 medium-sized onion, peeled
> 1 quart water

$\longrightarrow$

¼ cup sugar
2 tablespoons lemon juice
1 teaspoon salt
2 eggs
½ cup heavy sour cream (optional)

Wash the sorrel thoroughly in cold water. Remove any stems that are not tender. Finely chop the remaining stems and sorrel leaves. Combine the sorrel, whole onion, water, and sugar in a 2-quart saucepan. Over high heat, bring to the boiling point; lower the heat and simmer gently for 20 minutes. Add the lemon juice and salt. Remove from the heat and let cool. With a slotted spoon remove the onion.

In a small mixing bowl beat the eggs well; add a little of the broth and continue to beat; slowly stir the egg mixture into the pot of soup. Blend well. Taste and adjust the seasoning with additional sugar, salt, or lemon juice if desired. Chill well. Makes 1 quart; serves 4 to 6.

Variations:
• Mix together the eggs and sour cream until blended. Add to the borsht and mix thoroughly. Chill and serve very cold in a glass or in a bowl. Garnish each serving with a hot boiled potato or a sliced hard-cooked egg.
• Add a tablespoonful of finely cut cucumber and a tablespoonful of finely cut scallion to each serving of chilled soup. Crest with a dollop of sour cream.

Vegetable Soup

2 medium-sized potatoes, peeled
1 small zucchini squash, unpeeled
2 large carrots, peeled
2 parsnips, peeled
1 small onion
3 scallions
2 stalks celery
3 tablespoons margarine

      6 cups water
      1 teaspoon sugar
      Salt and white pepper to taste

Dice the vegetables into a medium-sized bowl. Melt the margarine in a 3-quart saucepan over medium heat. Add the diced vegetables and sauté them for a few minutes. Add the water and the sugar. Cover and simmer for 20 minutes or until the vegetables are tender. Season to taste with salt and white pepper. Do not overcook. Serves 6.

Goldena Yoich

(Golden Chicken Soup)

Medical science has at last confirmed the fact that chicken soup, long associated with Jewish cooking, is a good antidote to the common cold. (Dr. Marvin A. Sackner studied the effects of chicken soup at the Mount Sinai Medical Center in Miami Beach, Florida, and in 1978 he published his findings in *Chest*, a publication devoted to pulmonary disorders.) One of mother's cardinal tenets of "what is good for you" has been proven true!

      1 chicken (4 to 5 pounds)
      4 quarts cold water
      2 to 3 stalks celery, including the leaves
      1 large onion
      1 parsnip, peeled
      3 carrots, peeled
      1 parsley root, peeled
      1 piece celery knob, peeled
      Salt and white pepper to taste
      A few sprigs of fresh parsley
      A few sprigs of fresh dill

Cut the chicken into quarters; place in a large pot with the cold water. Bring the water to the boiling point, then lower the heat and let simmer. Remove the scum as it rises. Cover the pot and cook for 1 hour. Add the vegetables, salt, and pepper and cook for an additional hour or until the chicken is tender when pierced with a fork. Remove the chicken and vegetables; strain the soup. Let the soup cool so that the fat can be skimmed from the top. Heat to serve. Yields 2½ to 3 quarts.

Variations:

•The vegetables can be tied together in a piece of cheesecloth to facilitate their removal.
• The vegetables can be used to make Soup Green Latkes (see Index for recipe).
• Purée the vegetables in a blender and return the purée to the soup. This gives the soup a creamy consistency.
• Add a dash of garlic powder to each serving of soup.

New England Fish Chowder

This hearty, tasty, thick soup, for which New England is known, can double as a main course for a dairy luncheon.

> 1 medium-sized onion, diced
> 1 tablespoon margarine
> 1 cup water
> ¾ to 1 pound codfish, cubed
> 1 medium-sized potato, peeled and cubed
> 1 stalk celery, sliced fine
> Salt and black pepper to taste
> 1½ cups milk

In a large, deep skillet or saucepan, sauté the onion in the margarine until light brown. Add the water, codfish cubes, potato cubes, and the celery. Simmer for about 45 minutes. Add the seasoning and the milk. Simmer for an additional 5 minutes. Serves 6.

Israeli Fruit Soup

Excellent as a first course for a brunch or light lunch. Try serving in a dish with the pieces of fruit floating in it, or purée the fruit and serve in a glass as a refreshing beverage.

   3 cups fruit, fresh or dried
   2 quarts water
     Sugar to taste
   3 cups orange juice
   3 tablespoons potato starch
     Cold water

Mix together and chop 3 cups of any combination of fruits, fresh
and/or dried. Boil the fruits together in a large saucepan with 2
quarts of water sugared to taste. When the fruits are soft, purée
them in the blender, or press the fruits through a sieve. Return
the purée to the saucepan over low heat; add the orange juice.
Dilute 3 tablespoons of potato starch in a little cold water and
add to the fruit mixture; stir well as you bring the soup to a boil.
Cool and refrigerate. Serve cold. Serves 6.

Variations:
• A little lemon juice may be combined with the orange juice.
• Garnish with slices of fresh strawberries or a dollop of sour
cream.

Knaidlach
(Matzo Balls)

   In the absence of legumes and cereals on Passover, knaidlach
(dumplings) are prepared. They come in a variety of forms, from
the common chicken soup variety to fruit knaidlach for dessert.
Some can complement meat meals, others dairy dishes.
   There are countless variations on the traditional Passover
soup knaidlach. Knaidlach may be featherlight or so firm that a
knife is needed to cut them; they may contain fat or may be fat-
free; they may be seasoned or unseasoned. The recipes that
follow offer a wide selection. The choice is yours to enjoy.
   Take heed. Be sure you have adequate soup in which to cook
knaidlach, as they absorb some of the broth while cooking. You
may substitute chicken broth prepared with chicken bouillon
cubes, or cook them in boiling water seasoned with salt. When
cooked, remove the knaidlach from the pot with a slotted spoon,
then transfer them to the cooked chicken broth.

Knaidlach—Featherlight:

These knaidlach may be enhanced by adding ⅛ teaspoon freshly ground black pepper, a dash of ginger, or 2 tablespoons finely minced parsley. For each egg use:

⅛ teaspoon salt
¼ cup matzo meal

Separate the eggs into 2 bowls. Beat the egg whites until stiff. Beat the egg yolks and salt until light. Combine the beaten egg yolks with the stiffly beaten egg whites. Gradually add the matzo meal. Stir until smooth. Let rest for 10 to 15 minutes.

Wet the hands with cold water. Form the mixture into small balls by rolling in the palms. Carefully drop the balls into boiling clear soup stock or salted water (1 teaspoon salt to 1 quart water). Cover and cook at a slow boil for 20 minutes. Knaidlach made with 2 eggs will serve 4 to 5.

Knaidlach—Medium-Firm:

2 tablespoons fat, melted
2 eggs, slightly beaten
½ cup matzo meal
¾ teaspoon salt
2 tablespoons soup stock or water
2 quarts water
1 teaspoon salt

In a medium-sized bowl, mix together the fat and the eggs. Add the matzo meal and the salt. When well blended, add the soup stock or water. Mix well. Cover the mixing bowl and refrigerate for at least 20 minutes.

With wet or greased hands, shape the matzo meal mixture into small balls. Bring the 2 quarts of water and the teaspoon of salt to a brisk boil in a 3-quart pot. Lower the heat and drop the matzo balls individually into the pot. Cover and cook for 30 to 40 minutes. With a slotted spoon, remove the knaidlach and drain. Transfer them to a pot of soup. Before serving, simmer the soup with the knaidlach for approximately 5 minutes. Serves 6 to 8.

Knaidlach—Very Firm:

These knaidlach are a perfect alternative to potatoes. Serve them with a pot roast. One teaspoon chicken soup mix will enhance the flavor.

> 1 cup matzo meal
> ½ teaspoon salt
> 3 tablespoons fat, melted
> 2 eggs, well beaten
> ½ cup water, approximately
> 2 quarts water
> 2 teaspoons salt

In a medium-sized bowl, blend the matzo meal with the salt and the fat. Add the well-beaten eggs. Mix thoroughly. Gradually add cold water to make a dough firm enough to be shaped into balls.

With wet hands, shape the mixture into balls and drop them into a 3-quart pot of boiling salted water or into boiling soup. Cover the pot and cook for 15 minutes. If cooked in water, drain well. Drop into soup a few minutes before serving. Makes 12 to 14.

Whole Matzo Knaidlach

> 6 matzos
>   Cold water
> 2 tablespoons fat
> 3 medium-sized onions, chopped
> 1 teaspoon salt
> ⅛ teaspoon white pepper
> ⅛ teaspoon ginger
> 3 eggs, separated
> 1 teaspoon finely minced parsley
> ½ to 1 cup matzo meal

Soak the matzos in a bowl of cold water for 5 minutes. Drain thoroughly. Force the drained matzos through a medium-fine sieve. In a medium-sized skillet, melt the fat and sauté the onions until limp and golden brown. Add the matzo paste, stirring over low heat until the mixture is dry.

Remove the mixture to a medium-sized bowl. Add the salt, pepper, ginger, well-beaten egg yolks, and parsley. Stir together for a few minutes. In a clean small mixing bowl, beat the egg whites until stiff; fold them into the egg yolk mixture. The dough should be of a consistency that can be formed into balls; fold in sufficient matzo meal to achieve this consistency.

Shape the mixture into walnut-sized balls, then chill for several hours. Drop the balls into a shallow saucepan containing simmering salted water (1 teaspoon salt to each quart of water), broth, or wine diluted with water (1 cup water to 3 cups wine). Place cover half over the saucepan and simmer for 20 minutes. Drain and serve with soup or with any desired sauce as an accompaniment for meat. Serves 6.

Frozen Uncooked Knaidlach

Your favorite cooked knaidlach may be frozen either in soup or individually. To freeze individually, place the knaidlach on a cookie sheet in the freezer until frozen. Then pack them in an airtight container, preferably an oblong one so they will not stick together. This recipe is for uncooked knaidlach that are frozen and ready to cook.

> 4 eggs, beaten
> ½ cup water
> ⅓ cup melted shortening
> 1 teaspoon salt
>   Dash of black pepper
>   Dash of garlic powder (optional)
> 1 cup matzo meal
>   Oil for the trays

In a medium-sized mixing bowl, combine the eggs, water, melted shortening, and the seasonings. Mix well. Add the matzo meal. Lightly oil plastic ice cube trays, the kind that pop out. Fill each section with a spoonful of the knaidel mixture, scraping off any excess. Freeze. When ready to use, loosen around each knaidel with the point of a knife and pop them into boiling salted water. Do *not* thaw before cooking. Cover and boil gently for 25 minutes. Makes approximately 18 to 20.

Versatile Potato Knaidlach

These dumplings may be served as a soup garnish. Or serve with a mushroom or chicken liver sauce to make an excellent side dish for meat. When prepared with fruit, this is a lovely dessert to serve after meat or dairy.

> 3 large raw potatoes, peeled
> 1 quart ice water
> 1½ cups matzo meal
> ¼ cup margarine or chicken fat, melted
> 3 eggs, well beaten
> ¼ teaspoon white pepper
> 1½ teaspoons salt
> ½ cup cool water
> 2 quarts simmering water with 1 teaspoon salt or 2 quarts simmering broth

Grate the potatoes into a bowl containing the ice water. Drain and squeeze the potato pulp as dry as possible. In a large mixing bowl, combine the grated potato pulp with the matzo meal, the melted and cooled margarine or chicken fat, the well-beaten eggs, the pepper, and the salt. Gradually add the cool water to make a manageable dough. Cover the dough and refrigerate for 1 hour. Shape the dough into approximately 24 walnut-sized balls. Chill for an hour or longer.

Drop the potato balls into a large saucepan containing the salted simmering water (or broth). Cover and simmer with the cover of the saucepan aslant for 25 to 35 minutes (test a knaidel after 25 minutes cooking time for consistency). Serves 6 to 8 as a soup garnish.

Variation:

To prepare these knaidlach as a dessert, shape the dough into 24 flat pancakes and arrange on a piece of wax paper. Before chilling, fill each with a pitted prune or 6 large plumped raisins mixed with a drop of honey, or place a teaspoon of your favorite jam on 12 of the flat patties. Top the filling with a second patty. Pinch the edges together and form rounded dumplings. Chill for

1 hour. Cook, as directed, in boiling salted water or in a mixture of half-water and half-wine.

Chicken Liver Balls

These are hearty dumplings that may be served as an accompaniment or as a main dish with a mushroom sauce.

½ pound chicken livers
1 cup matzo farfel
1 cup boiling water
1 egg, beaten
1 teaspoon minced onion
1 teaspoon salt
⅛ teaspoon black pepper

Broil the chicken livers and chop them fine. Place the matzo farfel in a medium-sized bowl and pour the 1 cup boiling water over the farfel. Stir together to form a paste. Let cool. Add the beaten egg, chopped livers, minced onion, and the seasoning. Shape the mixture into small balls. Cook in simmering soup for 15 minutes. Serve hot with the soup. Serves 6 to 8.

Liver Knaidlach

Beef or calves' liver may be substituted for the chicken livers.

½ pound chicken liver
1½ cups boiling water
1¾ cups matzo meal
4 tablespoons oil or chicken fat
1 large onion, minced
3 eggs, well beaten
1 teaspoon salt
¼ teaspoon white pepper
3 quarts water
2 teaspoons salt

Broil the liver and grind or chop fine. Pour the boiling water over the matzo meal in a large mixing bowl. Let stand to absorb all the water. In a small skillet, heat the oil or melt the chicken fat over medium heat. Add the minced onion and sauté until golden. Combine the sautéed onion with the cooled matzo meal mixture; add the well-beaten eggs, salt, and pepper.

Mix together until thoroughly blended. With wet hands, roll the liver mixture into small balls. Drop gently into 3 quarts of boiling salted water. Cover, reduce the heat, and simmer gently for about 25 minutes. Yields 24 to 28.

Luckshen I

(Noodles)

  2 eggs
  1 teaspoon salt
  1 tablespoon water
  ⅓ cup cake meal
  Cake meal for rolling

In a medium-sized mixing bowl, beat together the eggs, salt, and water very well. Add the cake meal and knead together. Roll out the dough as thin as possible on a board dusted with additional cake meal. Set aside to dry for about ½ hour. Roll up the dough as you would a jelly roll and slice into thin slices. Separate the strands and set aside to dry. Before serving, boil gently in salted water for 20 minutes. Drain well. Serves 6 or more.

Luckshen II

(Potato Flour Noodles)

  ½ cup potato starch
  ⅓ cup water
  Pinch of salt
  3 eggs, well beaten
  Grease for the skillet

In a small mixing bowl, mix the potato starch with the water and salt until completely dissolved. Add the well-beaten eggs and mix until smooth. In a lightly greased skillet over medium heat, fry thin pancakes (use 1 to 2 tablespoons of batter for each). Continue until the batter is all used up. Roll each pancake tightly and cut into thin strips. Add to boiling soup at serving time. Yields 10 "luckshen pancakes."

Farfel

5 to 6 eggs
⅓ cup water
1 box (16 ounces) cake meal

In a large mixing bowl, beat the eggs with the water; stir in the cake meal to make a stiff batter. Grate the stiff batter on a hand grater into a large shallow baking pan. Brown the particles in a preheated 275-degree F. oven for 1 hour, stirring frequently to expose all grains of dough. Turn the heat down to 200 degrees F. for another hour, until all the farfel are nicely browned. Cool thoroughly and store in a glass jar. Makes 1 pound.

Mandlen

(Soup Nuts)

Mandlen, like matzo balls and noodles, is a soup garnish that can transform a bowl of clear chicken soup into a more satisfying and filling soup. Sprinkle some chopped parsley or dill over all.

3 tablespoons oil
¼ cup water
½ teaspoon salt
Dash of white pepper
¾ cup matzo meal
2 eggs
Grease for the baking sheet

In a medium-sized saucepan, heat the oil, water, salt, and pepper to the boiling point. Add the matzo meal, mixing quickly until smooth. Remove from the fire and beat the eggs into the mixture 1 at a time; blend well after each addition. Lightly coat the hands with oil. Shape the mixture into ¼-inch balls. Place them on a well-greased baking sheet. Bake in a preheated 400-degree F. oven for 30 to 35 minutes, until golden brown. Yields 80 to 90 mandlen.

Potato Croutons

A crunchy and decorative complement for a bowl of vegetable soup.

> Raw potatoes, peeled
> Oil for the baking sheet
> Salt and pepper

Dice the raw peeled potatoes. Place on a lightly greased baking sheet in a preheated 400-degree F. oven, turning occasionally until the potatoes are nicely browned on all sides. Season with salt and pepper. Yield depends upon the size and number of potatoes used.

Toasted Egg Farfel

Toasted egg farfel sprinkled on a tossed salad adds a pleasing crunch. The farfel are deliciously crisp. If serving as a soup garnish, they will retain their crispness if added to the soup just before serving. Better still, have a bowl of toasted farfel readied to be passed around the table, enabling your guests to help themselves.

> 4 eggs
> ¼ cup water
> Salt to taste
> White pepper to taste
> 1 box (16 ounces) matzo farfel

In a large deep mixing bowl, beat the eggs very well with the water, salt, and pepper. Add the box of farfel and mix with a pastry blender or fork until all the farfel are coated with the egg. Place the farfel on a large cookie sheet. Bake in a preheated 400-degree F. oven, shaking and using a pastry blender or fork occasionally to separate the particles. Toast until all the particles are separated and nicely browned. Cool thoroughly and store in a jar. Serve with soup or as a "popcorn" snack. Makes 1 pound.

Toasted Farfel Knaidlach

For snacking, onion powder and/or garlic powder may be added to the egg mixture before these farfel balls are formed. They make an excellent substitute for popcorn balls, even though they are not as soft and airy.

3 eggs
½ cup water
   Salt to taste
   White pepper to taste
2 cups farfel
   Grease for the cookie sheet

In a medium-sized mixing bowl, beat the eggs well with the water, salt, and pepper. Add the farfel; mix well. Form the egg-coated farfel into small balls. Place them on a lightly greased cookie sheet. Toast in a preheated 350-degree F. oven, rotating them until the balls are lightly toasted on all sides. Serves 6.

Royale Custard

These custard cubes are flavorful tidbits that add eye appeal, flavor, and extra heartiness to any bowl of clear soup.

3 eggs
¾ cup clear chicken soup
   Grease for the baking dish

In a medium-sized mixing bowl, beat the eggs with the chicken soup. Pour into a flat greased baking dish so that the "custard" is about ½ inch deep. Set the baking dish into a pan of hot water (½ to ¾ inch) in a 350-degree F. oven for 30 minutes, until the custard sets. Remove from the oven and let cool. Cut the custard into desired designs, that is, diamonds, squares, etc. Toss the little shapes into soup before serving. Sprinkle the pieces with chopped parsley for color.

Einlauf

Einlauf is an easy-to-prepare soup garnish. The batter forms little egg drops; the taste is comparable to that of knaidlach.

> 2 eggs, well beaten
> ½ teaspoon salt
> Dash of white pepper
> 1 tablespoon finely minced parsley (optional)
> ½ cup water
> ⅔ cup matzo meal

In a medium-sized mixing bowl, combine the well-beaten eggs with the salt, pepper, minced parsley, and water. Add the matzo meal. Stir until smooth. Drop the batter, ¼ teaspoon at a time, into boiling soup. Cover the pot tightly and cook for 3 to 5 minutes. Sufficient for 2 to 3 quarts of soup.

Eggdrop for Soup

Good for wheat allergics.

> 2 tablespoons potato starch
> 2 tablespoons water
> 1 egg
> Dash of salt

In a small bowl dilute the potato starch with the water. Add the egg and salt and beat until smooth. Drop by the teaspoonful into boiling soup. Reduce the heat and cook covered for an additional 5 to 10 minutes. Serves 4.

Soup Swans

No garnish creates more interest than these Soup Swans when served afloat a bowl of clear chicken soup.

> ½ cup water
> ¼ teaspoon salt
> ¼ cup oil

→

½ cup matzo meal
2 eggs
    Grease for the baking sheet

Bring the water, salt, and oil to a full rolling boil in a medium-sized saucepan. Reduce the heat and pour in the matzo meal all at once. Cook, stirring briskly, until the mixture forms a smooth ball that leaves the sides of the pan. Remove from the heat. Cool slightly. Add the eggs 1 at a time, beating after each addition until the mixture is smooth and glossy.

On a lightly greased baking sheet shape the "body" of each swan, as follows: Spoon teaspoonfuls of dough onto the baking sheet, forming small oblong mounds. Allow 1 inch of space between each teaspoonful. With a pastry bag and a small writing tube, pipe an equal number of small swan necks (the swan neck is piped in a question mark shape).

Bake in a preheated 375-degree F. oven for 10 minutes, until the necks are golden. Remove the necks to a wire rack, lower the heat to 350 degrees F., and continue baking the remaining pieces for 20 to 25 minutes, until well puffed and brown. Let cool. Make a hole in 1 end of each puff and insert the neck into position. Float a swan in each bowl of soup just before serving. Makes 12 to 14.

3
Poultry and Stuffings

When one thinks of poultry, chicken is the dish that invariably comes to mind first. Chicken's popularity is due, in part at least, to its versatility. It can be enhanced by many different flavorings, and each nationality has incorporated its favorite seasonings into the preparation of its favorite chicken dishes. Be that as it may, one should not overlook the other varieties of poultry: squab, duck, goose, and the ever-popular American bird, the turkey.

In this chapter you will find a variety of recipes for chicken, turkey, and duck. Some, such as the Lemon Chicken, are easy to prepare. Others, such as the Stuffed Chicken Legs or Duck With Cherries, require time and/or patience, but the result will make the effort worthwhile.

This chapter also includes a host of stuffing recipes, ranging from the basic Farfel Stuffing to a Savory Fruit Stuffing.

Roast Stuffed Chicken

This roast chicken stuffed with a vegetable-rich dressing should arrive at the table elegantly garnished. Parsley and carrots add color to the encased filling. Serve the bird with accompaniments of contrasting color—cranberry sauce, beets, broccoli, etc.

⅓ cup oil or margarine
1 cup diced onions
2 large carrots, peeled and grated
¼ cup chopped celery
2 tablespoons chopped fresh parsley
3 eggs
1½ teaspoons salt
¼ teaspoon freshly ground black pepper
½ cup water
1 cup matzo meal
1 roasting chicken (5 pounds)
  Paprika
1 tablespoon fat
1 clove garlic, quartered

First prepare the vegetable stuffing. Film a large heavy skillet with the oil, or melt the margarine over moderate heat. Stir in all the vegetables except for the clove of garlic. Cook slowly until the vegetables are tender but not yet brown. Remove the vegetables from the heat.

In a large bowl, beat the eggs with the salt and pepper; add the water, cooked vegetables, and the matzo meal. Blend well. Stuff the chicken with the dressing, making sure not to pack the chicken cavity too tightly. Skewer the opening. Place the stuffed chicken on a rack in a roasting pan. Sprinkle the chicken with paprika. Massage the tablespoon of fat into the chicken skin.

Roast in a preheated 350-degree F. oven, allowing about 30 minutes per pound. After 1 hour of roasting, add the cut garlic clove to the pan. Baste frequently with the pan drippings. Test the legs for doneness. Serves 6.

Stuffed Broiler Quarters

Here is a recipe that requires some time and effort, but you will delight in the result.

1 egg
½ cup water
2 to 2½ tablespoons oil

→

    1 small onion, minced, or 1 tablespoon
      minced onion flakes
    ½ teaspoon salt
    ⅛ teaspoon white pepper
    1 cup matzo meal
    1 broiling chicken (2½ to 3 pounds),
      quartered
    2 tablespoons oil or margarine, melted
    Onion powder
    Garlic powder
    Paprika
    Grease for the pan

First prepare the stuffing. In a medium-sized bowl, beat the egg with the water, oil, onion, salt, and pepper. Add the matzo meal and blend well.

Loosen the skin of each chicken quarter by carefully inserting the fingers under the skin, separating it from the meat. Spoon a portion of the stuffing under the skin of each quarter. Return the skin to its original position.

Arrange the chicken, skin side up, in a greased 9 × 13-inch shallow pan. Brush the oil or melted margarine over the chicken quarters. Sprinkle with the onion powder, garlic powder, and paprika. Roast in a preheated 350-degree F. oven. After 30 minutes, baste the chicken with the pan drippings. Continue to roast for an additional 30 minutes or until the chicken is tender. Baste once or twice during the second half of the roasting period. Serves 3 or 4.

Marinated Glazed Chicken

    This is a simple and delicious yet inexpensive company dinner. The onion soup mix adds a zesty flavor to the marinade, and the basting sauce gives the chicken a rosy brown hue. A green salad and farfel complement the dish.

    1 bottle (8 ounces) Russian dressing
    1 package (2 ounces) dry onion soup mix
    1 jar (10 ounces) apricot preserves or 1 jar   ⟶

(10 ounces) orange marmalade
2 frying chickens (2 to 2½ pounds),
quartered

In a small bowl, thoroughly blend the Russian dressing, onion soup mix, and the preserves. Arrange the chicken in a single layer in a shallow baking pan, skin side up. Pour the dressing over the chicken and marinate overnight. Bake uncovered in a 350-degree F. oven for 1½ hours, basting every half hour. May be frozen and reheated. Serves 4 to 6.

Almond Chicken

Chicken:

1 frying chicken (3 to 3½ pounds)
1 egg, slightly beaten
1 tablespoon water
¾ cup matzo meal
2 teaspoons salt
⅛ teaspoon black pepper
¼ teaspoon ground ginger
¼ cup fat

Ginger-Date Sauce:

1 cup water
1 tablespoon potato starch
½ cup white wine
½ teaspoon grated lemon rind
1 teaspoon salt
⅛ teaspoon ginger
½ cup toasted slivered almonds
¼ cup chopped fresh dates

Disjoint the chicken. In a shallow bowl, beat the egg with the water. Combine the matzo meal, salt, pepper, and ginger in a shallow dish. Dip the chicken pieces into the egg mixture, then roll in the matzo meal to coat. Set aside for 10 to 15 minutes to allow the coating to set.

In a large skillet, fry the chicken in the hot fat until golden. Turn the heat down, cover the skillet, and cook for 40 to 45 minutes, until tender. Remove the chicken to a hot serving platter. Serve with the Ginger-Date Sauce.

To prepare the Ginger-Date Sauce, remove the excess fat from the skillet in which the chicken was fried. Combine the water and potato starch; stir into the skillet. Cook until thickened. Add the wine, lemon rind, salt, ginger, almonds, and dates. Simmer 5 minutes more to blend the flavors. Serve hot. Serves 4 to 6.

Pineapple-Coffee Chicken

An exotic blend of flavors makes these tender chicken quarters especially appetizing.

> 2 frying chickens, quartered
> 1 can (8¼ ounces) crushed pineapple
> 2 cups ketchup
> ¼ cup well-packed brown sugar
> 2 cloves garlic, crushed, or ½ teaspoon
>   garlic powder
> ½ teaspoon ground ginger
> 1 teaspoon salt
> ½ cup strong coffee

Arrange the chicken in a shallow baking pan. In a large bowl, prepare the marinade by blending the ingredients. Pour over the chicken. Cover the pan and refrigerate overnight. Turn the chicken several times during the marinating period. Bake in a 350-degree F. oven until tender, about 1 to 1½ hours. Baste frequently with the pan sauce. Serves 4 to 6.

Lemon Chicken

This is easy on the cook: only one skillet is used from start to finish. Serve with thick red tomato slices and hot fluffy seasoned mashed potatoes.

⅓ cup cake meal
1 teaspoon salt
1 teaspoon paprika
1 frying chicken (2½ to 3 pounds),
   disjointed
3 tablespoons lemon juice
3 tablespoons oil
1 chicken bouillon cube
¾ cup boiling water
¼ cup sliced green onion (optional)
2 tablespoons brown sugar
1½ teaspoons grated lemon rind
   Chopped parsley (optional)

In a paper or plastic bag, combine the cake meal, salt, and paprika. Brush the chicken with the lemon juice. Add 2 to 3 pieces of chicken to the bag and shake well; repeat until all the chicken is coated. In a large skillet, brown the chicken in hot oil.

Dissolve the bouillon cube in the boiling water; carefully pour it over the chicken. Stir in the onion, brown sugar, lemon rind, and any remaining lemon juice. Cover the skillet and reduce the heat. Cook the chicken over low heat until tender, 40 to 45 minutes. Taste and adjust the seasoning. Remove the chicken to a hot serving plate. Sprinkle with chopped parsley if desired. Serves 4.

Stuffed Boneless Hen

A splendid gourmet party dish, this golden brown hen should be brought to the table whole. Slice it before the admiring eyes of your guests, and serve with a spoonful of gravy over each portion.

1 Cornish hen (2 pounds) with gizzard
1 egg
¼ cup water
½ teaspoon salt
⅛ teaspoon white pepper
½ cup matzo meal

→

1 to 2 tablespoons oil or chicken fat
1 teaspoon paprika
Grease for the pan

Place the hen on a carving board, breast side down. Cut the skin from the neck to the tail. Carefully separate the skin from the hen in 1 piece, separating the wings and the drumsticks from the body at the joints but leaving them connected to the skin.

Remove all the meat from the carcass and pass the meat through a meat grinder. Finely dice the gizzard and add this to the ground chicken. Beat the egg with the water, salt, and pepper in a small mixing bowl. Add the egg-water mixture to the ground chicken. Stir in the matzo meal and mix well.

Spoon the mixture onto the inside of the hen skin and sew it together, reforming the shape of the chicken. "Darn" any holes in the skin. Place the chicken in a roasting pan. Pour boiling water over the hen; remove any pin feathers still adhering to the skin. Remove from the roasting pan and pat dry.

Massage the oil and paprika into the skin. Place the hen in a lightly greased 7 × 11-inch baking pan, sewn side down. Cover the pan with aluminum foil and roast in a preheated 350-degree F. oven for 1 hour and 15 minutes, until the hen is firm and golden. Serve hot, preferably with a gravy. Serves 4 to 6.

Variations:

• If the Cornish hen is not very meaty, ¼ to ½ cup of minced veal may be added to the prepared filling.
• One-quarter pound fresh mushrooms, sliced and sautéed in 2 tablespoons of melted chicken fat or oil until lightly browned, may be added to the chicken mixture.

Stuffed Drumsticks

An elegant party dish. Although the preparation is a little complicated, the finished dish is stunning.

6 large chicken drumsticks
1 cup dry white wine

→

   2 eggs
   ½ cup water
   2 tablespoons oil
      Salt to taste
      Freshly ground black pepper to taste
   1 small onion, grated
   1 cup matzo meal
   2 to 3 tablespoons margarine or oil
      Grease for the baking pan

In a shallow 7 × 11-inch pan, soak the drumsticks in the wine for 3 to 4 hours, turning occasionally. Drain off the wine and reserve. With a sharp knife, cut lengthwise along the inside of each drumstick. Carefully remove the bone and tendons. Take care to preserve the shape of the leg, keeping the meat in 1 piece.

In a medium-sized bowl, beat the eggs with the water, oil, salt, and pepper. Add the grated onion. Stir in the matzo meal. Let the filling rest for 5 to 10 minutes, to thicken.

Stuff each drumstick with the mixture and sew each to re-form the shape of the drumstick. Lightly brown the legs in a skillet with the margarine or oil over medium heat. Arrange the drumsticks in a lightly greased 7 × 11-inch baking pan. Pour the reserved wine into the baking pan. Cover tightly. Bake in a preheated 375-degree F. oven for 30 minutes. Uncover and continue baking for an additional 30 minutes, basting occasionally with the wine. Add additional wine as necessary for the basting. Excess filling may be shaped into balls and baked with the drumsticks. Serves 6.

Filling Variation:

   1 medium-sized onion, finely chopped
   2 tablespoons margarine or oil
   ½ pound chicken livers
   ½ teaspoon salt
      Dash of freshly ground black pepper
   1 cup blanched almonds, toasted and
      chopped, divided

In a small skillet, sauté the onions in the margarine or oil over medium heat until golden brown. Broil the chicken livers. Grind the chicken livers together with the sautéed onions. Add the salt, pepper, and ½ cup of the almonds.

Fill the drumsticks following the directions above, or sew up the drumsticks (after removing the bone and tendon), leaving a small opening on the top. Use a pastry bag to insert the filling into the drumstick cavity. Then sew up the opening. Bake as above. Serve the drumsticks hot, sprinkled with the remaining ½ cup of almonds.

Gedempte Chicken

(Chicken Stew)

This stew can be cooked in advance and reheated before serving.

> **1 frying chicken (3 pounds)**
> **1 teaspoon salt**
> **⅛ teaspoon white pepper**
> **¼ cup fat**
> **1 cup diced onions**
> **½ cup boiling water**
> **1 can (15½ ounces) tomato sauce with mushrooms**

Cut the chicken into serving pieces. Season the chicken with the salt and pepper. In a deep skillet, heat the fat over medium-high heat. Add the chicken pieces and brown lightly on all sides. Add the onions; continue to cook until the onions are tender but not brown. Add the water; cover and simmer for 10 minutes. Add the tomato sauce. Cover again and cook for 20 minutes or until the chicken is tender. Turn the chicken once during the last stage of the cooking. Serves 4 to 6.

Chicken à la King or Creole

This recipe is quite flexible: it may be prepared from a freshly cooked chicken or from leftover cooked chicken. Use the recipe to make chicken pies as well. Spoon the prepared chicken mixture into individual casseroles. The cooked carrots, sliced, are a welcome addition. Top each with seasoned mashed potatoes combined with a beaten egg. Bake in a 350-degree F. oven just long enough for a brown crust to form.

> 1 broiler chicken (approximately 3
>   pounds), cut up
> 1 whole onion
> 2 carrots, peeled
> 1 stalk celery
> 1 teaspoon salt
> 4 cups cold water
> 4 tablespoons chicken fat or oil, divided
> 2 tablespoons chopped onion
> 2 to 3 cups chicken stock or chicken broth
>   prepared from a bouillon cube
> 1½ tablespoons potato starch
> ¼ teaspoon salt
> ¼ teaspoon paprika
> ½ cup dry white wine (optional)
> 1 teaspoon lemon juice
> ¾ pound fresh mushrooms, sliced, or 8
>   ounces canned mushrooms, drained
> 2 tablespoons chopped green pepper (for
>   creole only)

A la King Method:

Place the chicken, whole onion, peeled carrots, celery stalk, and salt in a 2-quart saucepan. Cover with the cold water. Bring to a boil and remove the scum. Turn down the heat; simmer until the chicken is tender. Strain the broth into a 4-cup glass measure. Let the chicken cool until easy to handle. Slip the skin from the chicken. Remove the meat from the bones. Dice the chicken into bite-sized pieces. Set aside.

In a large skillet, melt 2 tablespoons of the chicken fat over moderate heat, or heat 2 tablespoons of oil. Add the onion and sauté until light brown.

Combine 2 cups of the cooled chicken stock with the potato

starch, salt, and paprika. Stir until completely blended. Pour the mixture into the skillet. Add the wine if desired. Cook until smooth and thick. Add the lemon juice. Remove from the heat.

In a separate skillet, sauté the sliced mushrooms in the remaining fat or oil until tender. Transfer the mushrooms to the sauce in the first skillet. Add the diced chicken; mix through and reheat. If the chicken-mushroom mixture is too thick, slowly add a little more of the chicken stock. Nice to serve in a large cream puff. Serves 6 to 8.

Creole Method:

Follow the same method as above, but add the chopped green peppers when sautéing the onions.

Barbecued Fried Chicken

⅓ cup cake meal
1 teaspoon salt
1 frying chicken (2½ to 3 pounds), cut up
3 to 4 tablespoons oil
1 cup catsup
½ cup water
½ cup chopped onion
1 small clove garlic, minced
1 teaspoon Zing flavor enhancer
¼ teaspoon black pepper
3 tablespoons lemon juice

In a paper or plastic bag, combine the cake meal and salt. Add the chicken pieces, a few at a time; shake to coat. In a large skillet, brown the chicken pieces in hot oil over medium-high heat.

In a small saucepan, combine the catsup, water, onion, garlic, flavor enhancer, and pepper; heat to boiling; reduce the heat and simmer uncovered for 20 minutes. Remove from the heat and add the lemon juice; mix well. When the chicken is browned, add the sauce to the chicken. Cover, and cook slowly for 35 to 40 minutes, until tender. Turn the chicken frequently during the cooking. Adjust the seasoning and serve. Serves 4.

Orange Braised Duck

When the occasion demands an extra-special poultry dish, serve this Orange Braised Duck. The glistening brown duck portions teamed with orange gravy results in a very lively dish.

Apricot preserves may be substituted for the orange marmalade. If desired, add ½ cup sauterne wine to the orange juice marinade and reduce the chicken broth by ½ cup.

> 2 large ducks, quartered
> 2 cups orange juice
> 1 teaspoon salt
> ¼ teaspoon white pepper
> 2 cups chicken broth
> 1 cup orange marmalade
> 2 to 3 tablespoons potato starch
> ¼ cup cold water

In a large mixing bowl, marinate the duck quarters in the orange juice in the refrigerator for about 12 hours, turning the quarters occasionally. Drain off the orange juice and reserve.

Prick the skin of the duck repeatedly with a fork to let the fat drain out during the roasting. Place the duck on a rack in a roasting pan. Roast in a preheated 400-degree F. oven. Drain the fat as it accumulates in the pan. When the duck is brown and most of the fat is cooked out, reduce the heat to 325 degrees F. Remove the rack from the roasting pan and place the duck in the bottom of the pan. Season the duck with the salt and pepper. Mix the reserved orange juice with the chicken broth. Pour over the duck. Cover well. Bake for 1½ hours or until tender. Remove the duck from the roaster and keep warm. Skim off and discard any fat in the gravy. Add the marmalade to the gravy and stir until dissolved. Pour the gravy into a saucepan.

Mix the potato starch with the cold water. Add to the gravy in the saucepan. Cook until thickened, stirring frequently. Pour the sauce over the duck and serve; or place the duck on a platter and serve the sauce in a gravy boat. Serves 4 to 8

Duck With Cherries

Consider preparing this dish for guests. It is impressive, delicious, and may prove to be a new eating experience for many.

> 1 duckling (5 pounds)
> Salt
> Freshly ground black pepper
> Ground ginger
> 1 can (16 ounces) sweet cherries, drained,
>   syrup reserved
> ½ cup red wine, sweet or dry
> 1 tablespoon potato starch
> ¼ cup cold water

Sprinkle the duckling inside and out very lightly with salt, pepper, and ginger a day ahead of the actual cooking so that the seasonings have time to penetrate.

Put the duck in a roasting pan. Prick the skin of the duck with a fork to let the fat drain out during the roasting. Roast the duck in a very hot (450 degrees F.) oven for 15 minutes. Remove from the oven and pour off all the fat. Reduce the heat to 325 degrees F. and roast for 15 minutes, then drain off the accumulated fat once again. Continue to roast for 1 hour and 45 minutes.

Heat the reserved cherry syrup in a small saucepan. Baste the duck with a few teaspoons of the heated syrup every 15 minutes while the duck is in the final roasting period. Add the drained cherries to the wine. Place the cherries in the wine in a small saucepan and poach for about 3 minutes.

Remove the duckling to a hot serving platter; add the wine and cherries and any remaining syrup to the drippings in the roasting pan. Tip the pan back and forth so that the wine and cherries mingle with the juices in the pan. Blend the potato starch and water; add to the mixture in the roasting pan. Cook over medium heat, stirring until the mixture has thickened. Serve with the duckling. Serves 4.

South African Roast Turkey

This unusual roast turkey recipe originated in South Africa. The turkey is roasted in a savory liquid, and you'll note that the roasting method is not conventional.

> **1 turkey (12 to 14 pounds)**
> **2 whole carrots, peeled and cut lengthwise**
> **4 stalks celery**
> **2 cups tomato juice**
> **1 cup sherry**
> **1 teaspoon paprika**
> **2 teaspoons salt**
> **½ teaspoon freshly ground black pepper**
> **6 cups water**

Place the turkey in a large roasting pan. Stuff the turkey with the carrots and celery. In a large mixing bowl combine the remaining ingredients until thoroughly blended. Pour the mixture over the turkey in the roasting pan. Roast in a preheated 375-degree F. oven for 3 hours. Turn the turkey every half hour. The skin will be crisp but the meat moist. Serves 14 to 16.

STUFFINGS

Almost everyone has a favorite stuffing, but a new dressing can make a different treat of roast chicken, turkey, or duck. A poultry stuffing with subtle seasoning, unusual texture, and unexpectedly complementary flavor can contribute greatly to the finished dish. And besides adding flavor and interest, ofttimes the stuffing serves as an extender.

Stuffing expands during cooking, and room must be left for expansion. It is therefore advisable never to pack stuffing too tightly.

Almost any stuffing left over after filling a bird can be baked separately in a covered casserole. For a moister stuffing, add a little broth or water to the casserole before baking. Use a preheated 350-degree F. oven.

Basic Farfel Stuffing

The variations to this basic stuffing will add pleasurably to your stuffing repertoire.

> ¼ cup chopped onion
> 1 cup diced celery
> ¼ cup oil or shortening
> 4 cups matzo farfel
> ¼ cup chopped fresh parsley (optional)
> 1 egg
> 1 cup chicken broth or water
> 1 teaspoon salt
> ¼ teaspoon white pepper
> 1 teaspoon paprika

In a large skillet, sauté the onion and the celery in oil or shortening over low heat until tender. Add the farfel; stir until lightly browned. Add the parsley. In a small bowl, beat the egg with the chicken broth or water, salt, pepper, and paprika. Stir this into the farfel; continue to cook over low heat until the liquid is absorbed. Let cool before spooning into the bird. Do not pack the stuffing. Adequate for a large capon or small turkey.

Variations:

Mushroom: Sauté ½ cup sliced fresh mushrooms with the onions and celery. Add to the dressing.

Giblet: Cook the giblets in a saucepan with water to cover until tender. Mince the giblets and add to the dressing. Use the cooking water as the liquid in the stuffing.

Liver: Broil chicken livers. Dice them and add to the dressing.

Matzo Meal Dressing

> 1 small onion, diced
> 3 tablespoons oil or shmaltz (chicken fat)
> 3 eggs, separated

   ½ cup matzo meal
   ¾ cup water
   1 small carrot, peeled and grated
   1 teaspoon salt
     Dash of white pepper

In a small skillet, brown the diced onion in the oil or shmaltz over medium heat. Set aside.

In a small bowl, beat the egg yolks until light. In a separate large bowl, beat the egg whites until stiff. Whisk the egg yolks into the stiffly beaten egg whites. Fold into the matzo meal. Add the browned onion, any remaining fat in the skillet, the water, grated carrot, salt, and pepper to the egg mixture. Stir thoroughly and pour into the chicken cavity. Don't fill the chicken cavity completely with dressing, as it will expand during the roasting. Sew up all skin openings to seal in the dressing. Adequate for a 5-pound chicken.

Roulade Matzo Stuffing

   This stuffing may be used for any meat dish, such as veal birds, steak roulades, or stuffed chops. Spread the dressing on thin slices of veal or steak, roll up, skewer or fasten with toothpicks, then proceed with the recipe. Chops must be thick enough to enable a slit to be made down one side, into which the stuffing is inserted.

   4 matzos
   ¼ cup water
   2 eggs, well beaten
   1 teaspoon salt
   ¼ teaspoon white pepper
   ¼ teaspoon ginger
   1 tablespoon chopped fresh parsley
   2 tablespoons chopped onion

Crumble the matzos into a large bowl. Sprinkle with the water. Add the remaining ingredients and blend thoroughly. Adequate for 6 or more chops.

Savory Fruit Stuffing

½ cup minced onion
½ cup shortening or oil
7 cups matzo farfel
1 egg
2 cups water or chicken broth
1 teaspoon salt
¼ teaspoon white pepper
½ tablespoon paprika
1 jar (1 pound) stewed prunes, drained,
   pitted, and chopped
2 cups peeled and diced apples
½ cup raisins

In a large skillet over medium heat, sauté the onion in the oil
until tender. Add the farfel; stir until lightly browned. In a small
bowl, beat the egg with the chicken broth and the seasoning. Stir
the mixture into the farfel and continue to cook over low heat
until the liquid is absorbed. Remove from the heat. Stir in the
chopped prunes, apples, and raisins. Cool before spooning into
the bird. Do not pack the stuffing. Adequate for a 10 to 12-pound
turkey.

Mushroom Stuffing

½ pound fresh mushrooms, thinly sliced
1 medium-sized onion, grated
2 tablespoons fat
1 teaspoon salt
2 eggs, separated
⅜ cup water
⅜ cup matzo meal
   Dash of white pepper
1 tablespoon chopped fresh parsley

In a medium-sized skillet, sauté the mushrooms with the grated
onion in the fat over medium heat until tender; add the salt. Set
aside to cool.

In a small bowl, beat the egg whites until stiff. In a separate bowl, combine the egg yolks and water. Fold the yolk mixture into the stiffly beaten egg whites. Gradually fold in the matzo meal and pepper. Fold in the mushroom mixture and chopped parsley. Spoon into the bird. Adequate for a 5 to 6-pound capon.

Raw-Potato Stuffing

1 large onion, chopped
6 tablespoons melted margarine or oil, divided
5 large potatoes, peeled and coarsely shredded
3 to 4 tablespoons minced fresh parsley or minced celery tops
1 teaspoon salt
½ teaspoon paprika

In a small skillet over medium heat, sauté the chopped onion in 2 tablespoons of melted margarine or oil until golden brown. Combine the onions with the potatoes, minced parsley or celery tops, and the seasonings in a large mixing bowl. Pour the remainder of the oil or margarine over the potato mixture; mix well. Spoon into the bird. Adequate for a 4 to 5-pound bird.

Shake-and-Bake Mix

A shake-and-bake mix seasoned to your own liking. Equally good for fish, chops, and chicken.

1 pound matzo meal (about 4 cups)
1 tablespoon salt
1 tablespoon paprika
1 teaspoon white pepper
½ cup oil

Optional Seasonings:
Garlic powder, onion powder, Zing flavor enhancer, sugar

Combine the matzo meal, salt, paprika, and pepper in a deep bowl. Stir in the oil and blend with a pastry blender or 2 forks until evenly distributed. Add additional seasonings to taste. Store in a tightly covered container. Yields about 4 cups.

To Use:

Measure out the mix into a plastic bag. Moisten pieces of chicken with a bit of water and shake them in the bag, a few pieces at a time. Arrange the chicken, skin side up, in a single layer on a nonstick baking pan. Bake in preheated 375-degree F. oven for about 45 minutes, until tender and brown. Or dip the chicken into an egg beaten with a little water (1 to 2 tablespoons), then into the coating mix, and proceed as above.

4

Meat Specialties

History suggests that meat was a staple in the diet of our ancestors. We know that in Temple days the lamb was roasted and offered as a sacrifice. Today, meat is considered a valuable source of high-quality protein so essential to our health.

Besides the many cuts of beef, lamb, mutton, and veal available, adventure and delicious eating can be found in the variety meats. Brains, tongue, liver, sweetbreads, etc., may be prepared in many delicious ways, and the preparation is relatively simple.

Use the recipes in this chapter to make your holiday fare refreshingly different.

Gourmet Brisket

An Italian court once ruled that wine is indispensable in cooking. In a marinade, wine not only adds richness to the meat, it helps tenderize it as well. Prepare this brisket and see if you do not agree that your roast is more tender and flavorful as a result of the overnight marinating.

>   3 pounds brisket
>   1 envelope (2 ounces) onion soup mix
>   1 clove garlic, quartered
>   ½ cup dry red wine
>   Salt and black pepper to taste

Place the brisket in a medium-sized roasting pan. In a medium-sized mixing bowl, prepare the marinade by thoroughly blending the onion soup mix, garlic, wine, salt, and pepper. Pour the marinade over the brisket. Refrigerate overnight, turning the meat occasionally.

To roast, cover the roasting pan tightly with aluminum foil and roast in a 375-degree F. oven until tender, approximately 2½ hours. Serves 6.

Brisket in a Blanket

You can serve this brisket with additional accompaniments. Place twelve to fourteen pitted prunes and two large peeled carrots in a saucepan; cover with boiling water and cook until tender. After placing the almost-cooked brisket in the center of the pudding, arrange the cooked prunes around the meat. Decorate the outer edge with sliced carrots. Lovely to look at, delicious to eat.

> 2 to 3 pounds brisket
> 4 cups cubed raw potatoes
>   Cold water
> 3 eggs
> 1 large onion, quartered
> 1½ teaspoons salt
> ¼ teaspoon white pepper
> ⅛ cup oil
> ⅓ cup potato starch
> 3 sprigs parsley, stems removed
>   Grease for the pan

Cook the brisket as you usually do until nearly done (or see Boiled Brisket of Beef recipe). Prepare the pudding as described below and pour it into a hot greased 3-quart baking pan or casserole. In the center of the pudding place the almost-cooked brisket. Bake in a preheated 350-degree F. oven for 45 minutes or until the pudding is nicely browned. Serves 6 to 8.

Potato Pudding:

To prepare this pudding, place the raw cubed potatoes, a few cubes at a time, into a blender container; add cold water to cover. Process at high speed just a few seconds until the potatoes are grated. Drain the potatoes well. Put them in a large bowl. Place the remaining ingredients in the blender container and process until the parsley is chopped. Combine the drained potatoes with the batter from the blender and mix thoroughly. Continue as above.

Boiled Brisket of Beef

"Boiled beef" is a misnomer for the favorite dish. If beef were to be boiled, the flavor and texture would be inferior. Actually, boiled brisket is simmered.

> 3 pounds brisket of beef
> 2 carrots, peeled and quartered
> 2 stalks celery
> 1 large onion, peeled and studded with 2
>   whole cloves
> 1 parsnip, peeled and quartered
> 1 celery root, peeled and quartered
> 1 bay leaf
> 1 sprig parsley
>   Salt and black pepper to taste
>   Cold water

Put the meat in a large pot. Add the carrots, celery, the large onion studded with the cloves, parsnip, celery root, bay leaf, parsley, and the salt and pepper to taste. Cover with cold water. Bring the water to a boil. After a few minutes of boiling, skim off the foam. Cover the pot; lower the heat. Simmer for 2½ hours or until the meat is fork-tender. When the meat is cooked, remove from the heat and carefully remove the beef from the soup stock.

To serve, slice the beef, and serve it hot or cold with horseradish or with the vegetables strained from the broth. (The brisket broth, if not used as gravy, may be served separately as a soup course, with a portion of the cooked vegetables diced into it.) Or slice the beef and cover with Onion Sauce. Serves 6 to 8.

Onion Sauce:
>   1 tablespoon margarine
>   1 medium-sized onion, chopped
>   2 tablespoons potato starch
>   1¼ cups brisket stock, cooled

Heat the margarine in a small pan over low heat; add the chopped onion and sauté until golden brown. Dissolve the potato starch in the cooled brisket stock; add to the onions; stir well. Simmer gently for 15 to 20 minutes, until thickened, stirring occasionally.

Beef à la Stroganoff

>   2 tablespoons shortening or margarine
>   3 large onions, minced
>   1 pound mushrooms, sliced
>   1½ to 2 pounds shoulder steak
>   1 cup fresh beef or chicken stock, or
>   broth made with 1 bouillon cube
>   2 tablespoons ketchup
>   Salt and pepper to taste
>   1 tablespoon potato starch
>   2 to 3 tablespoons cold water

Heat the fat in a large skillet. Add the minced onions and the sliced mushrooms. Sauté for 10 minutes over medium heat. Cut the steak into strips about 2 inches long and ½ inch wide. Add to the pan. Sauté for an additional 10 minutes. Add the stock, ketchup, and salt and pepper. Bring to a boil. Cover the pan and simmer until the meat is tender. Dissolve the potato starch in a small amount of cold water; add to the meat and continue to cook until thickened. Serve with riced potatoes. Serves 4 to 5.

Steak Roulade

Elegant enough to serve to company. Simple enough for a home-style meal. Your choice: steak or thin slices of veal. Both work equally well.

> **1 shoulder steak for each serving (or veal)**
> **1 recipe Roulade Matzo Stuffing (see Index)**
> **Grease for the pan**

Pound the steak thin. Spread some matzo stuffing over the steak and roll up. Tie each steak securely with thread in 2 or 3 places, or fasten with toothpicks. In a skillet, sear the meat rolls on all sides. Place in a greased roasting pan. Add ½ cup hot water to the pan and bake covered at 325 degrees F. for 1 hour. Add more water if necessary. Serve with tomato sauce.

Spicy "Spareribs"

> **3 pounds lean short ribs**
> **Salt and black pepper to taste**
> **1 can (10½ ounces) tomato sauce**
> **3 tablespoons cider or wine vinegar**
> **1 small onion, finely chopped**
> **1 stalk celery, finely chopped**
> **1 clove garlic, mashed, or a dash of garlic powder**
> **2 tablespoons brown sugar**

Place the short ribs seasoned with salt and pepper in a shallow roasting pan. Bake uncovered in a 350-degree F. oven for 1 hour. Remove from the oven and drain off the fat. In a small bowl, thoroughly blend the tomato sauce with the remaining ingredients; pour the mixture over the ribs. Return to the oven and bake for 30 to 45 minutes, basting occasionally. Serves 4 to 5.

Veal Ragout

Veal was very popular in Europe, primarily because farmers found it economically wise to dispose of their calves while still young, thus sparing themselves the expense of feeding the animals until maturity. Ironically, veal is now a comparatively expensive meat, yet because of its relatively low cholesterol and calorie content, its popularity is on the rise.

There are many ways to prepare veal. One of these is as a ragout, a seasoned stew of meat and vegetables.

> 2 pounds veal, cubed
> 2 tablespoons oil
> ½ teaspoon salt
> Black pepper to taste
> 1 tablespoon potato starch
> ½ cup consommé or water
> 2 cups stewed or canned tomatoes
> ½ cup sweet red wine
> 1 large onion, chopped

In a large skillet, brown the veal in the oil over medium-high heat. Sprinkle with salt and pepper. In a large mixing bowl, combine the potato starch, consommé, tomatoes, and wine; mix well. In the bottom of a medium-sized casserole place the chopped onions. Arrange the veal cubes on top of the onions; pour the sauce over the veal. Bake uncovered in a 375-degree F. oven for 1 hour, basting occasionally. Adjust the seasoning and serve. Serves 6.

Creole Veal Chops

Easy to make, even easier to eat, this veal dish is ever so tender and succulent.

> 6 large veal chops
> ½ cup matzo meal
> Oil
> 1 can (11 ounces) tomato sauce with
> mushrooms

———▶

½ cup minced onions
½ cup finely sliced celery
½ cup finely sliced green pepper
Oil for the skillet

Dredge the veal chops with the matzo meal. In a large skillet, brown the veal chops in a small amount of hot oil. Remove the chops to a large baking pan. In a medium-sized mixing bowl, combine the tomato sauce with the remaining vegetables; spoon this over the veal chops. Cover the pan and bake in a 350-degree F. oven for 1 hour or until tender. Serves 6.

Variation:

Substitute large shoulder lamb chops for the veal chops. Eliminate the preliminary browning of the chops. Bake in the tomato sauce that has been combined with the remaining vegetables.

Veal Scallopine

The most popular cut of veal is the tender escalope. Escalopes are thin slices of veal which are boneless, skinless, and gristle-free. The Germans call it *schnitzel*, the Italians *scallopine*.
A crisp mixed green salad is excellent with this dish.

3 tablespoons margarine
1½ pounds thin veal cutlets
½ pound fresh mushrooms, sliced
1 cup chicken bouillon prepared from a
dry soup mix or a bouillon cube
½ cup chopped onions
1 tablespoon chopped fresh parsley
1 large clove garlic, minced
½ teaspoon Zing flavor enhancer
Dash of freshly ground black pepper
½ teaspoon paprika
1 tablespoon potato starch
¼ cup water
2 tablespoons dry white wine

Melt the margarine in a large skillet over medium heat. Brown the veal and the mushrooms. Add the chicken bouillon, onion, parsley, garlic, flavor enhancer, and pepper. Cover and cook over low heat for 30 minutes or until the veal is tender. Stir occasionally. In a measuring cup, blend the paprika with the potato starch and the water. Gradually stir the mixture into the sauce in the skillet. Heat, stirring until thickened. Add the wine and cook 5 minutes longer. Serves 5.

Veal "Parmesan"

> 2 cups matzo meal
> Salt, white pepper, and paprika to taste
> 4 veal chops
> 2 eggs, well beaten
> 4 tablespoons oil
> ½ cup each of chopped onions, celery,
> green pepper, tomatoes, mushrooms
> ½ cup mayonnaise
> ¼ cup ketchup

Season the matzo meal with salt, pepper, and paprika and place on a large flat dish. Dip the veal chops into the matzo meal, then into the beaten eggs, and back again into the matzo meal. Set the coated veal chops onto a baking sheet to rest for ½ to 1 hour so that the coating can set.

In a large heavy skillet, heat the oil over medium-high heat. Add the veal chops and sauté until golden brown on both sides. Transfer the veal chops to a rectangular baking pan large enough to accommodate the chops.

In a medium-sized bowl, toss the chopped vegetables lightly. Divide into 4 equal parts and top each of the chops with the vegetables. In a small bowl, mix the mayonnaise with the ketchup until smooth. Spoon the dressing over the vegetable mixture. Bake in a moderate oven, 350 degrees F., until golden brown. Serves 4.

Variation:
Substitute eggplant slices for the veal chops and proceed as above.

Stuffed Breast of Veal

The meat stuffing in the breast of veal is a wonderful extender for the dish. You may substitute your favorite savory matzo stuffing.

½ to 1 pound ground veal or ground beef
1 egg, beaten
1 teaspoon salt
½ teaspoon freshly ground black pepper
2 tablespoons chopped fresh parsley
2 to 3 hard-cooked eggs
1 breast of veal with pocket for stuffing
4 tablespoons oil, divided
2 onions, sliced
1 clove garlic, quartered (optional)
Paprika

In a medium-sized mixing bowl, mix the ground veal or beef with the beaten egg; add the salt, pepper, and parsley. Place the stuffing on a piece of wax paper and divide it into 2 equal portions. Shape each half to fit the veal pocket. On half of the stuffing arrange the whole hard-cooked eggs, topping the eggs with the second half of the stuffing. Place the stuffing into the veal pocket and fasten the opening of the veal pocket with skewers.

Put 2 tablespoons of the oil in a roasting pan. Place the stuffed veal in the pan; arrange the sliced onions around the veal; add the clove of garlic. Brush the remaining oil on top of the veal breast. Sprinkle with paprika and roast in a 350-degree F. oven for 2½ to 3 hours, until the veal is brown and tender. Baste frequently. Slice carefully between the ribs before serving.

Note:

• The amount of ground veal or beef and the number of hard-cooked eggs needed depends on the size of the veal breast used.
• The number of servings this recipe yields depends on the size of the veal breast used. A 5-pound breast of veal, for example, will serve approximately 6 to 8.
• This breast of veal *cannot* be frozen because of the hard-cooked eggs in the filling.

Mock Gefilte Fish

These veal cakes look amazingly similar to gefilte fish cakes, hence the name. Garnished with a sliced carrot and served with horseradish, the difference is indistinguishable.

>   ¾ pound veal
>   2 onions, divided
>   1 egg
>   1 tablespoon matzo meal
>   Salt and white pepper to taste
>   1 carrot, peeled and sliced
>   3 potatoes, peeled and quartered
>   2 cups water

Grind the veal with 1 onion. Add the egg, matzo meal, salt, and pepper. Dice the second onion into a medium-sized pot; arrange the sliced carrots on top. Shape the veal into cakes and place them on top of the carrots. Add the quartered potatoes. Add the 2 cups of water and season with additional salt and white pepper. Bring to a boil. Reduce the heat and cook for 2 hours. Serve hot or cold. Serves 3 to 4.

Jellied Veal Loaf

This veal loaf is a modern-day version of p'tcha (calves'-foot jelly).

>   1 veal knuckle bone
>   1 pound veal shoulder
>   1 large onion, sliced
>   2 bay leaves
>   1 teaspoon salt
>   1 clove garlic, minced, or ½ teaspoon
>   garlic powder
>   2 stalks celery
>   Water
>   3 to 4 hard-cooked eggs, sliced

Have the butcher saw the veal knuckle bone into 3 or 4 pieces. In a 3-quart pot, simmer the bones, veal shoulder, sliced onion, bay leaves, salt, garlic, and celery in water to cover for about 2 hours. Remove the bones. Strain the broth and set aside.

Grind or chop the meat. Arrange slices of hard-cooked eggs in the bottom of a 2-quart mold. Add the chopped meat to the broth; taste and adjust the seasoning. Pour the broth over the sliced eggs and chill. When ready to serve, unmold onto a platter. Serves 6.

Hamburger Popovers

Popover:

> **2 eggs**
> **2 teaspoons oil**
> **⅔ cup water**
> **½ teaspoon salt**
> **⅛ teaspoon white pepper**
> **½ cup cake meal**

Hamburger:

> **½ pound ground beef or veal**
> **1 egg**
> **1 tablespoon matzo meal**
> **1 tablespoon finely chopped onion or ⅛ teaspoon onion powder**
> **Oil for the muffin cups**

In a medium-sized mixing bowl, prepare the popover batter by beating the eggs with the oil, water, and seasonings. Stir in the cake meal. Blend well. Let rest for 30 to 45 minutes.

Thoroughly blend the hamburger ingredients in a small bowl. Shape the mixture into 12 balls; set them aside on a dish.

Grease and heat twelve 2½-inch muffin cups. Pour the batter into the heated cups. Put a meatball in each muffin cup. Bake in a preheated 450-degree F. oven for 35 minutes. Serves 3 to 4.

Yorkshire Meat Pie

>**2 eggs**
>**2 teaspoons oil**
>**⅔ cup water**
>**½ teaspoon salt**
>**½ cup cake meal**
>**1 small onion, thinly sliced**
>**¼ pound mushrooms, thinly sliced, or 1 can (4 ounces) sliced mushrooms, drained**
>**2 tablespoons margarine, divided**
>**1 pound ground beef (veal may be substituted)**
>**1 cup leftover diced cooked vegetables**
>**¼ teaspoon salt**
>**⅛ teaspoon black pepper**

Beat the eggs with the oil, water, and salt in a medium-sized bowl until well blended. Stir in the cake meal. Beat until the batter is smooth. Let rest while preparing the meat filling.

Sauté the onion and mushrooms in 1 tablespoon of margarine in a large skillet over medium heat until tender. Add the meat; cook until browned, breaking up the meat with a fork as it cooks. Remove from the heat. Stir in the vegetables; season with the salt and pepper. Blend well.

Melt the remaining tablespoon of margarine in a 10-inch quiche pan or pie plate set into a preheated 425-degree F. oven. Pour the prepared batter into the hot dish. Spoon the meat-vegetable filling evenly over the batter to within 1 inch of the edge. Bake for 30 minutes or until brown and puffy. Serve in wedges with a mushroom sauce. Makes 4 generous servings.

Note: If no leftover vegetables are on hand, precook 1 cup of fresh vegetables (diced carrots, diced celery, broccoli cuts, etc.) until tender. Drain well.

Sweet-Sour Meatballs

Meatballs:
> 1 pound ground beef
> ½ cup water
> ½ cup matzo meal
> 1 medium-sized onion, grated
> 1 egg
> 1 teaspoon salt
> ⅛ teaspoon freshly ground black pepper

Sauce:
> ½ cup sugar
> 2 cups boiling water
> ½ teaspoon salt
> ⅛ teaspoon white pepper
> 1 cup peeled and sliced tomatoes or 1 cup
>   canned tomatoes
> 1 tablespoon chopped green pepper
> 1 onion, chopped
> 1 teaspoon citric acid

Mix the ground meat, water, matzo meal, grated onion, egg, salt, and pepper in a medium-sized mixing bowl. Form the mixture into balls about 2 inches in diameter. Set aside.

To prepare the sauce, in a medium-sized saucepan melt the sugar over low heat until the sugar turns light brown. Very carefully pour in the boiling water. Add the remaining ingredients and bring to a boil. Add the meatballs and bring to a boil once again. Reduce the heat, cover, and simmer for about 1½ hours. Taste and adjust the seasoning. Yields 8 to 10 meatballs.

Beef Pinwheels

A meat roll that will be remembered. Easy to prepare, delicious, and different. And you can vary the filling. Try all-potato or all-carrot.

> 1 pound ground beef
> Salt and black pepper to taste
> 1 egg
> 2 tablespoons melted fat
> 6 tablespoons matzo meal
> 2 tablespoons water
> 1½ cups seasoned mashed carrots
> 1½ cups seasoned mashed potatoes
> Grease for the baking sheet

In a medium-sized mixing bowl, combine all ingredients except the potatoes and the carrots. Place the meat between 2 pieces of wax paper. Pat it into a rectangle about ½ inch thick. Remove the top sheet of wax paper; spread half of the crosswise surface with the mashed carrots and the other half with the potatoes. Roll the meat firmly, jelly roll fashion, starting with the end covered with the potatoes. Transfer the roll, seam side down, onto a lightly greased baking sheet. Bake at 350 degrees F. for approximately 45 minutes. Slice and serve with a mushroom sauce. Serves 6.

Stuffed Baked Potatoes

This meal-in-itself combines a baked potato with the meat. A tossed salad makes an appropriate side dish.

Filling:

> 1 pound ground beef
> 2 tablespoons water
> 2 tablespoons matzo meal
> 1 tablespoon grated onion
> 1 egg, beaten
> 1 teaspoon salt
> ⅛ teaspoon white pepper

Potatoes:

> 6 Idaho potatoes
> 1 teaspoon salt
> ½ teaspoon white pepper
> Paprika
> ¼ cup oil
> 1 to 2 tablespoons hot water

In a bowl, combine the ground beef with the water, matzo meal, grated onion, egg, salt, and pepper. Mix well.

Peel the potatoes and ream them from end to end with an apple corer. Stuff the holes of the potatoes with portions of the ground meat mixture.

Mix the salt and pepper with the oil and brush this on the potatoes; sprinkle the filled potatoes with paprika. Arrange the potatoes in a shallow baking pan. Bake for 45 minutes to 1 hour at 360 degrees F. Baste the potatoes several times with the pan drippings or with the oil and 1 to 2 tablespoons of hot water. Serves 6.

Variations:

• Stuff each potato with a frankfurter or with your favorite salmon patty recipe. Bake as above.
• Do not peel the potatoes. Brush them with melted shortening. To serve, slice each potato into thick slices and serve with a pat of margarine.

Holishkes

(Stuffed Cabbage)

Holishkes is one of the many names by which stuffed cabbage is known. Other appellations for this dish are *praakes, holipce, galuptze, holubtsi,* and *gelubtsky*. The Sephardim replace the cabbage leaves with grape leaves and the dish is known as *dolmades*.

Holishkes is excellent prepared a day in advance. To reheat, skim off any fat that may have congealed on the surface; simmer slowly. Do not bring the cabbage rolls to a boil. Interestingly, holishkes is considered by many a traditional food for Sukkot, the Feast of Booths.

> ½ cup matzo farfel
> 1 cup tomato juice
> 1 pound ground beef
> 1 egg, beaten
> 1 onion, grated
> 1 carrot, peeled and grated
> 10 to 12 large cabbage leaves

⟶

¼ cup lemon juice
½ cup brown sugar
1¼ cups tomato sauce
½ cup raisins
Hot water

In a medium-sized bowl, soak the matzo farfel in the tomato juice until softened. Combine the ground meat and the beaten egg with the farfel. Add the grated onion and the grated carrot.

Blanch the cabbage leaves in boiling water until softened. Drain the water from the cabbage leaves. Place a tablespoonful of the meat mixture in the center of each cabbage leaf. Fold in the sides of the leaf to cover the meat; roll up.

Shred the remainder of the cabbage into a large heavy saucepan. Arrange the cabbage rolls over the shredded cabbage, seam side down. Combine the lemon juice, brown sugar, tomato sauce, and raisins in a 4-cup measure. Pour the mixture over the cabbage rolls. Add enough hot water to cover the rolls. Cook over moderate heat for 30 minutes; reduce the heat and simmer for an additional hour. Taste and adjust the seasoning. Baste occasionally. Serves 5 to 6.

Optional:
• After cooking for 1 hour, set the pot into a preheated 350-degree F. oven for ½ hour to brown on top. Turn to brown the underside as well.
• For a more robust gravy, place 2 large meat bones in the bottom of the heavy saucepan; then add the shredded cabbage and the stuffed cabbage rolls. Tuck thin wedges of a large peeled and cored apple between and around the cabbage rolls before pouring in the sauce and the hot water.

Stuffed Cabbage Crown

An unusual cabbage dish. A head of cabbage is stuffed with a savory filling. The entire stuffed cabbage is then steamed and is later served in wedges.

1 pound ground beef
¼ cup matzo meal
1 teaspoon salt
¼ teaspoon black pepper
1 egg, well beaten
1 cup tomato juice or water
2 tablespoons grated onion
1 cabbage (about 3 pounds)
2 tablespoons margarine
1 tablespoon potato starch
A few tablespoons of cold water
Salt and pepper to taste
Paprika

In a large mixing bowl, combine the beef, matzo meal, salt, pepper, and egg. Mix until very well blended. Gradually beat in the tomato juice or water, a small amount at a time, until the mixture is smooth and pastelike. Stir in the onion.

Trim off the outside leaves of the cabbage. Cut off a 1-inch-thick slice from the core end; set aside.

Remove the core from the cabbage and hollow out the cabbage, making a shell about ½ inch thick. Spoon the meat mixture into the shell; fit the cut slice of cabbage back into place; secure it with string.

Place the stuffed cabbage, core end down, into a large pot; pour in boiling water to cover about three-fourths of the cabbage. Cover and simmer for 1½ hours, until the cabbage is tender. With 2 large spoons, lift the cabbage from the water carefully and set aside; keep hot while preparing the gravy.

In a small saucepan, melt the margarine over low heat. Blend the 1 tablespoon of potato starch in a small amount of cold water, add 1½ cups of the liquid in which the cabbage was cooked and pour this mixture into the saucepan with the melted margarine. Cook, stirring constantly, until the gravy thickens. Cook 1 minute longer. Season to taste with salt and pepper; color with paprika.

Place the stuffed cabbage on a heated serving platter; remove the string. To serve, cut the cabbage into wedges. Spoon the gravy over all. Surround the wedges with coarsely chopped cooked cabbage.

To prepare coarsely chopped cabbage, while the stuffed head of cabbage is cooking, coarsely chop the cut-out pieces from the cabbage and cook separately in boiling water seasoned with salt and pepper until tender. Drain well. Serve with the stuffed cabbage. Yields 4 generous portions.

Shish Kebab

Shish kebab has its origin in the Middle East. Legend has it that Turkish soldiers cooked chunks of freshly killed lamb on their swords over a fire. *Shish* in Turkish means "skewer," and *kebab*, "roast meat." The Russian *shashlik* and *shish kebab* are one and the same, pieces of meat roasted on a skewer. However, shish kebab may be cooked in a casserole on top of the stove or in the oven.

Although lamb is the meat most often used for shish kebab, other meats, such as beef, are sometimes substituted. The marinade of oil, herbs, spices, and an acid such as vinegar or lemon juice makes less expensive cuts of meat tender, at the same time adding flavor.

> ½ cup medium-dry Concord wine
> ¼ teaspoon black pepper
> 1 large onion, finely minced
> ¼ cup oil
> 2 tablespoons cider vinegar
> 2 pounds boneless shoulder of lamb, cut
>   into 1¼-inch cubes
>   Thick tomato wedges
>   Small white onions, parboiled
>   Whole mushroom caps
> 1 green pepper, cut into ¼-inch squares

To prepare the marinade, mix the wine, pepper, minced onion, oil, and vinegar in a large mixing bowl. Place the lamb cubes in the marinade; refrigerate for several hours, preferably overnight. Using 10 or 12-inch skewers, arrange the meat and the vegetables alternately, starting and ending with meat. Broil slowly until the meat and vegetables are tender, turning periodically. Baste occasionally with leftover marinade. Serves 5 to 6.

Variation:
Serve over savory matzo farfel or mashed potatoes.

Stuffed Shoulder of Lamb

> 1 cup chicken broth or broth made with a
>   bouillon cube
> ¼ cup oil
> ¼ cup grated onion
> 1 tablespoon minced fresh parsley
> ⅛ teaspoon white pepper
> ½ teaspoon salt
> 3 cups matzo farfel or 5 whole matzos,
>   crushed
> 1 lamb shoulder, boned
>   Salt, pepper, and paprika

In a medium-sized bowl, combine the chicken broth with the oil, grated onion, parsley, pepper, and salt; blend well. Add the matzo farfel or crushed matzos; stir well. Let rest for 15 minutes to absorb the liquid.

Stuff the pocket of the lamb roast with the matzo mixture. Sew up the opening, or close with a skewer. Place in a roasting pan. Sprinkle with additional salt, pepper, and paprika. Roast at 325 degrees F. for 30 to 35 minutes per pound. Makes 3 servings per pound.

Crown Roast of Lamb

A party-perfect lamb roast filled with a delicious stuffing and elegantly served. This recipe works equally well with veal.

Note: In ordering lamb for your crown roast, allow 1 or 2 ribs per serving and ask that the ends of the rib bones be "frenched" (meat removed from the ends of the bones).

½ cup chicken fat or margarine
½ pound mushrooms, sliced
½ cup chopped onion
½ cup chopped celery
3 cups matzo meal
1 teaspoon salt
¼ teaspoon white pepper
1 crown roast of lamb

In a large skillet, melt the chicken fat or margarine over medium heat; add the mushrooms, onions, and celery. Cook the vegetables until tender, stirring occasionally. Remove from the heat. Add the matzo meal, salt, and pepper; mix well. Place the lamb on a rack in a shallow roasting pan. Fill the center of the lamb crown with the mushroom mixture.

Cut a strip of foil 12 inches wide and long enough to enclose the roast with a slight overlap. Fold the foil lengthwise. Wrap tightly around the bone edge of the roast, folding over the bones to prevent charring. Or, wrap each rib end with aluminum foil to prevent charring.

Roast in a slow oven, 300 degrees F., allowing 30 or 35 minutes per pound, or until a meat thermometer inserted in the thickest part of the roast registers 170 to 180 degress F., depending upon the desired degree of doneness.

Serve the showy crown roast on a large heated platter. Garnish with pineapple-peach chutney-filled pear halves. Cover the rib ends with cherry tomatoes, cooked small white onions, roasted small white potatoes, or colorful paper frills.

Cut down between the ribs, dividing the roast into chops. Serve each person 1 or 2 chops plus a hearty spoonful of the stuffing. Serves 6 to 8.

Variations:
• If a dressing isn't used, place the roast upside down in the roasting pan. The fat from the roast will baste the rib ends, so

they need not be covered. To serve, fill the center of the crown with seasoned fluffy mashed potatoes sprinkled with paprika and garnished with tiny carrots.

• If desired, place small peeled potatoes in the roasting pan before placing the pan in the oven. Roast them with the meat; baste frequently. The roasted potatoes substitute for the mashed potatoes.

Stuffed Chops

>4 thick (1 inch) lamb or veal chops
>Salt and white pepper to taste
>2 tablespoons fat
>½ cup minced onion
>½ cup minced celery
>8 large prunes, pitted and chopped
>¼ cup matzo meal
>1 tablespoon lemon juice
>Grease for the baking pan

Rub the surface of the chops lightly with salt and pepper. Cut a pocket in the side of each chop. Set aside on a dish. Melt the fat in a skillet over medium heat. Sauté the onion and celery in the fat until the vegetables are tender. Remove from the heat. Stir the chopped prunes, matzo meal, and lemon juice into the vegetables. Blend thoroughly. Divide the filling and stuff the pocket of each of the 4 chops. Fasten the chops with toothpicks or small skewers so the filling doesn't run out.

Transfer the chops to a very lightly greased shallow baking pan. Bake in a preheated 375-degree F. oven for 45 minutes to 1 hour, until the chops are nicely browned. Serves 4.

Liver Pie

>2 onions, diced
>3 tablespoons oil
>¼ pound liver, broiled
>6 medium-sized potatoes

➡

    3 eggs
    Salt and freshly ground black
    pepper to taste
    Grease for the pie plate

Sauté the onions in hot oil in a medium-sized skillet over medium heat until golden. Grind the onions with the broiled liver.

Peel and boil the potatoes until tender. In a bowl, mash the potatoes very fine. Blend well with the eggs and the salt and pepper. Spread half of the potato mixture into a greased 8-inch or 9-inch pie plate. Cover with the liver mixture. Top the liver with the remainder of the potato mixture. Score the top with a fork to make a design. Bake at 350 degrees F. for 20 to 30 minutes. Serve hot with a gravy liberally laced with sautéed sliced mushrooms. Serves 4.

Chopped Liver and Potato Patties

    ¾ pound liver
    4 medium-sized potatoes, peeled and
    quartered
    1 small onion
    1 egg, well beaten
    Salt and black pepper to taste
    ¼ cup matzo meal
    Oil for frying

Broil the liver, then grind it. In a food processor or blender, finely chop the peeled and quartered potatoes together with the onion. Add to the ground liver. Stir in the beaten egg, salt and pepper, and matzo meal.

In a large skillet, heat the oil over medium-high heat. Drop the liver mixture by rounded tablespoonfuls into the hot oil. Fry over medium heat until the patties are browned on both sides and the potatoes are cooked through, about 3 minutes on each side. Yields 4 to 6 servings.

Stuffed Miltz

Variety meats, which are any of the edible animal organs, such as the liver, kidneys, heart, etc., are an excellent source of vitamins and minerals. They are also very tasty.

Here, the distinctive flavor and texture of miltz (spleen) is enhanced by your favorite stuffing.

> 1 beef miltz
> 1 clove garlic or ⅛ teaspoon garlic powder
> 4 onions
> ½ teaspoon salt
> 2 tablespoons shortening
> Your favorite stuffing (1 to 2 cups, depending on the size of the miltz pocket)
> Boiling water (optional)

Have the butcher cut a pocket in the miltz. Trim away the fat and any loose skin. Mince the garlic; slice the onions; combine with the salt and shortening. Place the mixture in the bottom of a roasting pan. Prepare your favorite stuffing and fill the miltz with it. Fasten the opening with skewers or toothpicks. Place the miltz on the bed of onions. Prick the miltz in several places with a fork. Roast in a 350-degree F. oven for about 50 minutes, until firm and brown. Baste occasionally, adding a little boiling water if necessary. Serves 4.

Brains in Tomato Sauce

For psychological reasons, brains are not everyone's dish. But those who enjoy sweetbreads (the thymus gland), a most delectable variety meat, brains are an excellent, less expensive substitute. They resemble sweetbreads in flavor and texture and can be used interchangeably.

> 2 cups cooked brains
> 2 tablespoons margarine
> 2 tablespoons chopped onion

———————➤

> 2 cups cooked tomatoes or 1 can (16
> ounces) tomatoes
> ½ cup chopped celery
> ½ tablespoon potato starch
> 1 to 2 tablespoons cold water
> Salt and freshly ground black pepper to
> taste

To prepare the cooked brains, soak them in cold salted water (1 tablespoon per quart of water) for ½ hour. Drain. Carefully remove the skin and membranes. Cut away the opaque white bits at the base of the brain, or remove the membranes after blanching the brains.

Place the brains in a saucepan of gently boiling acidulated water (1 tablespoon lemon juice and 1 teaspoon salt per quart of water) to cover. Reduce the heat and simmer for 20 minutes. Drain well. Cover with cold water to cool. Drain thoroughly. Set aside.

Melt the margarine in a large skillet over medium heat. Add the onions and sauté until brown. Add the tomatoes and celery. Cover and simmer for 20 minutes. Dissolve the potato starch in the cold water. Add to the skillet along with the salt and pepper. Stir until thickened. Cut the brains into serving pieces and add to the sauce. Simmer until heated through. Serve on a mound of matzo farfel. Serves 4.

"Creamed" Sweetbreads

The minced fresh parsley can be used as an ingredient in the preparation, or it can be used to garnish each portion before serving.

> 4 pairs cooked calves' sweetbreads
> (thymus gland)
> 4 tablespoons chicken fat or margarine,
> divided
> 1 cup diced onion
> 1 pound mushrooms, sliced
> 2 tablespoons potato starch
> 1 teaspoon salt

→

¼ teaspoon white pepper
½ teaspoon paprika
3 tablespoons minced fresh parsley

Wash the sweetbreads and prepare them in the same manner as the brains. However, reserve 2 cups of the stock in which the sweetbreads are cooked. Remove the membrane and dice the sweetbreads. Set aside in a bowl.

Melt 2 tablespoons of the chicken fat or margarine in a large skillet over medium heat. Brown the onions in the skillet. With a slotted spoon, remove the onions and reserve in the same bowl with the sweetbreads. Melt the remaining chicken fat or margarine in the skillet. Cook the mushrooms in the melted fat for 5 minutes. Mix the potato starch with the reserved stock until smooth; stir into the mushrooms. Cook over low heat for 5 minutes, stirring constantly. Add the browned onions, prepared sweetbreads, salt, pepper, paprika, and parsley; heat thoroughly, stirring gently. Adjust the seasoning to taste. Serve hot over cooked farfel, in a croustade, or in large puff shells. Serves 8 to 10 as an appetizer.

Tongue en Casserole

20 slices (¼ inch thick) cooked tongue
2 tablespoons margarine or oil
2 tablespoons diced green pepper
½ cup diced celery
½ cup sliced onion
1 tablespoon potato starch
1 cup tomato juice
Salt and black pepper to taste

Arrange the tongue in a 1-quart casserole. In a medium-sized skillet, heat the margarine or oil over medium heat. Add the green peper, celery, and the onion. Sauté for about 5 minutes, stirring occasionally. In a small bowl, blend the potato starch with the tomato juice, salt, and pepper. Add to the skillet. Simmer over medium heat for 5 minutes. Pour the sauce over the tongue. Bake in a moderate oven, 350 degrees F., for 1 hour Serves 4 to 5.

Tongue With Sweet-Sour Sauce

4 pounds tongue
1 large onion, sliced
2 bay leaves
Cold water
½ cup chopped onions
3 tablespoons oil
¼ cup potato starch
½ cup honey
½ cup raisins
½ teaspoon salt
½ teaspoon ginger
1 lemon, sliced

In a large pot, place the tongue, sliced onion, and the bay leaves. Cover with cold water. Bring to a boil. Cover and simmer for 2 to 3 hours, until tender. Remove the pot from the heat. Cool the tongue in the stock, then drain and reserve 2 cups of stock for the sauce. Peel and slice the tongue. Set aside on a platter.

In a small saucepan, sauté the chopped onions in the oil over medium heat until tender. Dissolve the potato starch in the cooled tongue stock and add to the onions, stirring to keep smooth. Add the honey, raisins, salt, and ginger. Continue cooking over medium heat until the sauce has come to a boil and thickened. Add the sliced lemon and continue cooking for 5 minutes. Serve the sauce over the sliced tongue. Serves 8 to 10.

Beef Tongue Polonaise

Tongue:

1 beef tongue, about 3 pounds
1 bay leaf
1 medium-sized onion, sliced
1 clove garlic
Boiling water

Sauce Polonaise:
> ½ **cup sugar**
> **3 tablespoons currant jelly**
> ¼ **cup orange juice**
> **2 tablespoons lemon juice**
> ½ **cup sliced blanched almonds**
> **Boiling water**
> ⅓ **cup raisins**

Place the tongue in a deep pot. Add the bay leaf, onion, garlic clove, and boiling water to cover. Simmer covered until the tongue is tender, about 3 hours. Remove from the water and cool for 15 minutes. Trim off the bone and the gristle. Using a sharp knife, slit the skin on the underside; loosen it around the thick end, grasp the skin firmly, and pull it off. Set aside while you prepare the sauce.

To prepare the sauce, in a small heavy skillet over moderate heat, melt the sugar until golden and syrupy. Stir constantly to prevent burning. Use a whisk to blend in the jelly and juices. In a small pan cook the almonds in boiling water to cover for 15 minutes. Thoroughly drain the almonds and combine with the raisins. Add to the caramel mixture. Simmer for about 15 minutes, until very hot, thick, and smooth. For a very thick sauce, mix 1½ teaspoons potato starch with 3 tablespoons water; stir this into the sauce. Cook over low heat until thick and clear.

Slice the tongue and arrange the slices in a heated casserole. Spoon sauce over and around the tongue. Serve hot. Serves 6 to 8.

Cholent

Cholent, a forerunner of our modern casserole, is said to have originated either in Italy or France.

The etymology of the word *cholent* is not clear. Some say it derives from the French word *chaleur* or *chaud*, meaning "hot"; others say it is from the German-Yiddish words *shule ende*, meaning "end of synagogue services." Indeed the preparation we today call "cholent" is a hot dish served as the first meal of the day on Saturday following the "end of synagogue services."

There are several varieties of cholent. Some are made with meat and can serve as a meal-in-one; others are meatless and are served as a side dish.

It is partly the manner in which cholent is cooked that makes it a delectable dish. During the cooking, a delightful aroma permeates the house, making all present anxious to partake in the meal at which it will be featured.

> 1 to 2 onions, sliced
> 1 pound chuck
>   Salt and black pepper to taste
> 5 large potatoes, peeled
>   Boiling water

Knaidel:

> 2 eggs, well beaten
> 2 tablespoons oil
> 2 tablespoons broth or water
> 1 teaspoon salt
>   Dash of black pepper
> ½ cup matzo meal

Place the sliced onion in a large heavy pot. Season the meat with salt and pepper and place it on top of the onions. Arrange the peeled potatoes around the meat.

To prepare the knaidel, combine the beaten eggs, oil, broth or water, salt, and pepper in a medium-sized bowl; mix well. Add the matzo meal. Let rest until firm enough to form a ball. The mixture may be refrigerated. Place the knaidel in the meat pot, on the side. Add boiling water to cover the contents of the pot. Bring to a boil, cover tightly, and set into a 225 to 250-degree F. oven overnight; or set it on a *blech* (a metal sheet or asbestos pad that is set over the stove burner during the Sabbath). Use low heat, and let the cholent cook overnight. Serves 5 to 6.

Variations:

• Sliced carrots and meat bones may be added to the meat in the pot. Season with salt, pepper, garlic powder, and paprika. The knaidel may be omitted.

• Make a vegetable knaidel:

1 large carrot, peeled
1 large potato, peeled
1 small onion
¼ to ½ cup oil
¾ cup potato starch
  Salt and white pepper
  Water

Grate the vegetables into a medium-sized bowl. Combine with the oil and potato starch. Season to taste with the salt and pepper. Add enough water to form a dough. Form the dough into a roll. Wrap the roll in aluminum foil and place it in the pot of cooking cholent.

Potato Cholent

2 to 2½ pounds short ribs, plate, or
  brisket of beef
2 medium-sized onions, sliced
6 medium-sized potatoes, peeled and
  quarterd
¾ to 1 cup matzo farfel
1 tablespoon salt
¼ teaspoon freshly ground black pepper
  Boiling water

Cut the meat into serving-size pieces. In a large Dutch oven, arrange a few of the onion slices, some of the potatoes, and a portion of the matzo farfel. Season with some of the salt and pepper. Top with several pieces of meat. Continue layering the ingredients until all are used up. Carefully add boiling water to cover. Bring to a boil; remove any scum that may rise to the surface. Cover tightly and let cook overnight over low heat on a *blech* (a metal sheet or asbestos pad) placed on the stove. Or cook in a 225 to 250-degree F. oven overnight. It is the very slow simmering that gives this dish its mouth-watering succulence. Serves 4 to 6.

5

Fish Specialties

It has often been said that fish nourishes the brain. Be that as it may, we do know that fish is a primary source of protein and essential vitamins and minerals.

A few hints on preparing fish: Fish should never be boiled; it should be poached, that is, cooked gently in seasoned water or fish stock. When cooking fish (gefilte fish, for example) in a fish stock, prepare the stock according to recipe directions. Bring the stock to a boil and let boil for 10 to 15 minutes. Turn the heat down, carefully add the prepared fish, and simmer until done.

Gefilte Fish I

Gefilte literally means "stuffed" or "filled." Originally, "gefilte fish" referred only to a chopped fish mixture encased in a fish skin. Today, however, what we call "gefilte fish" is merely a chopped or ground fish mixture formed into patties or a loaf.

> 1½ pounds whitefish, filleted
> 1½ pounds yellow pike, filleted
> Fish leavings from the whitefish and
>   pike purchased for the recipe
> 3 medium-sized onions, divided
> 3 teaspoons salt, divided
> ½ teaspoon white pepper, divided

⟶

2 teaspoons sugar, divided (optional)
5½ cups water, divided
3 eggs, slightly beaten
1½ tablespoons potato starch
1 carrot

Make a fish stock using the fish heads, bones, and skins: Slice 2 onions into a deep 3-quart saucepan; arrange the leavings on the onions; add 1½ teaspoons salt, ¼ teaspoon pepper, 1 teaspoon sugar, and 5 cups water. Bring to a boil.

Prepare the fish patties by grinding the fish fillets together with the remaining onion. Transfer the grindings to a wooden chopping bowl. Add the remaining ½ cup of water, the eggs, ¼ teaspoon of pepper, 1½ teaspoons of salt, the potato starch, and 1 teaspoon of sugar. Chop all the ingredients very well until a smooth pastelike mixture is formed.

Wet the hands with cold water and form the fish mixture into 12 patties the size of golf balls; drop individually into the boiling stock. Add the carrot. Reduce the heat and simmer for 2 hours in a partially covered saucepan. Cool slightly. Remove the fish balls and carrot to a platter. Mash the solids in the stock and strain the stock over the fish. Chill in the refrigerator. Garnish the fish with sliced carrot and serve with fresh horseradish. Serves 12 as an appetizer; 4 as a main course.

Gefilte Fish II

In this recipe reserved strips of fish skin may be wrapped around a few of the fish patties before poaching. This will add variety to the fish platter.

1½ pounds whitefish
1½ pounds pike
1 tablespoon coarse salt
3 medium-sized onions, divided
2 medium-sized carrots
1 quart cold water

8 almonds
⅓ cup cold water
2 eggs
1 teaspoon salt
¼ teaspoon white pepper
2 tablespoons matzo meal
Watercress or parsley for garnish

Clean and fillet the fish the day before cooking. Sprinkle with coarse salt. Refrigerate overnight. Retain the heads, skins, and all large bones.

Finely slice 2 of the onions into a 4-quart saucepan. Cut the carrots into round slices and add to the saucepan. Cover with the 1 quart of cold water. Add the fish leavings. Bring to a boil over high heat; reduce the heat and cook at a slow boil for about 10 minutes.

Prepare the fish forcemeat by washing off the fish fillets; drain well. Pass the fish through a meat grinder along with the remaining onion and the almonds. Place the mixture in a wooden chopping bowl. Add the ½ cup of water, eggs, salt, pepper, and matzo meal. Chop briefly, then mix thoroughly until the mixture is thick.

Wet the hands with cold water. Shape the fish mixture into patties about the size of cupcakes; gently place the patties into the boiling water. Cover the pot, and after the contents comes to a boil, reduce the heat to low and let simmer for 1 hour. Taste the broth for seasoning; additional salt or pepper may be desired. Continue to cook for an additional hour. Do not remove the cover from the pot for at least 1 hour after cooking.

When the pot has cooled, remove the patties carefully and arrange them attractively on a platter; place a slice of carrot atop each fish patty. Garnish with the remaining carrot slices and watercress or parsley. Strain the liquid into another bowl and serve warm, cold, or congealed, along with the fish patties. Serves 6 to 8.

"Padded" Gefilte Fish

The addition of the hard-cooked eggs and the baked potatoes adds body to the dish and extends the number of servings. Note that there is no matzo meal used here.

> 1 pound carp fillets
> 2 hard-cooked eggs
> 1 small onion
> 2 medium-sized potatoes, baked
> 2 raw eggs
>   Salt, black pepper, and sugar, to taste
> 1 large onion
> 2 stalks celery
> 3 to 4 carrots
>   Dash of paprika
>   Water

Mince the fish, hard-cooked eggs, and small onion in a medium-sized bowl. Transfer to a wooden chopping bowl. Remove the jackets from the potatoes; add to the fish. Add the raw eggs and salt and pepper to taste. Chop well to blend all the ingredients. Let the mixture rest until it thickens.

Slice the large onion, celery, and carrots into a 6-quart saucepan. Add salt, pepper, sugar, and a dash of paprika; fill the pot three-fourths full with water. Bring to a boil. Form the fish mixture into balls; carefully place them in the saucepan and bring to a boil. Turn the heat down and simmer for 45 minutes. Adjust the seasonings. Cool. Serve on a bed of lettuce garnished with the sliced carrots. Serves 4 to 6.

Baked Gefilte Fish

This gefilte fish is less time-consuming to prepare than the traditional version, which is simmered in a stock.

> 3 pounds pike and carp or pike and
>   whitefish
> ½ pound flounder fillets

$\longrightarrow$

> 1 large onion
> 1 large carrot
> 1 celery stalk
> 1½ teaspoons salt
> ½ teaspoon freshly ground black pepper
> ½ cup matzo meal
> 2 eggs, well beaten
> Grease for the pan

Fillet the pike and carp or pike and whitefish. Grind the fish fillets together with the onion, carrot, and celery. Transfer the ground fish to a wooden chopping bowl; chop by hand for a few minutes. Add the salt, pepper, matzo meal, and eggs. Mix thoroughly. Transfer the fish mixture to a greased 12-inch loaf pan, or form into 2 loaves and place in a greased 9 × 13-inch baking pan. Bake in a preheated 450-degree F. oven for 15 minutes; lower the heat to 325 degrees F. and bake 30 minutes longer. Serves 8 to 10.

Roast Gefilte Fish

This recipe is truly gefilte fish, as fish forcemeat is used as a filling between the skin and bone.

Fish:

> 5 pounds carp, sliced
> 1 pound whitefish fillets
> 2 onions
> 4 eggs
> ¼ cup cold water
> 2 teaspoons salt
> ¾ teaspoon black pepper
> ½ teaspoon sugar (optional)
> 3 tablespoons matzo meal

Stock:

> Fish heads and bones
> 1 stalk celery, sliced

→

   2 large carrots, sliced
   3 onions, sliced
   2 teaspoons salt
   ¾ teaspoon black pepper
   ½ teaspoon paprika
   2 quarts cold water

Fillet each slice of carp, leaving the bone and skin intact with a pocket to fill. Refrigerate the fish while preparing the stock and filling.

Place the stock ingredients in a large pot; cover with cold water (about 2 quarts). Bring to a boil over high heat. Reduce the heat and simmer while preparing the fish filling.

Grind the fish and onions with the fine blade of a food chopper. Turn the fish into a wooden chopping bowl. With a hand chopper gradually chop in the eggs, adding the water, salt, pepper, and sugar. Chop until the mixture is very light and soft; it should feel slightly sticky. Add additional water if necessary. Stir in the matzo meal and let stand for 15 minutes.

Wet the hands with cold water and fill the pocket in each slice of carp with the fish mixture. Carefully place slices of the fish into the cooking fish stock. If necessary, add additional water to cover the fish. Adjust the seasoning. Cover and cook at a very slow boil for 2 hours. The liquid should be reduced by half.

Carefully remove the slices of fish from the broth and place them on a large baking sheet. Roast in a preheated 400-degree F. oven until nicely browned. Let cool, then chill. Strain the broth to jell. Discard the skin and bones.

Serve the fish cold. Garnish with the sliced carrots and sliced onions from the broth, along with a serving of jellied broth. The number of servings depends upon the thickness of the slices of the fish purchased. Five pounds of carp will serve 8 to 10.

Note: If fish roe is available, add it to the fish stock to cook.

Variation:
Prepare the fish as above but eliminate the roasting. Simply cook the fish until done.

Gefilte Fish Mold

An attractive way to prepare a classic gefilte fish recipe. A real conversation piece.

>   3 pounds fish fillets (white, carp, pike),
>   reserve the trimmings
>   2 onions
>   3 eggs
>   Salt and black pepper to taste
>   ¼ cup cold water
>   Pinch of sugar
>   2 tablespoons matzo meal
>   1 teaspoon salt
>   Grease for the mold

Pass the fish fillets and onions through a grinder; repeat. Then chop the fish very fine in a wooden chopping bowl; add the eggs, salt, pepper, cold water, and pinch of sugar; continue to chop until well blended. Add the matzo meal; mix. Lightly grease a large fish mold and pour in the fish mixture. Place the fish mold in a large pan and pour boiling water around the mold, making sure the water does not cover the mold. Add 1 teaspoon of salt to the water. Cover the pot and steam for 3 hours. Add more hot water during the cooking if necessary. Cool and unmold the fish onto a large platter. Features of the fish can be made with vegetables: i.e., carrot circles for the eyes, a slice of green pepper for the mouth. Slice to serve. Serves 8 or more.

Note: The fish trimmings—heads, bones, and skin—can be cooked separately in a saucepan with diced onions, a stalk of celery, and 2 carrots to make a fish broth.

Baked Carp

When purchasing the carp, have the fishman split the underside of the fish from head to tail and remove the entrails and the fins.

>   1½ to 2 pounds carp
>   1½ teaspoons salt, divided

→

¼ cup matzo meal
3 tablespoons oil, divided
¼ cup lemon juice
2 tablespoons finely chopped fresh parsley
2 tablespoons sugar
¼ cup toasted slivered almonds

Thoroughly clean the inside of the whole fish. Wash the fish in cold water; pat dry. Sprinkle the cavity with ½ teaspoon of the salt. Season the matzo meal with the remaining salt. Coat the fish with the matzo meal mixture.

Brown the fish on both sides in 2 tablespoons of oil in a large skillet over medium heat. Transfer the fish to a baking pan large enough to accommodate the whole fish. Combine the remaining oil, lemon juice, parsley, and sugar in a large measuring cup. Pour the mixture over the carp. Sprinkle the fish with the slivered almonds. Cover the pan and bake in a preheated 350-degree F. oven for 30 minutes. Nice to serve with lemon shells stuffed with beet horseradish. Serves 3 to 4.

Knoble Carp

3 pounds carp, sliced
1 teaspoon onion powder
1 teaspoon garlic powder
1 tablespoon coarse salt
⅛ teaspoon black pepper
1 teaspoon paprika
4 large cloves garlic, sliced

Clean and wash the slices of carp. Mix together the onion powder, garlic powder, salt, pepper, and paprika. Rub the mixed seasonings onto each slice of fish. Layer the fish in a glass bowl, placing slices of garlic between the layers. Cover the bowl and refrigerate for a day or 2.

Remove the fish from the refrigerator; remove the slices of garlic from the fish. Place the fish slices on a greased broiler rack and broil for 10 to 12 minutes on each side, depending on the thickness of the fish slices. Serve cold.

Variation:

To bake rather than broil, place a small amount of oil (1 to 2 tablespoons) in a baking pan and heat it in the oven. Arrange the slices of fish in the pan and bake in a preheated 375-degree F. oven for 30 to 40 minutes, turning once. Drain the fish on paper towels. Serve cold. Serves 6 to 8.

Baked Knoble Carp

Team this dish with a fresh vegetable salad. Serve a fruit dessert and a beverage to make a well-rounded luncheon or dinner.

> 4 teaspoons garlic powder
> 4 teaspoons paprika
> Salt and black pepper to taste
> Oil
> 8 slices carp, thickness as desired. Each slice can weigh from ¼ to ½ pound or more.
> 2 to 3 onions
> 3 to 4 cloves garlic, sliced
> Hot water

Mix together the garlic powder, paprika, salt, and pepper. Add sufficient oil to form a paste. Rub the paste well into each slice of carp. Place in a bowl and refrigerate overnight.

Grease a 9 x 13-inch baking dish with a thin film of oil. Arrange the carp, sliced onions, and sliced garlic in the dish. Add enough hot water to prevent the fish from burning. Bake in a preheated 350-degree F. oven for 45 minutes. Add additional boiling water as necessary. Serve hot or cold. Serves 8.

Tuna-Nut Puffs

These puffs may be made with a teaspoonful of batter to yield many tiny puffs, which are ideal crunchy hot hors d'oeuvres. For an excellent luncheon dish, serve large puffs with a creamed mushroom sauce.

1 can (7 ounces) tuna fish, drained, liquid
   reserved
⅓ cup chopped toasted almonds
   Water added to reserved tuna liquid to
   make 1 cup
½ cup oil
1 teaspoon salt
1 tablespoon minced fresh parsley
   (optional)
1 very small onion, finely grated
⅛ teaspoon freshly ground black pepper
1 cup matzo meal
4 eggs
   Grease for the baking sheet

Finely chop the tuna in a wooden chopping bowl. Add the chopped almonds. Mix together and set aside.

Into a medium-sized saucepan, pour the cup of tuna liquid and water mixture; add the oil, salt, parsley, grated onion, and pepper. Bring to a boil. Add the cup of matzo meal all at once. Beat rapidly over low heat until the mixture leaves the sides of the pan and forms a smooth compact ball. Set aside to cool a bit.

Add the eggs, 1 at a time, beating hard with a spoon after each addition, until the mixture is shiny. Add the tuna fish mixture. Blend thoroughly.

Drop the mixture by the heaping tablespoonful onto a greased baking sheet. Do not crowd them; leave room for expansion.

Bake in a preheated 450-degree F. oven for 10 minutes. Turn the heat down to 350 degrees F. and continue baking for an additional 30 to 45 minutes, until brown. Serve hot. Yields 22 to 24 puffs.

Tuna-Stuffed Squash

6 medium-sized summer squash
1 medium-sized carrot
1 small onion

⟶

> 1 stalk celery, finely diced
> 1 can (7 ounces) tuna fish, drained
> 1 egg, well beaten
> 1 can (10½ ounces) tomato sauce
>   Water
> 1 tablespoon oil
> 1 tablespoon brown sugar

Wash and peel the squash. Cut off the necks and scoop out the insides of the squash with an apple corer. Line the bottom of a 9 × 13-inch baking pan with the squash necks and the scooped-out pulp. Grate the carrot and onion into a small bowl. Add the celery; add the drained tuna and beaten egg; chop all the ingredients together very well. Fill each squash with a portion of the tuna filling and arrange them in the baking pan.

Into a medium-sized bowl, pour the can of tomato sauce; add 1 can's worth of water, the oil, and the brown sugar. Pour the tomato sauce mixture over the squash. Cover and bake in a 350-degree F. oven for 30 minutes. Uncover, turn over the squash, and continue to bake uncovered for an additional 30 minutes. Serves 6 as an appetizer; 3 as a main dish.

Tuna-Stuffed Cabbage Rolls

> 8 to 10 cabbage leaves
> 1 can (7 ounces) tuna fish, drained and
>   chopped
> 2 carrots, divided
>   Dash of onion powder
> 1 egg, well beaten
> 1 medium-sized onion
> 1 stalk celery
> 1 ounce (⅛ cup tightly packed) raisins
> 1 can (10½ ounces) tomato sauce
>   Water
> 1 tablespoon brown sugar

In a small saucepan, cook the cabbage leaves in a small amount of boiling water until softened.

In a medium-sized mixing bowl, place the chopped tuna. Grate 1 of the carrots. Add the grated carrot, onion powder, and the beaten egg to the tuna.

Dice the onion. Slice the celery stalk and the remaining carrot. Arrange the vegetables in the bottom of a 2-quart saucepan. Chop 1 or 2 of the cabbage leaves; add this and half of the raisins to the saucepan.

Divide the tuna mixture among the remaining cabbage leaves, placing a portion in the center of each leaf. Roll up and tuck in the ends. Arrange the tuna rolls in the pan. Pour the can of tomato sauce and 1 can's worth of water over the rolls. Add the 1 tablespoon of brown sugar and the remaining raisins. Cover and bring to a boil. Turn the heat down to low and simmer for 1 hour. Taste and adjust the seasoning. Serves 8 to 10 as an appetizer; 4 to 5 as a main dish.

Note: Cabbage leaves can be easily removed from the cabbage if the head of cabbage is frozen, defrosted, and cored. To loosen the leaves even more, place the entire cored head of cabbage in hot water over low heat for 10 minutes. If this method is used, eliminate the cooking of the leaves until softened.

Tuna Fish Soufflé

Here, a small can of tuna fish is transformed into a delicious Passover fish soufflé.

>1 can (7 ounces) tuna fish, finely minced
>1 stalk celery, finely diced
>1 onion, diced, or ½ teaspoon onion powder
>2 to 3 tablespoons mayonnaise
>3 matzos
>8 slices American cheese
>4 eggs
>2½ cups milk
>Grease for the pan

In a medium-sized mixing bowl, prepare a tuna fish salad using the tuna fish, celery, onion or onion powder, and mayonnaise.

Grease a 9-inch square pan. Put a piece of matzo in the bottom of the pan; cover with 4 slices of the American cheese and half of the tuna fish mixture. Repeat: a layer of matzo, American cheese, and the remaining tuna fish mixture. Cover with the third piece of matzo. In a small bowl, beat the eggs with the milk; pour over the top matzo. Refrigerate overnight. Bake in a 325-degree F. oven for 45 to 50 minutes, until the custard is set. Remove from the oven and let set for 10 minutes before cutting. Serves 4 to 5.

Tuna Fish Quiche

Basically, a quiche is a pastry shell filled with a savory egg-and-cream custard to which numerous ingredients may be added, including fish and a variety of vegetables. This quiche is a treat for luncheon or supper.

> 1 quiche crust (see Gefilte Fish Quiche
> recipe below or consult the Index for
> Basic Pizza Dough)
> 2 eggs
> ½ cup milk
> ¾ cup mayonnaise
> 1 can (7 ounces) tuna fish, drained and
> chopped
> 1 small onion, chopped
> ½ pound Swiss cheese, grated, divided
> Matzo meal (optional)

Prepare the quiche shell and prebake until set, 20 to 25 minutes. In a medium-sized mixing bowl, beat the eggs, milk, and mayonnaise until well combined. Sitr in the chopped tuna fish, chopped onion, and all but one-fourth of the grated cheese. Pour the mixture into the prepared crust. Sprinkle the top with the remaining cheese and 1 to 2 tablespoons of matzo meal. Bake in a preheated 350-degree F. oven for 1 hour. Serves 4 to 6.

Variation:

> 3 eggs, beaten
> 1 cup sour cream

———▶

¼ cup onions sautéed in 2 tablespoons
   butter
1 cup grated Swiss cheese
1 can (7 ounces) tuna fish in water,
   undrained

In a large mixing bowl, thoroughly blend all the ingredients. Pour the mixture into the prepared crust. Bake in a 350-degree F. oven for 40 minutes or until golden.

Gefilte Fish Quiche

The crust recipe for this quiche can be used for other quiches as well.

Crust:

1¼ cups matzo meal
⅓ cup potato starch
⅔ cup soft margarine
3 tablespoons ice water, approximately

Filling:

2 jars (15½ ounces each) unsalted gefilte
   fish
1½ cups shredded American cheese
4 eggs, well beaten
1½ cups milk or light cream
1 teaspoon grated lemon rind
¼ teaspoon black pepper

To prepare the crust, combine the matzo meal with the potato starch in a medium-sized mixing bowl. Cut in the margarine with a pastry blender or 2 knives until the particles are very fine. Add ice water, 1 tablespoon at a time, until all the particles are moistened. Wrap the dough in wax paper and chill for about 1 hour. Roll out the dough between 2 sheets of wax paper large enough to fit the bottom and sides of an ungreased 11½-inch flat pan with straight sides (large layer pan). Remove the top sheet of wax paper. Press the pastry into the pan; trim the edges.

To prepare the filling, drain the fish and discard the broth. Cut the fish into small pieces and put the fish pieces through a food mill or sieve. Sprinkle the cheese evenly over the bottom of the pastry shell. Top with the mashed fish. Combine the remaining ingredients in a medium-sized mixing bowl. Blend well and pour over the fish. Bake in a 325-degree F. oven for 40 to 45 minutes, until set. Remove from the oven and let rest for 10 minutes before cutting into wedges. Serves 8 to 10.

Fish Loaf

3 tablespoons butter
¼ cup chopped onions
1 tablespoon potato starch
1½ cups tomato juice
1 tablespoon lemon juice
1½ cups cooked fish, flaked, variety of your choice
1½ cups matzo meal
2 eggs, slightly beaten
Oil and matzo meal for the pan

In a large skillet, melt the butter over low heat; sauté the onions for 5 minutes. Remove the pan from the heat. Dust the onions with the potato starch. Gradually add the tomato juice. Return the skillet to the heat and cook for a few minutes, stirring to avoid lumps. Add the lemon juice and cook a few minutes longer. Remove from the heat. Add the fish and matzo meal; mix well. Add the beaten eggs and blend well.

Generously oil and dust with matzo meal a 5 × 9-inch loaf pan. Pour the fish mixture into the pan and bake in a 350-degree F. oven for 35 to 40 minutes. Let stand for 5 minutes before unmolding and slicing. Serves 6.

Sweet-and-Sour Fish

In this unusual dish brook trout is combined with sweet and spicy ingredients. Carp, a plump, firm fish, also takes this kind of treatment well; it may be substituted for the trout.

2 medium-sized onions, sliced
3 cups water
1 teaspoon salt
3 to 3½ pounds brook trout, cut into 2-inch slices
5 tablespoons lemon juice
⅓ to ½ cup honey
⅓ cup raisins
½ teaspoon ground ginger
Lemon slices and parsley sprigs for garnish

Place the onions, water, and salt in a 4-quart saucepan. Bring to the boiling point over high heat; lower the heat and simmer for 15 minutes. Carefully add the fish slices to the saucepan; add the lemon juice, honey, raisins, and ginger. Simmer for 15 minutes or until the fish is tender. Adjust the seasoning, adding more salt and honey to taste. Do not overcook.

Remove the fish from the saucepan and arrange the slices on a large serving platter. Garnish with lemon slices and sprigs of fresh parsley. The fish is best served chilled. The liquid in which the fish was cooked may be boiled down and used as a sauce. Serves 6.

Baked Fish Roll-Ups

These tender fillets, pinwheeled with a spinach filling and baked with a slice of tomato, may be served with tomato sauce. If using a mushroom filling, serve the fish rolls with a mushroom gravy.

1 cup chopped cooked spinach, well drained
2 eggs, well beaten
½ cup matzo meal
Salt and white pepper to taste
8 flounder fillets
8 slices tomato
Butter or margarine

In a medium-sized mixing bowl, mix the spinach with the eggs, matzo meal, and seasoning. Divide the mixture over the fillets; roll up each fillet jelly roll fashion. If necessary, fasten with toothpicks. Place the fish fillets seam side down on a well-greased 9 × 13-inch baking dish. Place a slice of tomato on top of each fillet. Dot each roll with butter or margarine and bake for 30 minutes in a 325-degree F. oven. Serves 8.

Variation:

In place of spinach, sauté onions and sliced fresh mushrooms in margarine or butter until the onions are golden brown. Proceed as above.

Seafood Cocktail

Fish:

> 1 pound firm white-meat fish (haddock, halibut, or sole)
> 1 to 2 teaspoons salt
> 1 quart water
> Lettuce

Sauce:

> ½ cup ketchup
> 2 to 3 tablespoons horseradish (freshly grated if possible)

Cut the fish into chunks. In a 2-quart saucepan, poach the fish chunks in salted water until the fish flakes easily with a fork. Drain well and reserve.

To prepare the sauce, in a small bowl mix the ketchup with a small amount of horseradish. Add the horseradish a little at a time to arrive at the taste desired.

Line coupe or small sherbet glasses with lettuce. Arrange fish chunks around the sides and place a teaspoon of sauce in the center of each glass. Serves 4 to 5.

Sauce Variation:

Mix ½ cup red horseradish, well drained, with 2 to 3 table-spoons mayonnaise.

Sweet-Sour Borsht-Fish

An old favorite with a new flavor. This refreshing combination of fish and beet borsht can be made superbly with any white-meat fish.

Abby Belkin, wife of the late Dr. Samuel Belkin, president of Yeshiva University, shared this recipe with me. It was passed on to her by her grandmother.

Coarse salt
12 slices striped bass
2 medium-sized onions, sliced
2 small lemons, peeled and sliced
¾ teaspoon cinnamon
Scant ½ teaspoon ginger
1 teaspoon salt
¼ teaspoon white pepper
2 tablespoons sugar
1 jar (32 ounces) beet borsht
Water
1 egg, beaten

Salt the fish and refrigerate for several hours; rinse and drain. Line the bottom of a flat-bottomed 2½ to 3-quart saucepan with the onion and lemon slices; top with the sliced fish.

In a small bowl, combine the cinnamon, ginger, salt, pepper, and sugar. Sprinkle portions of the mixture over each slice of fish. Strain the jar of borsht. Combine the borsht with water in equal amounts to adequately cover the fish in the saucepan. Start with 1 cup of each and continue adding until the fish is covered. Cover the saucepan; bring to a boil over medium heat. Reduce the heat; simmer for 1 hour. Taste frequently and adjust the seasoning, adding additional sugar, salt and pepper as needed to suit the family palate.

Carefully lift the slices of fish with a wide slotted spatula; place in a shallow pan large enough to accommodate the fish slices arranged in a single layer. Strain the fish broth. Reserve ½ cup; pour the remainder back into the saucepan. Cool the reserved broth; gradually add to it the beaten egg. Beat well. Pour the combined mixture into the saucepan. Bring to a rapid boil over medium-high heat; boil for 1 minute. Pour the hot broth over the fish slices. Refrigerate. Serve cold. Serves 12.

6

Dairy Specialties

Passover dairy fare need not be served exclusively at breakfast or lunch. A well-planned dairy dinner can provide a welcome change from the usual, more filling meat meal.

Dairy foods are among the most protein-rich, and they harmonize perfectly with other protein foods such as fish and eggs. So, plan your meals to include some dairy specialties.

The recipes in this chapter are for a variety of dairy dishes. Some will undoubtedly become favorites, but don't neglect to consult Chapter Five, Fish Specialties, and Chapter Seven, Vegetable Specialties, for other *milchig* recipes.

Farfel Breakfast Cereal

¾ cup milk
1 teaspoon butter or margarine
⅛ teaspoon salt
1 teaspoon sugar (optional)
½ cup matzo farfel

Place the milk, butter or margarine, salt, and sugar in a small saucepan. Scald over medium heat. Add the matzo farfel and stir for 3 minutes. Serve as a breakfast dish. Serves 1.

Granola

This versatile concoction can easily be adapted to personal taste. The only basic ingredients are the matzo farfel and coconut. Cashew nuts and walnuts are equally crunchy and are delectable substitutes for the almonds. Chopped dried apples, apricots, peaches, dates, or prunes may be substituted for the raisins or may be used in combination with them.

An all-honey syrup works as well as the brown sugar-honey combination, and oil may be substituted for the margarine.

Delicious flavor variations can be achieved by making additions to the simmering syrup before coating the granola. For cinnamon flavor add 1 to 2 teaspoons ground cinnamon; for chocolate flavor add ⅛ to ¼ cup carob powder; for orange flavor add 1 to 2 teaspoons finely grated orange rind. Vanilla sugar is also a welcome addition.

Granola may be served with milk as a breakfast cereal, or sprinkle it over cooked Passover cereal. It is also a great snack food as well as a handy topping for cottage cheese or just about any dessert.

> 2½ cups matzo farfel
> 1 cup shredded fresh coconut
> 1 cup coarsely chopped blanched almonds
> ¼ cup (½ stick) margarine
> ¼ cup brown sugar
> ¼ cup honey
> ½ teaspoon salt
> ½ cup raisins
> Grease for the cookie sheet

Preheat the oven to 325 degrees F. Combine the matzo farfel, coconut, and chopped nuts in a medium-sized bowl. Spread the mixture on a lightly greased cookie sheet. Bake for 15 to 20 minutes, tossing several times until the mixture is lightly toasted.

Meanwhile, in a 2-quart saucepan combine the margarine, brown sugar, honey, and salt. Bring to a simmer for a few minutes, stirring constantly. Remove from the heat. Add the lightly toasted farfel-coconut-nut mixture to the syrup mixture.

Mix well, tossing the ingredients as if you were making a tossed salad, until everything is coated evenly.

Spread the coated granola on the cookie sheet. Increase the oven temperature to 350 degrees F. Return the cookie sheet to the oven and continue to toast for an additional 20 to 25 minutes, until the ingredients are golden brown. Stir frequently to prevent burning.

Remove the cookie sheet from the oven. Transfer the granola to a large mixing bowl. Stir in the raisins. With a flexible spatula break up any large lumps into small pieces. Cool thoroughly and store in an airtight container. Yields about 4½ cups.

Breakfast Matzo Fry

Did you ever think about the meaning of the word "breakfast"? It means you've been fasting all night and the time has come to "break-fast," to start refueling your body for the day ahead.

A breakfast consisting of a glass of juice, an adequate portion of this matzo fry, plus a cup of your favorite beverage is an excellent way to start the day. This recipe will serve four, but the dish will be more successful if each serving is individually prepared in a small skillet. To determine the quantity of ingredients required for one serving, simply divide by four.

> **4 eggs**
> **1 teaspoon salt**
> **1 cup milk**
> **8 matzos, broken into large pieces**
> **(fourths)**
> **4 tablespoons butter for frying**

In a large bowl, beat the eggs with the salt. Stir in the milk and the matzo pieces. Cover tightly and refrigerate overnight. At breakfast time, melt the butter in a large skillet over medium heat. Pour in the matzo-egg mixture and cook for a few minutes, until the batter is nicely browned. Turn with a cake turner to brown the other side. Remove to a hot plate. Cut into quarters and serve with honey or a favorite jam. If you prefer not to refrigerate the ingredients overnight, soak the broken matzo in the milk-egg mixture for a few minutes, to moisten it, before frying. Serves 4.

Matzo Brei

Matzo is Passover's most versatile food. It turns up at breakfast, lunch, and dinner—either whole or crumbled into matzo farfel or ground into matzo meal. Of all the dishes prepared with matzo, one of the most popular is matzo brei, which is basically softened matzo that is fried with eggs. Matzo brei can be fried pancake-style, crusty on both sides, or the matzo-egg mixture can be scrambled, making it light and fluffy.

This basic four-egg matzo brei can be served plain for breakfast or in a more elaborate version for lunch or dinner. Add vegetables or cheese, as you would to any omelet. Try sliced mushrooms (about 1 cup), chopped onions (1 medium-sized), or the cheese of your choice (about 1 cup, shredded).

> 4 matzos
> 3 cups water
> 4 eggs
> ½ cup milk
>   Salt and white pepper to taste
> 3 tablespoons butter

Break the matzos into small pieces and soak them in the water in a large bowl until soft but not soggy. Drain well. In a separate large bowl, beat the eggs with the milk, salt, and pepper. Add the matzos. Blend together.

Melt the butter in a large skillet over medium heat; add the egg mixture. Cook over medium heat. As the eggs begin to thicken and brown, stir from the bottom with a wide spatula or pancake turner, keeping the matzo in large scrambled pieces. If you prefer, cook the egg-matzo mixture as a large omelet, browning on both sides. Turn out onto a warm serving dish. Serves 4.

Variation:

Use 4 matzos to 1 egg and fry the mixture, like an omelet, in a medium-sized skillet until golden brown on both sides. This makes a crispy pancake-like dish.

Orange Matzo Brei

Turn this large pancake out onto a large serving dish, browned-side-up, by inverting the skillet. Slip the brei back into the skillet to brown the other side.

> **3 cups orange juice**
> **4 to 5 square matzos**
> **¼ cup raisins (optional)**
> **2 large eggs**
> **½ teaspoon salt**
> **1 tablespoon margarine**

In a medium-sized saucepan over low heat, heat the orange juice to just below the boiling point. Remove from the heat. Break the matzos into small pieces. Add the matzo pieces and raisins to the hot juice. Let soak until the matzos are soft. Drain the matzos in a colander or strainer. Using the back of a spoon, press out the excess orange juice. Reserve the juice for making Orange Sauce I (see Index for recipe).

Beat the eggs with the salt in a medium-sized mixing bowl. Add the well-drained matzos and raisins; mix thoroughly. Melt the margarine in a 10-inch skillet over medium heat. Add the matzo mixture; flatten with a spatula to form a large pancake. Cook over medium heat until browned on the bottom. Turn the pancake to brown the other side. Transfer to a large serving platter. Cut into wedges and serve with Orange Sauce I.

Variation:
Substitute apple juice for the orange juice. Serve with applesauce.

Matzo Brei Parmigiana

A matzo brei that is baked instead of fried. Almost as light and fluffy as a soufflé.

> **6 matzos**
> **2 cups water**

→

1 onion, chopped
1 clove garlic, minced
1 tablespoon oil
2 cups tomato sauce
1 tablespoon chopped fresh parsley
5 eggs
    Salt and black pepper to taste
    Grease for the casserole
½ cup diced hard cheese of your choice

Soak the matzos in the water in a large bowl until soft. Drain, then squeeze out the excess water. Set aside.

In a large skillet over low heat, sauté the onion and the garlic in the oil until golden. Add the tomato sauce and parsley. Simmer for 15 minutes. In a large mixing bowl, beat the eggs with the salt and pepper. Combine the reserved matzos with the beaten eggs. Stir to blend. Pour half of the egg-matzo mixture into a 2-quart greased casserole. Sprinkle with half of the diced cheese. Top with the remaining matzo mixture, then with the remaining cheese. Pour the prepared tomato sauce over all. Bake the casserole uncovered in a preheated 325-degree F. oven for 25 minutes. Serves 5 to 6.

Breakfast Pancakes

Avoid the monotony of eating matzo fry or matzo brei for breakfast each day. Prepare these matzo meal pancakes for a change of pace.

3 eggs, separated
½ cup matzo meal
½ cup water
½ teaspoon salt
1 tablespoon sugar (optional)
    Oil or butter for the griddle

In a medium-sized bowl, beat the egg yolks until light and thick. In a separate bowl, mix the matzo meal with the water, salt, and sugar until thoroughly blended. Fold into the egg yolks. Blend thoroughly.

In a clean medium-sized bowl, with clean beaters, beat the egg whites until stiff. Fold them into the yolk mixture.

Heat a pancake griddle over medium heat. Grease thoroughly with oil or butter. Drop the pancake batter onto the griddle by the tablespoonful. Do not crowd; the batter will spread somewhat. Cook until the bottom of the cakes are golden brown. Turn and brown the other side. Serve with sugar and cinnamon, jam, or pancake syrup. Serves 2 or 3.

Featherweight Cheese Pancakes

These pancakes are creamy and cheesy inside. Fruit syrup left over from canned fruit may be used as the syrup.

> 3 eggs, separated
> ¼ teaspoon salt
> ¼ cup cake meal
> ¾ cup cottage cheese
> Butter or margarine for the griddle

In a medium-sized mixing bowl, beat the egg whites until stiff but not dry. In a separate medium-sized bowl, with the same beaters, beat the egg yolks with the salt until light and lemon-colored. Stir in the cake meal and the cottage cheese. Fold the stiffly beaten egg whites into the yolk mixture. Drop by small spoonfuls onto a hot, lightly greased griddle. Cook over medium heat until golden brown on both sides. Serve at once with butter and syrup. Yields about 16 small pancakes.

Passover French Toast

Passover French Toast has several variations. For an orange-flavored toast, substitute one-half cup orange juice for the milk; add one teaspoon of grated orange rind. For a honey-sweetened toast, substitute three tablespoons of honey for the sugar. By cutting the slices of the sponge cake into fingers about one inch wide and preparing as directed, you can create French Toast Fingers.

       3 eggs
       ½ cup milk
       3 tablespoons sugar
       ⅛ teaspoon salt
       6 to 8 slices (½ inch thick) stale sponge
       cake
       Butter or margarine for frying
       Cinnamon and sugar (optional)

In a medium-sized bowl, beat the eggs with the milk. Add the sugar and the salt. Dip the sponge cake into the egg-milk mixture. Brown on both sides on a hot well-greased griddle or in a skillet. Sprinkle with cinnamon and sugar if desired. Serves 3 to 4.

Luncheon Omelet

An omelet for lunch takes little preparation and is light enough to please delicate tastes. This omelet may be served plain, with a filling, or with a cheese or fruit sauce.

Basic Omelet:

       4 eggs
       4 tablespoons milk or water
       Salt and white pepper to taste
       2 tablespoons butter or margarine

In a small bowl, beat the eggs until frothy. Add the liquid; season with salt and pepper. Beat until well blended. Heat a large heavy skillet until hot. Add the butter or margarine and swirl the pan to coat the entire surface. Do not brown the fat. Pour the egg mixture into the skillet. Cook slowly over low heat. When the eggs begin to set around the edges, lift the edges lightly with a knife or spatula, letting the uncooked part run underneath. Cook until the omelet has puffed.

To turn the omelet out, tip the pan; lift the edge with a spatula; fold the omelet over onto a plate, forming a half-moon. Serve plain or with any of the sauces or fillings below. Add the filling just before folding the omelet over through the middle and tipping it onto the serving plate. Serves 3.

Tomato Sauce:

In 1 tablespoon of hot fat in a small skillet over medium heat, sauté 2 medium-sized fresh tomatoes that have been peeled, quartered, seeded, and sliced. Season with salt and pepper. Spoon over the omelet before folding. Canned tomato sauce may be substituted for the freshly-made sauce.

Onion Sauce:

In a small skillet over medium heat, sauté 2 medium-sized onions in 1 tablespoon of hot fat. Season with ¼ teaspoon salt. When the onions are limp, add 1 tablespoon of minced fresh parsley. For a dairy luncheon, the onions may be mixed with 2 to 3 tablespoons of sour cream before being served with the omelet.

Mushroom Sauce:

Sauté ¼ pound sliced mushrooms in 2 tablespoons of fat in a small skillet over low heat. Season to taste with salt and pepper. Add 3 tablespoons dry wine. Cover; cook over low heat for 3 minutes. Serve with the omelet.

Cheese Sauce:

In the top of a double boiler, over hot but not simmering water, place 1 cup creamed cottage cheese, 2 tablespoons sour cream, 1 tablespoon honey, and ½ teaspoon cinnamon. Stir to blend. Cover and let the flavors meld for 10 minutes. Serve the sauce with the omelet.

Cheese Filling:

Top the omelet with the thinly sliced or grated cheese of your choice before folding the omelet.

Jelly Filling:

Spread ¼ cup of jelly, jam, or marmalade over the omelet before folding.

Fruit Sauce:

Soak ¼ cup of seedless raisins, 6 to 8 dried apricots, and an equal number of pitted prunes in ¾ cup of hot water for ½ hour.

Drain. Chop the fruit in a small chopping bowl. In a saucepan over low heat, cook gently with a few tablespoons of sweet wine or hot water for 2 to 3 minutes. Serve the sauce with the omelet, with sour cream if desired.

Baked Eggs

Small wonder that eggs contain protein, vitamins, and minerals, for inside an eggshell are all the "components" of a complete chicken. And chicken is an undisputed source of high-quality protein, vitamins, and minerals.

A serving of these eggs, baked and sprinkled with grated cheese, plus a glass of milk, makes a delicious, nourishing lunch.

> 1 cup matzo farfel
> 1 teaspoon salt
> ⅛ teaspoon white pepper
> 1¼ cups tomato sauce with mushrooms
> 4 raw eggs
> Grated cheese of your choice (optional)

In a small bowl, combine the matzo farfel with the salt, pepper, and the tomato sauce. Divide the mixture evenly into 4 well-greased 8 or 10-ounce baking dishes. Make a well in the center of each dish and drop an egg into each depression. Bake at 350 degrees F. for 15 to 20 minutes, until the eggs are firm. If desired, sprinkle the top of each egg with grated cheese and bake until the cheese melts.

Cheese Puffs

> 2 cups milk
> 2 tablespoons potato starch
> 1 cup grated cheese
> 4 eggs, separated
> ¾ teaspoon salt
> ½ teaspoon white pepper
> Pinch of ginger
> Butter for the custard cups

In the top of a double boiler, combine the milk and the starch. Cook directly over medium heat; slowly bring to the boiling point, stirring well to prevent lumps. When the mixture begins to thicken, place the top of the double boiler over hot water; add the cheese and cook just until the cheese melts. Remove the double boiler from the heat; let cool. Add the egg yolks 1 at a time, beating well after each addition. Add the salt, pepper, and ginger. In a large bowl, beat the egg whites until stiff but not dry; fold them into the cooled cheese mixture.

Divide the batter between 6 large buttered custard cups, filling them about two-thirds full. Set the cups into a hot water bath. Bake at 350 degrees F. for 25 to 35 minutes, until firm. Let stand for 5 minutes before unmolding. Serves 6.

Cheese-Mushroom Puff

    2 tablespoons butter
    ½ pound fresh mushrooms, thinly sliced
    2 cups milk
    8 ounces Cheddar or American cheese,
        grated
    ½ teaspoon salt
    1/16 teaspoon white pepper
    3 eggs, separated
    2¾ cups matzo farfel
    Butter for the pan

Melt the butter in a large skillet over medium heat. Sauté the mushrooms over low heat for about 5 minutes. In a small saucepan, heat the milk to just below boiling. Stir in the cheese, salt, and pepper. Cool slightly. In a large mixing bowl, beat the egg yolks until light and creamy. Add the cheese mixture. Combine the matzo farfel with the mushrooms. Stir into the cheese mixture.

In a medium-sized bowl, beat the egg whites until stiff but not dry; fold them into the cheese-farfel mixture. Pour the mixture into a greased 7½ × 12-inch baking pan. Bake in a 375-degree F. oven for 30 minutes or until a knife inserted in the center comes out clean. Serves 4 to 6.

Pizza Soufflé

Butter for the pan
5 matzos
Water
1 can (10½ ounces) tomato sauce with
mushrooms
Onion powder (optional)
Garlic powder (optional)
½ to ¾ pound American or mozzarella
cheese, sliced
2 large eggs
1 cup milk

Lightly butter a 9 × 13-inch pan. Wet the matzos lightly with water. Fit 2½ matzos on the bottom of the pan. Cover the matzos with half of the tomato sauce. Arrange the sliced cheese over the tomato sauce. Cover the cheese with the remaining matzos. Pour the remaining sauce over the matzos. Sprinkle the top with onion and garlic powder. In a medium-sized bowl, beat the eggs well with the milk; pour over the matzos. Bake in a preheated 375-degree F. oven for 30 minutes or until the custard is set. Let rest for 10 minutes before cutting into serving portions. Serves 6 to 7.

Potato Soufflé

4 medium-sized potatoes
¼ to ½ pound American cheese, divided
Salt, white pepper, and paprika to taste
¼ cup milk
2 eggs, separated

Peel the potatoes and cook in a medium-sized saucepan until tender. Drain. Transfer the potatoes to a large mixing bowl; mash. Grate half of the cheese or cut it into small bits and mix with the hot potatoes. Add the salt, pepper, and paprika. Beat the potatoes until the cheese melts. Add the milk and egg yolks. Mix well.

In a small bowl, beat the egg whites until stiff; fold them into the potato mixture. Turn the potato mixture into a very lightly greased 1½-quart casserole. Sprinkle the remaining half of the cheese, cut fine or grated, over the potatoes. Bake in a preheated 425-degree F. oven for 20 minutes. Serves 4.

Spinach Lasagna

A Passover pasta dish featuring spinach, cottage cheese, mozzarella cheese, and tomato sauce.

> **Margarine or butter for the pan**
> **10 ounces frozen chopped spinach, thawed**
> **but uncooked**
> **1 egg, beaten**
> **½ cup cottage cheese**
> **6 to 8 ounces mozzarella cheese, grated**
> **11 ounces tomato sauce with mushrooms**
> **1 cup milk, divided**
> **8 ounces Passover noodles, uncooked**
> **Grease for the baking pan**

Lightly grease a 2-quart baking pan with margarine or butter. In a small bowl, combine the thawed spinach with the beaten egg, cottage cheese, and three-fourths of the grated mozzarella. Mix to blend.

In a separate small bowl, dilute the tomato sauce with ½ cup of the milk. In the prepared pan, alternate layers of tomato sauce, uncooked noodles, and the spinach mixture. Sprinkle the remaining grated cheese over all. Pour the remaining ½ cup of milk around the edges of the baking pan. Cover tightly; refrigerate for 1 to 2 hours. Bake covered in a preheated 350-degree F. oven for 1 hour and 15 minutes. Let rest for 10 minutes before cutting. Serves 6 to 8.

Matzo Meal Polenta

For an enjoyable taste experience, prepare this wonderfully nourishing dish. It combines batter cakes with a robust tomato-cheese sauce.

> 3 eggs, separated
> ½ cup water
> 1 teaspoon salt
> ⅛ teaspoon white pepper
> 1 cup matzo meal, divided
> 3 tablespoons butter
> 1 onion, finely diced
> ¼ to ½ pound mushrooms, thinly sliced
> 3 cups fresh tomatoes, diced
> ½ cup grated cheese of your choice

In a large bowl, beat the egg yolks until light. Add the water, salt, pepper, and half of the matzo meal. Blend together. In a separate bowl, beat the egg whites until stiff. Fold the egg whites into the yolk mixture; add the remainder of the matzo meal.

In a large skillet, melt the butter over medium heat. Drop the matzo meal mixture by the tablespoonful into the butter and fry on each side until light brown. Remove the batter cakes from the skillet and arrange them in a 9 × 13-inch baking pan.

Sauté the onion and the mushrooms in the skillet over medium heat, adding additional butter if necessary, until golden brown. Remove the skillet from the heat. Add the tomatoes and cheese to the pan; mix well. Pour the mixture over the batter cakes in the baking pan. Bake in a 325-degree F. oven for 45 minutes. Serves 4 to 6.

Variation:

Fry the entire batter as 1 cake. When cool, cut into pieces and arrange the pieces in the baking dish. Continue as above.

Tunaburgers

Served with a tossed green salad, this meatless burger makes a satisfying luncheon dish.

> 1 can (7 ounces) tuna fish
> 1 cup (4 ounces) cubed Swiss cheese
> ⅓ cup finely chopped celery

⟶

1 tablespoon chopped fresh parsley
(optional)
1 teaspoon grated onion
¼ cup mayonnaise
Butter
4 to 6 large Passover Rolls (see Index for
recipe)

Drain and flake the tuna in a small mixing bowl. Combine the fish with the Swiss cheese, celery, parsley, onion, and mayonnaise. Stir until well mixed.

Split and butter the Passover rolls. Divide the tuna mixture evenly among the buttered rolls. Wrap each roll in foil. Arrange the rolls on a small baking tray. Bake in a preheated 400-degree F. oven for 15 minutes or until the rolls are heated through and the cheese has melted. Makes 4 to 6 servings.

Baked Cheese Loaf

This cheese loaf, high in protein and easy to prepare, is a nice substitute for cheese blintzes. Chopped walnuts add a pleasant accent.

2 eggs
1 pound farmer cheese
¼ cup sugar
Dash of white pepper
½ cup raisins
Cinnamon
Grease for the pan

Beat the eggs in a medium-sized bowl. With a pastry blender, blend the cheese, sugar, pepper, and raisins into the eggs; or use a hand mixer to blend these ingredients very well. Taste for sweetness; add more sugar if necessary. Grease a 3 × 7-inch loaf pan. Pour in the cheese mixture. Sprinkle the top with cinnamon. Bake in a preheated 350-degree F. oven for 30 minutes. Serve hot or cold with sour cream and fresh strawberries. Serves 4.

Cheese Crumbettes

As a change of pace, serve these Cheese Crumbettes, which have the same taste appeal as blintzes. Serve with sliced strawberries and sour cream. These freeze very well. Defrost before reheating.

> 2 ounces soup nuts
> 1 tablespoon sugar
> 1 pound farmer cheese
> ½ pound cream cheese
> ½ cup sugar
> 2 eggs
> 1 teaspoon lemon juice
> 1 tablespoon potato starch
> Grease for the cookie sheet

First prepare the crumbs. Chop the soup nuts in a bowl. Mix in the 1 tablespoon of sugar. Set aside while preparing the cheese.

Press the farmer cheese through a food mill or strainer into a medium-sized bowl. Add the cream cheese. Blend. Beat in the sugar, eggs, lemon juice, and potato starch. Drop a tablespoonful of the cheese mixture into the crumb mixture to form an oblong pancake; turn to coat it on all sides. Transfer the pancake to a greased cookie sheet. Continue making pancakes until all of the mixture is used up. Bake in a preheated 350-degree F. oven for 15 to 20 minutes, until golden brown and crusty. Serves 6 to 8.

Variations:
• Use chopped egg kichel for the crumb coating. Omit the sugar.
• A dash of cinnamon can be added to the crumb mixture or a cinnamon-sugar combination sprinkled over the Cheese Crumbettes before baking.

Cheese Croquettes

These croquettes can be served as a main dish or as a snack with a cup of coffee. Serve warm—plain, with sour cream, or with applesauce.

> 2 cups cottage cheese, drained
> 2 cups mashed potatoes, cooled
> ½ cup minced onions (optional)
> 2 eggs, well beaten
> 1 teaspoon salt
> ¼ teaspoon white pepper
> 1½ cups matzo meal
> 2 eggs beaten with 2 tablespoons water
> Oil for deep frying

Combine the well-drained cottage cheese, mashed potatoes, and minced onions in a medium-sized bowl. Add the well-beaten eggs, salt, and pepper. Mix until thoroughly blended. Chill the mixture in the refrigerator for at least 1 hour. Shape the potato-cheese mixture into individual rolls about 1 inch in diameter and 3 inches long. Dredge the rolls with matzo meal. Dip into the egg mixture, then roll in the matzo meal. Arrange the rolls on a tray and refrigerate again for another hour. In a deep fryer, at 375 degrees F., fry the rolls in oil until golden brown. Drain on absorbent paper. Serves 6.

Cheese Kreplach

Inasmuch as kreplach are traditionally triangular in shape, you may wish to create more authentic-looking kreplach than this recipe yields. You may do so by gently pressing the filled and sealed dough into a triangular shape. Great care must be exercised so that the filling is not exposed.

Dough:

> 3 eggs
> 3 tablespoons milk
> 3 tablespoons butter or margarine, melted
> ½ teaspoon salt
> 1 cup matzo meal

Filling:

> ½ pound dry cottage cheese
> 1 egg yolk

→

    2 teaspoons sugar
    ½ teaspoon salt
    Dash of cinnamon
    Dash of white pepper

In a medium-sized bowl, beat the eggs, milk, melted butter or margarine, and salt until well blended. Gradually add the matzo meal. Let rest for 10 minutes while preparing the cheese filling.

Combine the cheese, egg yolk, sugar, salt, cinnamon, and pepper in a small bowl. Mix together with a spoon or fork until smooth. Taste and adjust the seasoning, adding more sugar if desired. Shape the matzo meal mixture into balls. With a finger moistened with cold water make a hollow in the center of each ball. Place 1 tablespoonful of the cheese filling in each hollow. Press the edges together and seal tightly.

Drop the balls gently into 2 to 3 quarts of boiling salted water (1 teaspoon salt to 1 quart of water). Cover the pot and cook for 15 to 20 minutes. Drain well. Serve with sour cream. Serves 3 to 4.

Matzos With Cottage Cheese Custard

    4 square matzos
    Lukewarm water
    1½ pounds cottage cheese
    ½ cup raisins
    ⅔ cup sugar, divided
    ½ teaspoon cinnamon
    Butter for the pan
    4 eggs, well beaten
    2 cups milk
    Juice and grated rind of 1 orange
    ½ teaspoon salt

Soak the matzos, 1 at a time, in lukewarm water in a shallow pan. Remove carefully; drain and press between paper towels to remove excess moisture. In a medium-sized bowl, combine the cheese, raisins, ⅓ cup of the sugar, and the cinnamon. Butter a 9-inch square baking pan. Place 1 soaked matzo in the pan. Cover with a third of the cheese mixture. Continue layering, ending with the matzo.

In a large mixing bowl, beat the eggs, milk, orange juice and rind, the salt, and the remaining ⅓ cup of sugar until smooth and well blended. Pour the mixture over the matzos. Bake in a preheated 375-degree F. oven for 1 hour or until puffed and brown. Yields 6 to 8 servings.

Fruited Farfel Custard

A delicious dessert to serve with a light dairy meal.

> 4 ounces egg barley
> 2½ cups scalded milk
> 6 tablespoons brown sugar
> 1 teaspoon salt
> 1 teaspoon vanilla flavoring or 1 envelope
> (.43 ounces) vanilla sugar
> 3 eggs, beaten
> ¾ cup cooked dried apricots
> ¾ cup raisins

Cook the egg barley according to package directions; drain. In a large bowl, combine the milk, sugar, salt, flavoring, eggs, apricots, and the raisins. Fold in the drained farfel. Pour the mixture into a buttered 1½-quart casserole. Set the casserole in a hot water bath and bake in a 350-degree F. oven for 1 hour. Serve with cream or a fruit sauce. Serves 4.

7

Vegetable Specialties

An astounding variety of fresh vegetables are kosher for Passover, and for the inventive cook the ways in which they can be prepared are infinite.

Vegetables should play a major role in Passover meal planning. Some vegetables need no dressing up; they rest on their own flavor laurels. Others can fit into the menu in various guises—in a "dressed" salad or a soup, in a main dish, relish, side dish, dessert, or in a memorable cake.

Dishes prepared with vegetables offer many taste delights, as evidenced by the recipes in this chapter. You don't have to be a vegetarian to enjoy them.

Beets With Orange Juice

Beets brighten meals with their rich red color. The beets in this dish can be cut into a variety of shapes.

> 2 tablespoons matzo meal
> ¼ cup sugar
> ½ cup orange juice
> 2 tablespoons shortening
> 3 cups sliced cooked beets

Combine the matzo meal, sugar, orange juice, and shortening in a mixing bowl. Add the sliced beets; stir until coated with the mixture. Turn the beets into a 1-quart casserole. Bake covered for 15 minutes in a preheated 350-degree F. oven. Serve with fish or poultry. Serves 4 to 6.

Beets in Honey Sauce

Sweet and tangy. Ideal for company.

2 cups diced or sliced cooked beets
1 tablespoon potato starch
½ teaspoon salt
1 tablespoon water or beet juice
2 tablespoons vinegar
¼ cup honey
1 tablespoon fat

Put the beets in a bowl; set aside while making the sauce. Combine the potato starch with the salt in a small saucepan. Stir in the water or beet juice. Add the vinegar, honey, and fat. Cook slowly over low heat, stirring constantly until thickened. Add the sauce to the beets. Let stand for at least 10 minutes to allow the flavors to meld. Reheat. Serves 4.

Broccoli Soufflé

2 packages (10 ounces each) frozen
chopped broccoli
3 eggs
Salt and white pepper to taste
1 tablespoon onion soup mix
½ cup mayonnaise
Grease for the pan
2 tablespoons matzo meal, divided

Cook the broccoli according to package directions. Drain thoroughly. Set aside. In a mixing bowl, beat the eggs very well with the salt, pepper, and onion soup mix; add the mayonnaise and continue beating until well blended. Stir in the cooked broccoli.

Grease a 7 × 11½-inch baking pan. Dust it lightly with 1 tablespoon of matzo meal. Pour in the broccoli mixture and sprinkle with the remaining tablespoon of matzo meal. Bake at 350 degrees F. for 40 to 50 minutes, until the top is golden. Serves 4 to 6.

Variation:

Prepare a cream sauce using ¾ cup of liquid from the drained broccoli (or milk for dairy), 1½ tablespoons margarine, and ¾ tablespoon potato starch. Add the cream sauce to the beaten eggs and proceed as above

Broccoli-Walnut Ring

Walnuts add a crunch to this luscious broccoli dish.

1 package (10 ounces) frozen chopped broccoli
1 clove garlic (optional)
2 tablespoons minced onion
¼ cup margarine
1½ tablespoons potato starch
1 cup water or bouillon made from a cube
3 eggs, separated
½ cup chopped walnuts

Grease a 1½-quart ring mold with softened margarine. Refrigerate while preparing the filling.

Cook the broccoli according to package directions, but add the garlic clove to the water. Drain well and discard the garlic.

In a 1-quart saucepan over medium heat, sauté the onion in the margarine until soft and golden. In a measuring cup, dissolve the potato starch in the water or bouillon; add to the onions. Cook over low heat, stirring until thick and smooth. Cool slightly.

In a mixing bowl, beat the egg yolks until light. Stir the yolks, broccoli, and walnuts into the onion mixture. In a separate bowl, with clean beaters, beat the egg whites until stiff. Fold them into the broccoli mixture. Spoon the mixture into the prepared ring mold. Set the mold into a hot water bath that reaches half way up the sides of the mold. Bake in a preheated 350-degree F. oven for

30 to 35 minutes, until firm. Let rest for 5 minutes before unmolding. Serves 4.

Variations:
• For dairy, substitute butter for the margarine and use milk as the liquid.
• To make a broccoli-cheese ring, substitute ⅓ to ½ cup of the grated cheese of your choice for the walnuts.

Baked Cabbage

Cabbage is very versatile. It can be used successfully in main dishes, side dishes, and salads. And as an added bonus, it is rich in calcium and vitamins A and C.

1 cabbage, approximately 3½ pounds
2 eggs
Salt and white pepper to taste
2 teaspoons matzo meal
Grease for the pan

Cut the cabbage in half, then cut each half into 4 or 5 wedges, but do not separate the wedges. Cook the cabbage over medium heat in a covered saucepan in a small amount of water, about 3 or 4 inches, until barely tender. With a slotted spoon, remove the cabbage; drain well. Separate the wedges.

In a shallow pan, beat the eggs with the salt and pepper. Add the matzo meal; stir to blend. Dip the cabbage wedges into the egg mixture and arrange in a greased 9 × 13-inch baking pan. Bake in a preheated 350-degree F. oven until nicely browned on both sides of each wedge. Serves 8 to 10.

Cabbage Patties

1 cabbage, approximately 3½ pounds
3 eggs
Salt and white pepper to taste
¾ cup matzo meal
Grease for the baking sheet

Core the cabbage and parboil in a covered pan in about 2 inches of water for 8 to 10 minutes. Remove from the water; drain well. Put the cabbage through the medium blade of a food chopper, or chop in a chopping bowl. Drain again. You should have approximately 4 cups.

With a rotary beater or electric mixer, beat the eggs well with the salt and pepper in a medium-sized mixing bowl. Add the beaten eggs to the chopped cabbage. Fold in the ¾ cup of matzo meal and let rest for about ½ hour.

Shape the mixture into patties and bake on a greased baking sheet at 400 degrees F. for 45 minutes, turning once. Should be nicely browned on each side. Serve hot. Serves 6 to 8.

Variation:

After chopping the cabbage, prepare a white sauce with 3 tablespoons of butter or margarine, 1½ tablespoons of potato starch, and 1 cup of milk or water from the cooked cabbage. Add to the cabbage with the 3 beaten eggs and 1½ cups (rather than ¾ cup) matzo meal. Season to taste; mix well. Chill for 1 hour. Shape into flat patties. Brown on both sides in hot fat over medium-high heat. Makes about 20 patties.

Carrot Patties in Raisin Sauce

Patties:

> 2 cups finely grated peeled carrots
> 2 cups matzo meal
> 2 eggs, well beaten
> ⅓ cup milk or orange juice
> 1 teaspoon cinnamon
> ½ teaspoon salt
> ½ teaspoon grated orange rind
> 2 tablespoons butter or margarine

Sauce:

> 1 tablespoon potato starch
> ⅓ cup water

→

⅓ cup orange juice
½ cup raisins
⅓ cup currant jelly
½ teaspoon grated orange rind

In a large bowl, combine the carrots, matzo meal, eggs, milk or orange juice, cinnamon, salt, and grated orange rind. Work the mixture with the hands until an evenly blended mass is formed. Shape the mixture into 8 to 10 patties.

Melt the butter or margarine in a large skillet over medium heat. Add the patties; sauté until golden on each side and cooked through. (Patties may be baked in a preheated moderate oven, 350 degrees F., on a greased baking sheet, for 10 to 15 minutes, until golden on each side and cooked through.)

To prepare the sauce, mix the potato starch with the water in a small saucepan. Stir in the orange juice, raisins, currant jelly, and grated orange rind. Cook over medium-heat, stirring frequently until the mixture thickens and boils. Spoon the sauce over the carrot patties before serving. Serves 4 to 5.

Candied Carrots

Can be prepared well in advance of Passover and refrigerated. Reheat before serving.

16 to 24 baby carrots
1 teaspoon salt for parboiling
3 tablespoons margarine
½ cup brown sugar
½ teaspoon salt

Peel the carrots. In a small saucepan over medium heat, parboil the carrots in salted water to cover. Cook until barely tender. Do not overcook. Drain. In a large heavy skillet, melt the margarine; add the sugar and salt; cook over low heat until the sugar dissolves. Add the carrots. Continue to simmer over low heat, shaking the pan occasionally to coat each carrot with the glaze. Serves 8.

Eggplant-Cheese Steaks

Many food authorities believe that the bitterness in eggplant can be reduced by sprinkling slices of the eggplant with salt and placing the slices in a colander or on a dish with a weighted plate set on top for several hours. If this procedure is followed, some excess liquid is extracted from the eggplant slices, and less fat is required to fry them. However, some of the nutrients are lost as well. Hence, it is not advisable to salt eggplant slices before preparing a recipe using sliced eggplant, such as this one.

In this recipe, eggplant and cheese team up with tomato sauce to make a savory and nourishing dish. Serve with a green salad.

> 1 medium-sized eggplant
> Sliced hard cheese of your choice
> 2 to 3 eggs
> ½ teaspoon salt
> Dash of white pepper
> 1½ cups matzo meal
> Oil
> 2 cups tomato sauce
> Dash of garlic powder (optional)
> Grease for the baking sheet

Peel the eggplant and slice it across the width into 8 to 10 slices. Place slices of hard cheese on half the eggplant slices. Cover each cheese-covered slice (the cheese should not extend beyond the edge) with another eggplant slice.

In a small bowl, beat the eggs with the salt and pepper. Place the matzo meal in a shallow dish. Dip each eggplant sandwich into the beaten eggs, then into the matzo meal. Place the coated sandwiches on a greased baking sheet and bake at 375 degrees F. for 35 to 45 minutes, until nicely browned, turning once.

Using a spatula, remove the eggplant. Serve hot with warm tomato sauce spooned over the steaks. Dust very lightly with garlic powder. Serves 4 to 5.

Variation:

The eggplant slices may be coated and fried individually before being used to make cheese sandwiches. Place the sandwiches in a baking pan in a single layer. Cover with tomato sauce and bake until the cheese melts and the sauce is hot. Serves 4 to 5.

Eggplant-Meat Steaks

This delicious *fleishig* variation on the Eggplant Cheese Steaks, above, features eggplant, meat, and tomato sauce.

>½ pound ground meat
>1 small onion, ground
>Salt and black pepper to taste
>1 egg
>2 tablespoons matzo meal
>2 to 3 fresh parsley leaves, finely minced
>½ clove garlic, puréed, or a dash of garlic powder (optional)
>1 medium-sized eggplant, peeled

In a small mixing bowl, combine the ground meat with the onion, salt, pepper, and egg. Stir in the matzo meal, minced parsley, and puréed garlic. Blend thoroughly.

Slice the peeled eggplant across the width. Form the meat into patties, 1 for each 2 slices of eggplant. Place a meat patty between each 2 slices of eggplant.

Coat the sandwiches as directed in the Eggplant Cheese Steaks. Fry the sandwiches in oil in a large skillet over medium heat, or bake on a greased baking sheet in a 375-degree F. oven. While the eggplant steaks are frying or baking, prepare the sauce.

Tomato Sauce:

>2 cans (10½ ounces each) tomato sauce
>Dash of sugar
>1 garlic clove, puréed, or ¼ teaspoon garlic powder (optional)
>1 to 3 teaspoons minced fresh parsley

In a mixing bowl, combine the tomato sauce with the sugar, puréed garlic, and minced parsley. Stir to blend. When the steaks are nicely browned on both sides, use a spatula to transfer them to a baking pan large enough to accommodate them in a single layer. Pour the tomato sauce over the sandwiches. Bake in a 350-degree F. oven for 30 minutes. Serves 4 to 5.

Rolled Stuffed Eggplant I

This is an impressive vegetable dish, ideal for buffet service. A crisp green salad is all that is needed as a complement.

> 1 eggplant, approximately 2½ pounds
> ½ pound dry cottage cheese
> 1 egg
> ¼ pound thinly sliced American cheese
> Grease for the pan
> 1 can (10½ ounces) tomato sauce with mushrooms
> 1 can (10½ ounces) milk, skim or whole.
> Use the tomato sauce can to measure.

Peel the eggplant and slice it lengthwise. Steam the slices in a vegetable steamer for 4 to 5 minutes, until softened. Drain well and pat dry.

In a small bowl, mix the cottage cheese with the egg. Place a tablespoonful of the cheese mixture on each slice of eggplant. Top the cottage cheese mixture with half-slices of American cheese. Roll up jelly roll fashion. Arrange the rolls in a greased 2-quart oblong baking pan. Cover the eggplant rolls with the remaining slices of American cheese. In a large measuring cup, dilute the tomato sauce with mushrooms with the milk; pour the sauce over the rolls. Cover the pan and bake at 350 degrees F. for 30 minutes, then uncover and bake for an additional 15 minutes.

Variation:
Rather than softening the eggplant by steaming, lightly fry each slice.

Rolled Stuffed Eggplant II

1 eggplant, approximately 2½ pounds
1 egg, slightly beaten
½ cup milk
2 teaspoons oil
½ cup cake meal
⅛ teaspoon salt
    Oil for the skillet
½ cup grated cheese of your choice
½ cup farmer cheese
2 tablespoons snipped fresh parsley
    Dash of white pepper
2 cans (10½ ounces each) tomato sauce
    with mushrooms

Peel the eggplant and slice lengthwise. Combine the egg, milk, and 2 teaspoons of oil in a shallow pan. Add the cake meal and salt; beat until smooth. Dip the sliced eggplant into the batter; cook on both sides in a skillet with a little oil over medium heat until soft. Drain on paper towels.

In a small bowl, combine the cheeses, parsley, and pepper. Blend thoroughly. Place 1 tablespoonful of the cheese mixture on each eggplant slice. Roll up jelly roll fashion. Pour half of the tomato sauce into a 2-quart oblong baking pan. Arrange the eggplant rolls in the pan, then cover with the remaining tomato sauce. Additional grated cheese may be sprinkled on top. Bake in a 375-degree F. oven for 30 to 45 minutes. Serves 6.

Potato Nests

During Passover, we rely heavily on potatoes as a substitute for pasta and the cereal products that are prohibited. Potato Nests are convenient "cases" for fillings of all kinds. For an impressive first course fill with chopped liver or tuna fish salad. For a hot appetizer, fill with sautéed chicken livers and serve.

Large potatoes
Fat for the skillet

Cook thinly sliced potatoes in a small amount of hot fat in a large skillet over medium heat until tender, not brown. Arrange the slices against the sides and bottom of muffin pans or custard cups. Bake at 450 degrees F. for 15 minutes. Three large potatoes yield 6 nests.

Potato Twirls

An unusual potato preparation. Spoon a creamed dish over them, or serve as a side dish.

Medium-sized potatoes
Oil for frying

Peel medium-sized potatoes. Cut them crosswise into ¾ to 1-inch slices. Starting at the outer edge, cut around and around in a continuous spiral. Reshape the spiral to its original form. Wipe dry.

Place a few of the spirals in the bottom of a frying basket. Immerse the basket in hot oil (380 degrees F.) deep enough to cover the potatoes. Cook until lightly browned. Drain on absorbent paper. Yield depends upon the size of the potatoes.

Potato Puff Shells

A combination of pâtè à choux (cream puff paste) and mashed potatoes. Recommended enthusiastically as a shell in which to serve liver sauté.

½ cup water
¼ cup oil
¼ teaspoon salt
½ cup matzo meal
2 eggs
1 cup mashed potatoes

→

Salt and white pepper to taste
1 egg
Grease for the baking sheet

Boil the water, oil, and salt together in a 2-quart saucepan over medium heat. Add the matzo meal all at once, stirring vigorously. Turn down the heat to low and continue to stir until the batter no longer adheres to the sides of the pan.

Transfer the batter to the bowl of an electric mixer. Add the 2 eggs, 1 at a time, beating well after each addition. In a separate bowl, season the mashed potatoes with the salt and pepper; add the 1 egg. Beat until very light and fluffy.

Combine both mixtures. Beat with the electric mixer until thoroughly blended. Drop by the tablespoonful onto a lightly greased baking sheet.

Bake in a preheated 450-degree F. oven for 10 minutes. Reduce the heat to 350 degrees F. and continue baking for an additional 30 to 40 minutes, until lightly browned. Yields 6 to 8 shells.

Potato Noodles

3 medium-sized potatoes
1 egg, well beaten
Salt and white pepper to taste
1 teaspoon grated onion
½ cup matzo meal, approximately
Butter for the baking pan
2 tablespoons melted butter
Milk

In a medium-sized saucepan, boil the potatoes in salted water until tender. Cool until the potatoes are easy to handle. Peel and pass through a food mill into a bowl. Cool slightly, then add the egg, salt and pepper, and grated onion. Mix well. Add just enough matzo meal to make a soft dough.

With floured hands, roll out pieces of dough into pencil-like sticks. Arrange in a buttered baking pan, leaving about ½ inch between each stick. Dot with the butter. Add enough milk to cover the top surface of the sticks. Bake in a moderate oven, 350 degrees F., for about 25 minutes, until delicately browned. Serves 4 to 6.

Potato Shalet

¼ cup oil, butter, or margarine
1 medium-sized onion, minced
1 teaspoon salt
¼ teaspoon black pepper
2 matzos, broken
　 Cold water
2 cups grated raw potatoes, undrained
2 eggs, well beaten
　 Grease for the pan

Place the fat in a 1-quart saucepan. Add the onion, salt, and pepper and cook over medium heat for 5 minutes, stirring all the while. Remove from the heat. Place the matzos in a bowl. Add cold water to cover. Let soak until soft but not mushy. Drain the matzo pieces well. Add the matzo and the grated potato to the onion mixture. Stir in the well-beaten eggs. Pour the mixture into a well-greased 1½-quart baking dish. Bake uncovered in a moderate oven, 350 degrees F., for 1 to 1½ hours, until nicely browned. Serves 4 to 6.

Mashed Potato Knaidlach

For a meat meal, bury a surprise in the center of each knaidel. Perhaps form the knaidel around a piece of broiled chicken liver.

2 cups mashed potatoes
1 tablespoon oil
1 tablespoon minced onion
1 egg, slightly beaten
1½ teaspoons salt
½ teaspoon white pepper
¾ cup matzo meal
2 quarts boiling salted water

Put the mashed potatoes in a mixing bowl. Add the oil, onion, and slightly beaten egg. Blend well. Add the salt, pepper, and matzo meal. Mix well. With wet hands, shape the potato mixture into balls. Cook covered in the 2 quarts of boiling salted water (1 teaspoon salt per quart of water) for 12 to 15 minutes. Using a slotted spoon, remove the knaidlach. Drain well.

Serve plain or with browned onions. Or brown the knaidlach in melted fat in a skillet over medium heat or in a 400-degree F. oven. Serves 4 to 6.

Top-Hat Tomatoes

Baked tomatoes filled with creamed spinach and crowned with a pastry "top hat." A distinctive vegetable dish.

> 6 medium-sized firm tomatoes
> 1½ cups creamed spinach (recipe below)
> ¼ cup water
> 2 tablespoons margarine
> ¼ cup matzo meal
> ⅛ teaspoon salt for the batter
> 1 egg
> 1 teaspoon sugar
> ½ teaspoon salt for the tomatoes

Cut off the tops of the tomatoes; scoop out the insides with a teaspoon. Turn the tomatoes upside down to drain. (Use the pulp in other cooking.) Prepare the creamed spinach. Keep hot. Bring the water and margarine to the boiling point in a small saucepan over medium heat. Add the matzo meal and salt all at once. Reduce the heat and cook, stirring vigorously for about 2 minutes, until the batter forms a thick smooth ball. Remove from the heat immediately. Cool slightly. Beat in the egg until the mixture is thick and shiny smooth.

Sprinkle the tomato cups with the sugar and salt. Fill each tomato cup with hot creamed spinach. Spread about 1 table-spoonful of the batter over the creamed spinach in each tomato, then use the remaining batter to form a mound on top of each (this gives the "top-hat" effect). Bake in a preheated 400-degree F. oven for 25 minutes or until the topping is puffed and lightly golden and the tomato cups are hot. Serves 6.

Creamed Spinach

> 1 pound fresh spinach or 1 package (10
> ounces) frozen chopped spinach
> 2 tablespoons margarine
> 1 tablespoon potato starch
> 2 tablespoons cold water
> ½ teaspoon salt
> ½ teaspoon sugar (optional)
> ⅞ cup liquid

If using fresh spinach, put the spinach in a saucepan. Cover and cook over low heat only in the water that clings to the leaves after washing. Cook until wilted and tender. Drain well, reserving the cooking liquid. Chop the spinach in a small bowl. (If using frozen spinach, cook according to package directions. Drain well, reserving the cooking liquid.)

Melt the margarine in a small saucepan. Remove from the heat. Dissolve the potato starch in the 2 tablespoons of cold water. Add to the melted margarine. Stir in the salt and sugar. Measure the liquid reserved from the cooked spinach; add water as necessary to make ⅞ cup. Pour the liquid into the flour mixture. Place the saucepan over medium heat. Cook, stirring constantly, until thickened and smooth. Add the cream sauce to the chopped spinach. Mix well. Makes 1½ cups.

Note: For dairy, substitute milk for the spinach liquid and butter for the margarine.

Spinach-Cheese Squares

> 2 cups cooked spinach
> 4 tablespoons butter
> 1 tablespoon minced onion

⟶

> 2 tablespoons potato starch
> 1 teaspoon salt
> ⅛ teaspoon white pepper
> 2 cups milk
> 1 cup grated American cheese
> 2 eggs, slightly beaten
>   Hard-cooked egg wedges (optional)

Drain the spinach well and chop in a wooden bowl. Melt the butter in a medium-sized saucepan over low heat; add the minced onion and cook until tender. Add the potato starch, salt, and pepper to the milk and stir to dissolve the potato starch.

Pour the milk mixture into the saucepan and cook until the sauce boils and thickens, stirring constantly. Add the cheese and stir until blended. In a mixing bowl, combine the sauce with the beaten eggs; stir in the chopped spinach. Turn the mixture into a buttered 8-inch square pan. Set the pan into a shallow pan of hot water and bake in a 350-degree F. oven for about 30 minutes, until firm. Cut into serving squares. Garnish with hard-cooked egg wedges if desired. Serves 6.

Stuffed Mushrooms

An easy garnish that adds a glamorous low-calorie touch to many fine dinners.

> 6 very large fresh mushrooms
> 4 tablespoons margarine or butter
> 1 tablespoon finely chopped onion
> ¾ cup matzo farfel
>   Salt and white pepper to taste
> 2 tablespoons red wine
> 2 tablespoons water

Wash and dry the mushrooms. Remove the stems carefully. Chop the stems fine in a wooden bowl. Melt the margarine or butter in a small saucepan; add the chopped stems and the onion and stir over medium heat for 5 minutes. Remove from the heat. Add the farfel and the salt and pepper. Stir to blend thoroughly. Grease a 6 × 10-inch baking dish. Arrange the mushroom caps in the dish, cap side up. Stuff the mushroom caps with the mushroom-farfel mixture, dividing evenly. Combine the wine with the water in a small dish. Spoon 1 teaspoonful of the mixture over each stuffed mushroom. Bake in a preheated 400-degree F. oven for 15 minutes. Serves 6.

French-fried Mushrooms

A medium-sized head of cauliflower can be substituted for the mushrooms. Separate the cauliflower into small flowerets and prepare in the same manner as the mushrooms.

> **1 pound medium-sized mushrooms**
> **¼ cup cake meal**
> **1 teaspoon salt**
> **¹⁄₁₆ teaspoon freshly ground black pepper**
> **2 eggs, well beaten**
> **¾ cup matzo meal**
> **Oil for deep frying**

Rinse, pat dry, and trim the mushrooms. Do not peel them; merely trim away a slice from the bottom of each stem; discard the trimmings. In a small bowl, combine the cake meal with the salt and the black pepper. Dredge the mushrooms in the cake meal mixture, then dip into the well-beaten eggs, then roll in the matzo meal.

Preheat the oil in a deep fryer to 365 degrees F. Place the mushrooms in the frying basket. Fry until golden brown—about 3 minutes. Drain on paper towels. Serve hot. Yields 25 to 35 mushrooms.

Scalloped Tomato Matzos

> **Grease for the pan**
> **4 slices Bermuda onion**
> **4 cups canned or fresh stewed tomatoes**

⟶

1 teaspoon salt
¼ teaspoon freshly ground black pepper
2 tablespoons sugar
3 matzos
3 tablespoons butter or margarine

Grease a 9 × 9-inch baking pan and line with the onion slices. In a small bowl, season the tomatoes with the salt, pepper, and sugar. Alternate layers of tomato and matzo over the onion slices, ending with matzo. Dot the top matzo with the butter or margarine. Cover the pan and bake in a preheated 375-degree F. oven for about 30 minutes, until heated through and the onions are tender. Serves 6.

Parsnip Fritters

2 large parsnips, peeled
  Boiling water
2 eggs
1 tablespoon oil
⅓ cup honey or ½ cup sugar
  Salt to taste
⅓ cup potato starch
½ cup matzo meal
  Oil or margarine for the skillet

In a saucepan over medium heat, cook the parsnips in a little boiling water until soft. Drain and mash well. (If the parsnips have woody cores, cut them in half lengthwise and remove the tough cores.) In a medium-sized mixing bowl, beat the eggs with the oil, honey or sugar, and salt until light. Mix in the mashed parsnips, potato starch, and matzo meal. Stir well. The batter should be firm enough to form patties, but not too heavy. Taste for sweetness; add more sugar if necessary.

Drop the batter by the tablespoonful into a large skillet lightly greased with oil or margarine. Brown as you would pancakes. Serves 4 to 5.

Variation:
Grate parsnips, uncooked, and proceed as above.

Zucchini Fritters

2 medium-sized zucchini
1 carrot, peeled
½ teaspoon salt
2 tablespoons minced onion
2 tablespoons minced fresh parsley
1 egg, beaten
½ cup matzo meal
Dash of freshly ground black pepper
Oil for the pan

Grate the zucchini and carrot into a bowl. Drain the mixture in a colander. Return to the bowl and add the remaining ingredients. Blend thoroughly. Drop by tablespoonfuls into hot oil in a large skillet and fry over medium-high heat until browned on both sides; or bake in a 400-degree F. oven on a greased baking sheet for 30 to 40 minutes, until browned on both sides, turning once. Drain on absorbent paper. Makes about 12 fritters; serves 4.

Vegetable Cutlets I

As a main dish, serve these colorful cutlets cloaked with a mushroom gravy. Or serve them plain as a side dish.

6 medium-sized potatoes, peeled
2 onions, chopped
¼ pound mushrooms, chopped
¼ cup margarine
2 eggs
Salt and white pepper to taste
2 cups diced cooked carrots
2 cups cooked broccoli cuts
1½ cups matzo meal, approximately
1 egg, well beaten

In a medium-sized saucepan, cook the potatoes in boiling salted water. Drain and mash them in a bowl. Sauté the onions and mushrooms in the margarine in a small skillet over medium heat until tender. Pour the mushrooms and onions over the potatoes; stir. Beat in the 2 eggs, salt, and pepper until well blended. Stir in the cooked carrots and the cooked broccoli cuts, cutting any remaining large broccoli pieces into smaller pieces. Add enough matzo meal so that the mixture can be formed into large patties. Shape the mixture into patties (12 very large or 18 medium-sized). Brush both sides with the well-beaten egg. Bake on a greased baking sheet in a preheated 350-degree F. oven for 45 minutes or until lightly browned, turning once. Serves 9 to 12, depending on the size of the patties.

Shortcut:

Prepare two 6-ounce packages of mashed potatoes with toasted onions, following package directions. Sauté drained mushrooms from one 4-ounce can. Proceed as above. For dairy, substitute butter for the margarine.

Vegetable Cutlets II

An array of vegetables goes into these cutlets, which are baked in a savory tomato sauce.

> 2 beets
> 2 carrots
> 1 parsnip
> 1 medium-sized sweet potato
> 1 medium-sized white potato
> 4 stalks celery
> 1 onion
> 1½ teaspoons salt
> ½ teaspoon freshly ground black pepper
> 1½ cups matzo meal
> 3 eggs, well beaten
>   Oil for frying
> 2 cups fresh stewed or canned tomatoes
> ¼ cup sugar
>   Juice of 1 lemon

Peel all the vegetables and pass them (except the tomatoes) through a food grinder or process in a food processor. Put the vegetable purée in a large mixing bowl. Add the salt, pepper, matzo meal, and the eggs.

Mix well. Shape the vegetable mixture into small rounds, as in making meat rissoles. Heat oil in a large skillet over high heat. Add the vegetable rounds and brown them on both sides in the hot fat. With a slotted spoon remove them to a 9 × 13-inch baking dish.

In a small bowl, combine the tomatoes with the sugar and lemon juice. Mix well. Pour the mixture over the vegetable rounds. Bake in a 350-degree F. oven for 30 minutes. Taste and adjust the seasoning. Serves 6 to 8.

Vegetable Quiche

The exact quantities of vegetables are not important in this versatile dish. Judgment must be exercised to determine the quantity and variety of vegetables desired.

> **1 recipe Basic Pizza Crust or Quiche**
> **Crust (see method)**
> **Peeled tomatoes**
> **Carrots**
> **Onions**
> **Celery**
> **Mushrooms**
> **Green pepper**
> **Margarine or butter**
> **1 tablespoon potato starch**
> **1 cup grated hard cheese of your choice**
> **2 eggs**
> **1 cup milk**
> **Salt and black pepper to taste**

Prepare the Basic Pizza Crust (see Index for recipe) or the Quiche Crust of the Gefilte Fish Quiche (see Index for recipe). Line a large quiche dish with the crust. Bake until set but not firm.

In a large skillet over medium heat, sauté the vegetables slightly in the margarine or melted butter. Arrange the vegetables on the set pizza crust. Sprinkle the potato starch and half of the grated cheese over the vegetables.

In a small bowl, combine the eggs with the milk; season with salt and pepper. Whisk until well blended. Pour the egg mixture over the vegetables. Sprinkle the remaining cheese over all. Bake in a preheated 350-degree F. oven until the top is nicely browned.

Green Pepper Horseradish Holder

When you need a garniture with character to serve with fish, prepare this green pepper holder for the horseradish.

Select a large green pepper with a flat bottom and a long stem. With a paring knife, cut in zigzag fashion all around the top of the pepper. Remove the cover. Seed the pepper and remove all inside membranes. Fill with horseradish and replace the cover. Place the filled holder in the center of a fish mold, or serve on a dish with a serving spoon on the side.

8

Side Dishes

A side dish enhances the main dish with which it is served. Although all the side dishes in this chapter can be served as accompaniments to main dishes, many can be served as main dishes or appetizers or hors d'oeuvres as well. An adequate portion of the Potato Varenekas, for example, can be a delightfully satisfying main dish, while the Miniature Potato Knishes make lovely hot hors d'oeuvres.

Many wonderful, distinctive side dishes can also be found in other chapters. Latkes and many kugels are excellent main dish complements (see Chapter Nine—Latkes, Fritters, and Kugels). Also consult Chapter Eleven, Foods With a Foreign Flavor, where you will find such Sephardi specialties as rollos (potato-meat dumplings) and a variety of burmuelos (pancakes). In Chapter Seven, Vegetable Specialties, you will find such delights as the Broccoli Soufflé and Baked Cabbage.

Miniature Potato Knishes

3 cups mashed potatoes
2 eggs, slightly beaten
2 tablespoons chicken fat or margarine
1 teaspoon salt
⅛ teaspoon black pepper

⟶

⅜ cup matzo meal
1 egg yolk beaten with 1 tablespoon
    water
Oil for the baking sheet

In a medium-sized bowl, combine the mashed potatoes with the eggs, chicken fat or margarine, salt, pepper, and matzo meal. Form into walnut-sized balls. Brush with the diluted egg yolk. Place on a well-greased baking sheet and bake in a preheated 400-degree F. oven for 20 minutes or until well browned. Makes approximately 42 miniature knishes.

Variation:

To make liver-filled knishes, prepare a filling by combining 1 chopped medium-sized onion sautéed in 3 tablespoons margarine with ½ pound of ground broiled chicken livers. Make a depression in the center of each walnut-sized ball, fill with the liver mixture, then brush with the diluted egg yolk. Arrange the knishes on a well-greased baking sheet and bake until browned.

Pareve Kishka

This is an excellent imitation of the derma prepared the year 'round. It is not quite as firm but is no less delicious to serve with roast chicken or turkey. It also makes a very nice hot hors d'oeuvre.

2 cups matzo meal
2 carrots, peeled and cut up
2 stalks celery
½ teaspoon white pepper
    Dash of garlic powder (optional)
1 large onion, cut up
½ cup oil or ½ cup melted shortening of
    your choice
1 egg, beaten
1 tablespoon sugar
1 teaspoon salt

Preheat the oven to 375 degrees F. Put the matzo meal in a medium-sized bowl. Thoroughly blend the remaining ingredients in the blender container. Pour the mixture over the matzo meal and mix well. Divide in half. Form into 2 rolls and place each on a piece of ungreased aluminum foil. Wrap each roll in the foil. Seal the foil and place on a baking sheet. Bake for 45 minutes to 1 hour. Remove the foil and slice. Serve hot. Serves 10 to 12.

Alternate Method:

Put the carrots, celery, and onion through a grinder. Add the beaten egg, oil or melted shortening, and seasonings; combine well. Pour the mixture over the matzo meal. Mix well and proceed as above.

Variation:

In place of the matzo meal, use matzo or matzo farfel crushed very fine.

Savory Matzo Farfel

The character of this savory side dish can be altered by stirring in one-quarter pound of minced liver. Any kind of liver can be used, even leftover chopped liver.

> 2 large onions
> ¼ cup margarine
> 3½ cups matzo farfel
> 1 teaspoon salt
> ¼ teaspoon pepper
> 1 teaspoon paprika
> 2½ cups boiling water or chicken broth

Mince the onions. In a large pan or skillet, melt the margarine and sauté the onions until tender. Add the matzo farfel and stir until lightly browned. In a large bowl, combine the seasonings with the boiling water. Add slowly to the skillet and cook over low heat, stirring frequently until all the liquid is absorbed. Serve as a side dish with meat or poultry. Serves 6.

"Spaghetti"

1 egg
½ cup water
1 teaspoon salt
⅛ teaspoon white pepper
1 cup sifted matzo meal
Oil
1 quart boiling water with 1 teaspoon salt

Using a rotary beater, beat the egg with the water and seasonings. Gradually stir in the matzo meal. Cover and refrigerate for at least 1 hour. Lightly grease the hands with oil. Pinch off a small piece of dough, the size of a green pea. Using the hands, on a rolling board (or on a clean flat surface) roll out the piece of dough into a pencil-like strand, as long and as thin as possible. Continue until all the dough is used up. Line up the strands on a baking sheet or flat plate. Store until ready to use. Covered with wax paper, these "spaghetti" strands can be refrigerated for up to 4 days.

To cook, add the "spaghetti" to 1 quart of boiling salted water and cook for 20 minutes. Drain well. Serve plain or with meatballs in tomato sauce. Serves 4.

Variations:

• To make Pretzel Sticks, nice to serve with a glass of cold milk, follow the above recipe, but do not boil. Heat ½ to 1 cup oil in a heavy skillet over medium heat. Add about half of the strands at a time and fry until golden brown. Turn the hot browned sticks into a paper bag with 1 teaspoon of salt. Close and shake the bag to coat the sticks evenly.
• To make Munchins, delicious to munch on or to serve in soup, cut the strands into shorter lengths, then fry. Serve plain in soup or salt them as you would the Pretzel Sticks. For a variation in seasoning, add a bit of onion powder or garlic powder to the salt in the bag before adding the Munchins.

Carrot, Sweet Potato, and Apple Tzimmes

The word "tzimmes" is used to identify several distinctly different preparations: a sweet casserole of vegetables, a sweet casserole of vegetables in combination with fruit, and a sweet casserole of vegetables and/or fruit with meat. Here, we have a vegetable-fruit combination.

3 carrots, peeled and sliced
4 sweet potatoes or yams, peeled and sliced
3 tart apples
Oil for the casserole
½ cup brown sugar or honey
⅛ teaspoon salt
⅛ teaspoon white pepper
3 tablespoons oil or margarine
1 cup water

In a medium-sized saucepan, cook the carrots and the sweet potatoes until tender. Peel, quarter, core, and slice the apples approximately ¼ inch thick. Lightly oil a 2½-quart casserole. Arrange in alternate layers the drained carrots, apples, and the drained sweet potatoes. Season each layer with some of the brown sugar or honey, salt, pepper, and oil or margarine. Add the water, cover, and bake in a preheated 350-degree F. oven for 30 minutes or until the apples are tender. Uncover and continue baking until the top is golden brown. Serves 6.

Variations:
• Add an 8-ounce can of crushed pineapple and reduce the amount of water by the amount of juice in the can.
• Substitute ½ pound of pitted prunes for the apples.

Carrot Tzimmes With Beef

Tzimmes was originally a traditional Sabbath dish, but it has become traditional holiday fare as well. On Rosh Hashanah, a carrot and honey tzimmes, a succulent combination symbolic of the wish for a good and sweet New Year, is served. The tzimmes of sweet potatoes and fruit served on Sukkot, the harvest festival, symbolizes the bounty of the harvest. Tzimmes has also become a favorite Passover side dish—for no reason other than that it has proven to be a wonderful *Yom Tov meichel* (a tasty holiday dish). It can be prepared in advance, be kept warm or reheated, and will still retain its luscious flavor. This tzimmes, prepared with meat, makes a substantial meal in itself.

> 2½ to 3 pounds beef (brisket)
> Salt and black pepper to taste
> 6 carrots, peeled and sliced
> 6 medium-sized sweet potatoes or 3 sweet
>   potatoes and 3 white potatoes, peeled
>   and cut into 1-inch rounds
> 1 tablespoon potato starch
> ¼ cup water
> 2 tablespoons chicken fat or shortening
> ½ to ¾ cup brown sugar, to taste
> Grease for the casserole

Season the meat with salt and pepper; cover with cold water and simmer in a medium-sized covered saucepan until tender, about 2½ hours. Add the vegetables after 2 hours. Remove the meat and vegetables and place them in a greased 3-quart casserole.

In a small saucepan, mix the potato starch with the ¼ cup of water. Gradually stir in 2 cups of the meat gravy and the chicken fat or shortening. Cook over medium heat, stirring until thick and smooth. Add the brown sugar. Taste and adjust the seasoning, adding salt and pepper as necessary. Pour this gravy over the meat in the casserole. Bake in a 350-degree F. oven until nicely browned, about 30 to 45 minutes. Serves 6.

Tzimmes With Matzo Balls

"Make a tzimmes over it!" This expression, in the vernacular, has come to mean "make much ado" about something or somebody. Your family and guests will surely "make a tzimmes" over this dish.

Matzo Balls:

> ½ cup hot water
> ½ teaspoon salt
> Dash of cinnamon
> ¼ cup oil or melted margarine
> 3 eggs, well beaten
> 1 cup matzo meal
> 2 quarts boiling water
> ½ teaspoon salt

Tzimmes:

> 2 pounds yams, cooked, drained, peeled,
> and sliced
> 1 pound prunes, cooked, drained, and
> pitted
> 1 pound small carrots, peeled, cooked, and
> drained
> 1 can (16 ounces) pineapple chunks,
> drained, juice reserved
> ½ cup brown sugar
> ½ teaspoon salt
> Grease for the baking pan

First, prepare the matzo balls. In a medium-sized bowl, combine the hot water, salt, cinnamon, and oil or melted margarine. Cool. Add the beaten eggs and matzo meal. Mix well. Refrigerate for 1 hour. Shape the mixture into balls and drop gently into the boiling water seasoned with the salt. Cook for 15 to 20 minutes, until firm. Remove immediately with a slotted spoon and drain.

Arrange the cooked vegetables and fruit in a lightly greased oblong pan. Sprinkle with the sugar and salt. Add the matzo balls. Pour the reserved pineapple juice over all. Bake in a preheated 400-degree F. oven for 30 to 40 minutes, until browned. Baste several times. Serves 6 to 8.

Variations:

- Arrange the yams, prunes, carrots, brown sugar, and matzo

balls in the pan. Pour an 8½ or 16-ounce can of undrained crushed pineapple over all; continue as per recipe. Your fondness for crushed pineapple will determine the size can you select.

• Slice the matzo balls. In a greased casserole, starting with the sliced matzo balls, alternate layers of the matzo balls, sliced yams, stewed prunes, sliced carrots, and sliced apples (2 large apples, peeled, cored, and sliced.) Sprinkle each layer with a portion of the sugar and the salt. Drizzle a teaspoon of oil over all. Repeat until the ingredients are used up, ending with the apples. Sprinkle with cinnamon. Bake in a 350-degree F. oven for 30 to 40 minutes, until hot and bubbly.

• As a shortcut use 2 cans of yams or sweet potatoes (32 ounces in all), drained; 1 jar (16 ounces) of prunes, drained and pitted; and 1 can (16 ounces) of small carrots, drained.

Varenekas

Little envelopes of potato dough encasing seasoned meat.

> 2 cups mashed potatoes
> 2 eggs, well beaten
> Salt and black pepper to taste
> ¼ cup cake meal
> 1 cup meat filling (recipe below)
> 1 egg, well beaten
> Matzo meal (optional)
> Grease for the baking sheet

Combine the mashed potatoes with the 2 well-beaten eggs and the salt and pepper. Mix together with the ¼ cup of cake meal.

On a piece of wax paper, form the dough into 8 to 10 flat round patties. Place a tablespoon of filling on half of each patty. Fold over the other half to cover the filling completely and form a half-circle. Pinch the edges together to seal. Dip each varenek in the well-beaten egg; coat with matzo meal if desired. Bake on a well-greased baking sheet in a 375-degree F. oven for about 20 minutes, until golden brown. Serves 4 to 5.

Meat Filling:

It does not matter what kind of meat is used. Leftover poultry can be used as well.

> **Leftover cooked meat to yield 1 cup ground**
> **2 to 3 tablespoons minced onion**
> **2 to 3 tablespoons minced celery**
> **Salt and black pepper to taste**
> **1 tablespoon chicken fat or oil**
> **1 egg, well beaten**

Grind enough leftover meat to yield 1 cup. Sauté the onion and the celery in the fat or oil until tender. Mix together with the meat, the salt, and the pepper. Add the egg to bind. This makes 1 cup of filling.

Liver and Potato Kugel

Whether you pronounce it "kugel" or "kigel," in the vernacular the word refers to a baked pudding. An infinite variety of kugels can be prepared, both sweet and savory, to be served hot or cold.

A savory potato kugel makes an excellent accompaniment to a meat roast. A sweet kugel may be served as a side dish or as a substitute for a dessert.

> **6 potatoes (about 3 pounds), peeled**
> **3 eggs, separated**
> **Salt and black pepper to taste**
> **3 tablespoons matzo meal**
> **2 to 3 medium-sized onions, chopped**
> **3 to 4 tablespoons margarine**
> **1 pound liver, broiled**
> **1 whole egg**
> **Grease for the pan**

Boil the potatoes in lightly salted water until tender; drain and mash in a medium-sized bowl. Beat the 3 egg yolks with the salt and the pepper; add to the potatoes along with the matzo meal.

Beat the 3 egg whites until stiff and fold them into the potato mixture.

Sauté the onions in the margarine in a small skillet; grind them together with the broiled liver. Thoroughly mix the liver with the whole egg.

Grease a 2-quart oblong baking pan. Put half of the potato mixture into the pan. Pat it down to cover the entire bottom of the pan evenly. Spread the liver mixture over it and cover with the remaining mashed potatoes. With a fork, score the top of the potatoes. Bake in a preheated 375-degree F. oven for 30 minutes or until browned. Serves 6 to 8.

Carrot Kugel

This kugel is very light, almost like a soufflé. The center might fall, but the taste will not be altered.

> **4 eggs, separated**
> **½ cup sugar**
> **1 cup tightly packed grated carrots**
> **¼ cup shredded peeled apple**
> **¼ cup sweet red wine**
> **2 tablespoons lemon juice**
> **½ teaspoon grated lemon rind**
> **⅓ cup potato starch**
> **Grease for the casserole**

In a large mixing bowl, beat the egg yolks with the sugar until light. Add the grated carrots, shredded apple, wine, lemon juice and rind, and the potato starch. Blend well. In another bowl, beat the egg whites until stiff; fold them into the yolk mixture. Turn into a well-greased 1½-quart casserole. Bake for 35 minutes in a preheated 375-degree F. oven or until nicely puffed and set. Serve hot or cold. Serves 6.

Carrot Ring

> **1 pound carrots, peeled**
> **½ cup matzo meal**

——➤

> ¼ cup potato starch
> ½ teaspoon salt
> ½ cup sugar
> 1 teaspoon cinnamon
> 1 teaspoon ground ginger
> Juice and grated rind of 1 large lemon
> ½ cup sweet wine
> 1 egg, well beaten
> ¼ cup raisins
> ¼ cup margarine, melted
> **Margarine for the mold**

On the fine side of a grater, grate the carrots into a bowl. In a large mixing bowl, blend together the matzo meal, potato starch, salt, sugar, cinnamon, and ginger. Add the grated carrots, the lemon juice and the grated rind, the wine, and the well-beaten egg. Mix well. Stir in the raisins and the melted margarine. Blend thoroughly.

Pour the mixture into a greased ring mold. Bake in a preheated 350-degree F. oven for 1 hour. Unmold onto a serving dish. Serves 6.

Noodle Kugel

Do not attempt to make this kugel with homemade noodles. The result will not be acceptable to any kugel *maven*.

> 1 box (8 ounces) Passover noodles
> 2 eggs
> ¼ cup white sugar and ¼ cup brown
> sugar, or ½ cup white sugar
> ¼ cup orange juice
> 2 heaping tablespoons orange marmalade
> 2 teaspoons cinnamon
> 1 cup raisins
> **Grease for the pans**

Cook the noodles according to package directions; drain. Beat the eggs and the sugar until light; add the orange juice, the orange marmalade, the cinnamon, and the raisins. Add to the noodles and mix well. Divide the mixture into 2 greased 8 × 8-inch pans and bake in a preheated 350-degree F. oven for 30 minutes or until browned on top. Makes 12 servings.

Mock Luckshen Kugel

The coarsely grated potatoes give this kugel the appearance of a luckshen (noodle) kugel.

> 6 raw potatoes, peeled
> Cold water
> 3 eggs, separated
> Salt and black pepper to taste
> 1 small onion, grated
> ¼ cup matzo meal
> Oil for the pan

Grate the potatoes on the coarse side of a grater into a medium-sized bowl with enough cold water to cover the grated potatoes. Beat the egg yolks well with the salt and the pepper. Drain the potatoes well; add the seasoned yolks, the grated onion, and the matzo meal. Beat the egg whites until stiff and fold them into the mixture. Pour into a well-greased 7 × 11-inch heated baking pan. Bake in a preheated 375-degree F. oven for 1 hour or until a nice brown crust has formed on top. Serves 8.

Carrot, Sweet Potato, and Apple Kugel

This kugel should not be confused with the Carrot, Sweet Potato, and Apple Tzimmes. The addition of matzo meal to the ingredients makes it possible to cut this kugel into serving portions. It makes a tasty side dish or an excellent dessert. Best served warm, not too hot.

> ½ cup margarine, melted
> 1 cup grated peeled sweet potatoes
> 1 cup grated peeled carrots
> 1 cup grated peeled apples
> ½ cup matzo meal

→

    2 tablespoons sweet wine
    ½ teaspoon cinnamon
    ½ cup white sugar
    ¼ cup brown sugar

Use some of the melted margarine to lightly grease a 7 × 11-inch baking pan. Combine the remainder of the margarine with the other ingredients; mix well. Pour the mixture into the pan. Bake at 375 degrees F. for 45 minutes or until brown. Makes 8 generous portions.

Variation:

    Add ½ cup chopped pitted prunes and ½ cup chopped raisins to the ingredients.

Cooked-Potato Knaidlach

    As a substitute for potato pancakes, try these knaidlach. Serve them plain or garnished with browned onions.

    6 medium-sized potatoes
    Boiling salted water
    1½ teaspoons salt
    Dash of freshly ground black pepper
    (optional)
    2 eggs, beaten
    ¾ cup matzo meal, approximately
    1½ quarts boiling water with 1 teaspoon
    salt
    Oil for the pan

Peel the potatoes. Boil the peeled potatoes in salted water until tender. Mash the potatoes, adding the salt and pepper. When cool, add the beaten eggs and enough matzo meal to hold the mixture together. Shape into balls and drop into the 1½ quarts of boiling water seasoned with 1 teaspoon salt. Boil for 20 minutes in a covered saucepan. Using a slotted spoon, remove the balls. Arrange the knaidlach in a 2-quart oblong baking pan greased with oil. Brown in a preheated 400-degree F. oven, turning to brown on all sides. Serves 4 to 6.

Zucchini Kugel

Nice to serve as a complement for meat and lovely as part of a vegetable platter. The ovo-lacto-vegetarian (whose diet includes eggs) will enjoy this dish immensely.

> 1 pound zucchini
> 1 tablespoon sugar
> ⅛ teaspoon salt
> ½ to 1 teaspoon cinnamon
> ½ cup raisins
> ¼ cup chopped walnuts
> 1 tablespoon oil or melted margarine
> 4 eggs, lightly beaten

Peel the zucchini and grate on the medium holes of a hand grater, or grate in a food processor. Let rest for 10 minutes; drain off the liquid. Add the remaining ingredients to the lightly beaten eggs; mix well. Add to the grated zucchini; mix lightly. Place the mixture in a lightly greased 8-inch square baking pan and bake in a preheated 400-degree F. oven for 25 minutes or until lightly browned. Serves 4 to 6.

Bananas Almondine

A nice change of pace from candied sweet potatoes. The unique flavor makes this an unusual dessert substitute when served warm.

> 4 firm, ripe bananas
>   Grease for the pan
> 2 tablespoons brown sugar
> 2 teaspoons unsweetened cocoa
> ¼ teaspoon cinnamon
> ½ cup brewed coffee
> 1 tablespoon Sherry wine
>   Sliced blanched almonds

Peel the bananas. Halve them lengthwise, then cut each half crosswise. Arrange the banana pieces in a greased 8 × 10-inch baking pan. Combine the remaining ingredients except the almonds; pour the mixture over the bananas. Sprinkle the almonds over all. Bake at 300 degrees F. for 20 to 30 minutes, until the bananas feel tender when pierced with a fork. Serves 8.

Peach-Potato Puffs

This sweet potato delight partners very well with roast chicken or turkey.

>   2 cups mashed sweet potatoes
>   1 teaspoon lemon juice
>   2 tablespoons brown sugar
>   ¼ teaspoon salt
>   Dash of ginger
>   2 tablespoons margarine, softened
>   6 canned peach halves
>   Margarine

In a medium-sized bowl, combine the sweet potatoes, lemon juice, brown sugar, salt, dash of ginger, and the margarine. Whip until fluffy. Pile some of the potato mixture into each peach half. Arrange the filled peach halves in a greased 6 × 10-inch baking pan. Dot with additional margarine. Bake in a preheated 400-degree F. oven for 20 minutes. Serves 6.

Pareve "Cheese" Blintzes

Serve these "cheese" blintzes with a meat main dish and be prepared for looks of surprise. The blintzes not only have the appearance of cheese blintzes when cut, but it is incredible how like farmer cheese the filling tastes.

Blintz Leaves:

>   3 eggs
>   ½ teaspoon salt
>   1½ cups water
>   1 tablespoon oil
>   ⅔ cup cake meal
>   Oil for the skillet
>   Margarine

Filling:

> 6 hard-cooked eggs
> 2 tablespoons lemon juice
> Dash of salt
> ½ tablespoon sugar

First prepare the blintz leaves. Beat the eggs, salt, water, and oil in a medium-sized bowl. Gradually add the cake meal, beating continuously until the mixture is smooth and free of lumps. It should have the consistency of light cream. If the batter thickens as it stands, thin it with additional liquid. Stir the batter periodically.

Heat a 7 or 8-inch lightly greased skillet over moderately high heat. Ladle in sufficient batter to thinly coat the bottom of the pan. Quickly rotate the pan to distribute the batter evenly. Tip out any excess batter. Return the pan to moderate heat. Cook until the bottom of the pancake sets and the edges start to leave the sides of the pan. Invert the skillet over a clean cloth. The pancake will fall onto the cloth cooked side up. Regulate the heat and cooking time so that each pancake will cook to a uniform gold color. Yields 10 to 12 leaves.

To prepare the filling, separate the whites of the eggs from the yolks. Put the whites through a food mill, or mash very fine. Add the lemon juice, a dash of salt, and the sugar. Place about 1 heaping tablespoonful of filling in the center of each pancake; fold in the side edges and roll up the pancake over the filling. Place in a well-greased baking pan large enough to accommodate the blintzes. Dot the top of the blintzes with margarine. Bake in a 350-degree F. oven for 30 to 45 minutes, until lightly browned. Serves 6.

Note: The yolks of the eggs may be prepared the same way, with a dash of cinnamon added.

Variation:

Prepare "cheese" by dropping bits of raw egg white into a saucepan of boiling water. The egg white will cook and look like cheese curd. Drain off the water very well. Prepare as above.

9

Latkes, Fritters, and Kugels

In this chapter there is a wide selection of recipes for latkes (pancakes), fritters (small cakes of fried batter, usually filled), and kugels (puddings). You will find everything from a simple matzo meal latke to the glorious latke known as the chremsel.

The kugel recipes have been selected for their outstanding *tam* (marvelous taste), and they may be served as a side dish, main dish, or dessert. Blintzes (crêpes), very delicate pancakes that are usually filled, are so versatile that an entire chapter (Chapter Ten) has been devoted exclusively to them.

Kartoffel (Potato) Latkes

These latkes are made from two forms of potatoes, raw and cooked. Served with a dollop of zesty sour cream or a side dish of applesauce, this is a nourishing luncheon dish.

> **4 medium-sized raw potatoes, grated**
> **1 cup mashed cooked potatoes**
> **2 eggs, well beaten**
> **Salt and white pepper to taste**
> **Fat for frying**

Press out the liquid from the grated potatoes and discard. In a medium-sized mixing bowl, combine the grated potatoes with the mashed potatoes, eggs, salt, and pepper. Shape the mixture into the desired size pancakes and fry in hot fat in a large skillet over medium-high heat until brown and crisp on both sides. Drain on paper towels. Serves 4 to 5.

Two-tone Latkes

    2 large potatoes
    1 large sweet potato
    1 medium-sized onion
    2 eggs
    1½ teaspoons salt
    Dash of white pepper
    ¼ cup matzo meal
    Oil for the skillet

Peel the vegetables. On the small openings of a grater grate the vegetables into a bowl, or pass them through the fine blade of a meat grinder. Add the eggs, salt, pepper, and matzo meal. Drop the batter by the tablespoonful into hot oil in a large skillet over medium-high heat. Brown on both sides. Drain on absorbent paper. Serves 4.

Walnut Latkes

    1 cup chopped walnuts
    2 cups mashed potatoes
    2 eggs, well beaten
    1 teaspoon salt
    ⅛ teaspoon white pepper
    ⅛ teaspoon cinnamon
    Oil for frying

In a medium-sized mixing bowl, combine the walnuts, mashed potatoes, eggs, salt, pepper, and cinnamon. Mix well. Heat oil in a large skillet over medium heat. Form the latkes into the desired size and fry in the heated oil until nicely browned on both sides. Drain on paper towels. Serve garnished with walnut halves. Serves 4 to 6.

Wine Latkes

3 eggs
¾ cup sweet red wine
½ cup matzo meal
Pinch of salt
1 tablespoon sugar
Grease for the skillet

Separate the eggs into 2 medium-sized bowls. Beat the yolks until light. Add the wine. Mix in the matzo meal. Set aside for 1 hour.

Beat the egg whites with the salt until frothy. Continue beating until stiff, gradually adding the sugar. Carefully fold the egg whites into the yolk-wine mixture. Drop by the tablespoonful into a hot well-greased skillet over medium-high heat. Brown on both sides. Serves 4 to 6.

Soup-Green Latkes

Greens from chicken soup (carrots,
parsnips, parsley root, dill, etc.)
1 package (3 ounces) potato pancake mix
2 to 3 eggs
Matzo meal
Salt and white pepper to taste
Grease for the baking sheet

Remove all the vegetables used in cooking chicken soup. Drain well and put through a food mill or grinder into a bowl (or mash them very well).

In another bowl, prepare the potato pancake mix according to package directions. Add the mixture to the vegetables. The number of eggs to be added (in addition to those called for on the pancake mix package) depends upon the amount of vegetables prepared. Add a sufficient amount of matzo meal to give the mixture body. Add salt and pepper to taste.

With a large spoon, form latkes on a greased baking sheet and bake in a 400-degree F. oven until nicely browned, turning once. Or fry in hot oil. Yield depends upon the amount of vegetables used. Soup greens used to make approximately 3 quarts of soup yields 12 or more servings.

Potato Pancakes

These potatoes need not be peeled before grating.

> 3 cups coarsely shredded potatoes
> 2 eggs
> 1½ teaspoons salt
> ¼ teaspoon white pepper
> 1 heaping tablespoon matzo meal
> Fat for frying

Put all the ingredients in a medium-sized mixing bowl. Blend well. Drop by the tablespoonful into heated fat in a large skillet over low heat. Fry the pancakes slowly until browned on both sides. Drain on paper towels. Alternatively, the potato mixture may be baked in the form of a pudding in a well-greased 1-quart baking dish in a 375-degree F. oven for 45 minutes to 1 hour, until the top is browned and crisp at the edges. Serves 4 to 5.

Potato-Apple Pancakes

These are lovely party-fare pancakes when served topped with sour cream and with additional applesauce on the side.

> 1 package (3 ounces) potato pancake mix
> 1 egg
> ½ cup applesauce
> ½ cup cold water
> Melted butter or margarine
> Sour cream (optional)

In a small mixing bowl, combine the pancake mix with the egg, applesauce, and cold water. Mix until well combined. Let the batter stand for 10 minutes.

Heat a griddle or heavy skillet. Brush with melted butter or margarine. Use about 1 tablespoonful of batter for each pancake. With a spatula, spread the batter into a 3-inch circle. Cook on each side over medium heat for about 2 minutes, until golden brown. Serves 4 to 6.

Farfel Pancakes I

½ cup farfel
1 cup milk
2 eggs
½ cup matzo meal
½ teaspoon salt
2 tablespoons melted butter
Butter or margarine for the griddle

In a small bowl, soak the farfel in the milk. In a medium-sized mixing bowl, beat the eggs until light. Add the soaked farfel, matzo meal, salt, and butter. Beat well.

Heat a pancake griddle over medium heat. Liberally grease the griddle with butter or margarine. Drop the pancake batter onto the griddle by the tablespoonful. Cook until the bottom of the pancakes are golden brown. Turn and brown the other side. Serve with honey or preserves. Serves 4 to 6.

Farfel Pancakes II

2 cups matzo farfel
2 eggs
1 teaspoon salt
1 cup water
Fat for the skillet

Put the farfel in a medium-sized bowl. In a medium-sized mixing bowl, beat the eggs with the salt and water; pour over the farfel. Mix well.

Heat the fat in a large skillet over medium-high heat. Drop into the hot fat by the tablespoonful. Fry until golden brown on both sides. Serves 4.

Farfel-Cheese Pancakes

> 5 cups matzo farfel
> 1 cup hot water
> 3 eggs, well beaten
> 1 tablespoon melted butter or margarine
> 3 heaping tablespoons cottage cheese or
>   cream cheese
>   Fat for frying

Place the farfel in a large bowl. Pour the hot water over the farfel; let stand until the water has been absorbed. Add the eggs, butter or margarine, and cheese. Mix well.

Melt about 3 tablespoons of fat in a large skillet over medium-high heat. Drop the pancake mixture into the skillet by the tablespoonful. Brown on both sides. Drain the pancakes on paper towels. Serve hot with jam, preserves, or honey. Yields about 36 small pancakes or 24 large ones.

Variation:
Use 4 crumbled matzos in place of the matzo farfel.

Cheese Pancakes I

The cottage cheese adds high-quality protein to these pancakes.

> ½ pound cottage cheese
> 4 eggs, well beaten
> 1 teaspoon butter
> 2 teaspoons sugar, or to taste
> ½ cup matzo meal
>   Butter or margarine for frying
>   Sugar and cinnamon

In a large bowl, combine the cheese with the eggs. Slowly stir in the remaining ingredients. Mix well. In a large skillet over medium-high heat, melt a liberal amount of butter or margarine. Fry the pancakes in the fat until light brown on both sides. Drain on paper towels. Sprinkle with sugar and cinnamon. Serve hot. Serves 4.

Variations:

- Separate the eggs. Mix the yolks with the cheese and fold in the stiffly beaten egg whites.
- Use ½ pound of farmer cheese, 3 tablespoons of melted butter or oil, and ¼ teaspoon of cinnamon.

Cheese Pancakes II

A cheese pancake that will be as welcomed at breakfast as at lunch or dinner. For breakfast or lunch, serve sprinkled with sugar and cinnamon; for dinner, top with crushed strawberries or hot sliced peaches.

>   8 ounces sour cream
>   8 ounces cottage cheese
>   ½ to ¾ cup matzo meal
>   4 egg yolks, well beaten
>   1 tablespoon sugar
>   ½ teaspoon salt
>   4 egg whites, stiffly beaten
>   Butter for the griddle

In a large mixing bowl, combine the sour cream with the cottage cheese until well blended. Stir in the matzo meal, egg yolks, sugar, and salt. Fold in the stiffly beaten egg whites. Refrigerate the mixture and allow to rest for several hours or overnight. Cook quickly on both sides on a buttered griddle over medium heat. Makes 12 to 14 four-inch pancakes.

Matzo Meal Pancakes

Vary the taste of these pancakes by substituting apple juice for the milk. Or substitute pineapple juice for the milk and 1 cup of drained crushed pineapple for the applesauce in the topping.

Pancakes:

> 3 eggs
> 1 cup milk
> ½ teaspoon salt
> ½ teaspoon sugar
> 1 cup matzo meal
> Butter for the skillet

Topping:

> 1 cup sour cream
> 1 cup thick applesauce
> 1 teaspoon cinnamon

In a large bowl, beat the eggs with the milk, salt, and sugar. Add the matzo meal; beat until well blended. Melt the butter in a large skillet over medium heat. Drop the pancake mixture into the hot butter by the tablespoonful. Brown on 1 side, then turn to brown the other side.

In a small bowl, combine the cream, applesauce, and cinnamon. Spoon the topping over the pancakes. Serves 4.

Orange-Matzo Pancakes

To prepare these as hors d'oeuvre pancakes, a plättar, a skillet with separate 2½-inch depressions, would be very convenient.

> 6 eggs, separated
> 2 tablespoons sugar
> 1 teaspoon salt
> 1 cup orange juice
> 1½ cups matzo meal
> Fat for the skillet

In a large bowl, beat the yolks until light and fluffy. Beat in the sugar, salt, and orange juice. Blend well. Stir in the matzo meal.

In a separate large bowl, beat the egg whites until stiff but not dry. Fold the whites into the egg yolk batter. Spoon a rounded tablespoonful of batter into a well-greased skillet or griddle over medium heat. Cook on both sides until lightly browned. Serve with orange sugar (see Index for recipe). Yields about 48 small pancakes.

Pancake Specials

For an intriguing contrast of flavors, serve with hot honey or syrup to which a few drops of lemon juice has been added.

>   3 eggs, separated
>   ½ cup matzo meal
>   ½ cup water or milk
>   ½ teaspoon salt
>   1 tablespoon sugar
>   Oil or butter for the griddle

In a medium-sized mixing bowl, beat the egg yolks until light and thick. In a small bowl, mix the matzo meal, water or milk, salt, and sugar until thoroughly blended. Fold the mixture into the egg yolks. Beat until smooth and thoroughly blended. In a separate bowl, beat the egg whites until stiff but not dry. Fold them into the yolk mixture.

Heat a pancake griddle over medium heat. Oil or butter the griddle thoroughly. Drop the pancake batter onto the griddle by the tablespoonful. Cook until the bottom of the cakes are golden brown. Turn and cook the other side. Serve hot with sugar or jam. Yields about 12 pancakes.

Variations:

Apple Pancakes: Add ½ to 1 cup pared, cored, and chopped apples to the batter. Serve sprinkled with sugar and cinnamon. Apple juice may be substituted for the water.

Blueberry Pancakes: Sprinkle the pancakes with berries before turning.

Banana Pancakes: Add ½ to 1 cup very thinly sliced bananas to the batter.

Nutty Pancakes: Fold ½ cup chopped nuts into the batter, or sprinkle chopped nuts over the pancakes before serving.

Sandwich-fashion: Eliminate the sugar from the batter. Place a thin slice of cheese between 2 thinly baked pancakes, sandwich-fashion, and have a lovely luncheon dish.

Pineapple Pancakes: Add ½ cup well-drained canned crushed pineapple or pineapple chunks to the batter. Pineapple juice may be substituted for the water in the recipe.

Chremslach

Chremslach (singular, *chremsel*) are basically matzo meal pancakes. However, chremsel batter may be prepared in countless ways. More often than not, chremslach are prepared as sweet pancakes containing fruit, or they are filled with a sweet filling. The chremslach may be fried in hot oil or in a hot oil-honey mixture; or they may be baked and then coated with honey. Chremslach may be served as an accompaniment to a meal, as the climax to a meal, or as dessert.

> 6 eggs
> ½ cup sugar
> ¾ cup chopped walnuts
> Juice and grated rind of ½ lemon
> 1 cup matzo meal
> 6 tablespoons honey
> 6 tablespoons fat

Separate the eggs into 2 bowls. Beat the egg yolks and sugar until very light and fluffy. Beat the egg whites until stiff; fold them into the beaten yolks. Slowly fold in the nuts, lemon juice and rind, and the matzo meal.

Melt the honey with the fat in a large heavy skillet over medium heat. Drop the batter into the skillet by the tablespoonful. Brown on both sides. Serves 6 to 8.

Baked Chremslach

Batter:

> 1 cup water
> ½ cup oil
> ½ cup sugar
> ¼ teaspoon cinnamon
>   Juice and rind of 1 orange
>   Juice and grated rind of 1 lemon
> 2 cups matzo meal
> 2 eggs

In a medium-sized saucepan, boil the water and the oil together. Add the sugar, cinnamon, orange juice and rind, lemon juice and rind, and the 2 cups of matzo meal. Stir briskly. Remove from the heat and mix well. Add the eggs, 1 at a time; stir to blend. Let rest while preparing the filling.

Filling:

> 1 bag (12 ounces) pitted prunes
> ¼ cup raisins
> ¼ cup finely ground nuts
>   Dash of ginger
>   Grease for the pan
> 6 tablespoons honey
> 6 tablespoons oil
>   Finely chopped nuts

Grind the prunes and the raisins together. Stir in the finely ground nuts and dash of ginger. Blend thoroughly. Wet the hands with cold water. In the palm of 1 hand, form a thin patty with some of the batter. Place a spoonful of the prune mixture on the patty. Roll the patty over the filling to completely enclose it. Repeat until the batter and prune mixture have all been used up.

Place the patties in a well-greased baking pan and bake in a preheated 350-degree F. oven for 45 minutes, turning once. Heat the honey and the fat in a large heavy skillet over medium heat. Place the baked chremslach in the skillet. Fry in the honey mixture until browned on both sides. Remove the skillet from the heat. Roll each of the chremslach in chopped nuts. Makes 24 chremslach.

Variation:

Use a 25-ounce jar of stewed prunes. Drain, pit, and chop or mash the prunes very well. Continue to prepare the filling as above.

Cherry Chremslach

Batter:

>6 tablespoons margarine
>2 cups hot water
>Juice and grated rind of 1 lemon
>3½ cups matzo meal, divided
>4 eggs, separated
>1 cup sugar
>¼ teaspoon cinnamon
>¼ teaspoon salt
>Grease for the baking sheet

Filling:

>¾ cup cherry preserves
>½ cup chopped nuts
>2 tablespoons matzo meal

Topping:

>Honey and toasted slivered almonds or
>the chopped nuts of your choice, or
>cinnamon and sugar

In a large mixing bowl, combine the margarine, hot water, and lemon juice and rind. Gradually stir in half of the matzo meal to make a stiff batter. In another large bowl, beat the egg yolks with the sugar and cinnamon until light and creamy; stir this into the stiff batter. Add the remaining matzo meal. Mix well. In a large clean bowl, beat the egg whites with the salt until stiff. Fold this into the matzo meal mixture. Let rest for 10 to 15 minutes. Meanwhile, combine the filling ingredients.

Form the batter into small balls, making a depression in the center of each to accommodate the filling. Tuck ½ teaspoon of the filling mixture into each ball and enclose smoothly.

Flatten the chremslach into pancakes and bake on a well-greased baking sheet in a 375-degree F. oven until golden brown. (Chremslach may also be deep-fried in oil.) Drain on paper towels. Serve topped with honey and the nuts of your choice; or sprinkle with cinnamon and sugar. Makes 24 to 30 small chremslach.

Filling Variations:

Apple Filling:
> 1 cup chopped apples
> ½ cup chopped almonds
> 3 tablespoons sugar
> 2 tablespoons matzo meal
> Dash of cinnamon

Orange Filling:
> 1 cup orange marmalade
> 2 tablespoons matzo meal
> ½ cup chopped nuts

Raspberry Filling:
> 1 cup raspberry preserves
> 2 tablespoons matzo meal
> ½ cup chopped nuts

Select-a-Flavor Fritters

Fruit fritters to end a meal. The batter blends nicely with any fruit. Select your favorite flavor and enjoy. Best served hot.

> 3 eggs
> 2 tablespoons oil
> ½ teaspoon salt

→

½ cup water
1 tablespoon sugar
1 cup matzo meal
Fat for frying
Cinnamon sugar (see Index for recipe)

In a large mixing bowl, beat the eggs with the oil, salt, water, and sugar. Add the matzo meal and mix well. Select a flavor from the variations below and add to the batter. Stir until the fruit is incorporated.

Drop batter by tablespoonfuls into hot fat (375 degrees F.) in a deep fryer; fry until golden brown. Or fry like pancakes in a large heavy skillet with at least 1 inch of hot oil. Remove with a slotted spoon and drain on paper towels. Sprinkle with cinnamon sugar. Yields 12 to 14.

Flavor Variations:

Apple: 3 tart apples, peeled, cored, and thinly sliced or chopped. Add a dash of cinnamon. Substitute apple juice for the water.

Pear: 1 to 2 cups chopped peeled and cored pears.

Banana: 2 large bananas, sliced

Pineapple: 1 to 2 cups drained pineapple tidbits or 2 cups grated fresh pineapple. Substitute pineapple juice for the water.

Brandy: A few tablespoons of brandy may be added to the batter, in which case an equal quantity of water must be omitted.

Tips on Frying Fritters:

Keep the temperature of the fat constant (375 degrees F.) Fritters will be greasy if the temperature is too low; the outside of the fritters will be dark and the centers undone if the temperature is too high. Keep the grease clear by removing batter particles with a slotted spoon.

Dried Fruit Fritters

Fritters are best served hot. These, however, are a culinary delight when served cold with a fruit sauce.

>   2 matzos
>   2 cups cold water
>   2 eggs
>   ¼ cup sugar
>   ⅔ teaspoon cinnamon
>   ⅓ cup ground walnuts or blanched
>   almonds
>   ⅔ cup finely diced mixed dried fruits
>   ½ cup sifted matzo meal
>   ¼ cup oil
>   Cinnamon sugar (see Index for recipe)

Soak the matzos in a small bowl with cold water to cover. Drain and squeeze dry. Separate the eggs into 2 medium-sized bowls. Beat the egg yolks with the sugar and cinnamon until light. Add the matzo and the ground nuts. Beat the mixture until thoroughly blended. Stir in the dried fruit and the matzo meal. Mix to distribute the fruit evenly throughout the batter. Beat the egg whites until stiff but not dry. Fold them into the batter.

Heat the oil in a large heavy skillet over medium heat. Drop the batter by tablespoonfuls into the oil. Fry the fritters until browned on each side. Drain on absorbent paper. Serve hot with cinnamon sugar sprinkled on top. Or serve cold with a fruit sauce. Serves 4.

Matzo Meal Kugel

A kugel that is equally delicious served plain, with fruit, or with sour cream or a sauce spooned over each portion.

>   2 eggs
>   ½ cup sugar
>   2 cups milk
>   4 tablespoons melted butter or margarine
>   1 cup matzo meal
>   ¼ teaspoon salt
>   ½ teaspoon cinnamon
>   ½ cup finely chopped nuts
>   Butter for the casserole or baking dish

In a medium-sized bowl, beat the eggs until frothy and light. Gradually add the sugar. Add the milk and melted butter or margarine. Stir in the matzo meal, salt, and cinnamon. Blend thoroughly. Fold in the chopped nuts. Pour the mixture into a well-buttered 2-quart casserole or baking dish. Bake in a 350-degree F. oven for 1 hour or until set and browned. Serves 6.

Matzo Kugel

The secret of this kugel is that all the apples are baked into it. Serve as a side dish or dessert.

> 4 square matzos
> Water
> 7 eggs
> 1½ cups sugar
> Juice of ½ lemon
> ⅓ cup margarine
> 1½ teaspoons cinnamon
> Salt to taste (optional)
> 4 large apples
> ½ cup raisins
> ¼ teaspoon salt
> Grease for the pan

Soak the matzos in a large bowl with water to cover. Drain and press out the excess water. Separate the eggs into 2 large bowls. Beat the egg yolks with the sugar until light and fluffy. Add the drained matzos, lemon juice, margarine, cinnamon, and salt. Beat until well combined.

Peel the apples and grate them into the yolk mixture; add the raisins and mix to blend. With an electric mixer at low speed, beat the egg white with the ¼ teaspoon salt until frothy. Increase to a high speed and beat until stiff peaks form. Gently fold the stiffly beaten egg whites into the yolk mixture. Lightly grease a 9¾ × 13¾-inch baking pan. Turn the mixture into the pan. Bake in a preheated 375-degree F. oven for 30 to 45 minutes, until nicely browned. Serves 12 to 14.

Scalloped Matzo Kugel

Stewed fruit makes a nice topping for this Scalloped Matzo Kugel.

>   4 eggs, divided
>   6 matzos, broken into pieces
>   1 pound creamed cottage cheese
>   ⅛ cup melted butter
>   ¼ cup sugar
>   1 teaspoon cinnamon
>   ½ cup raisins
>   Butter for the pan
>   1 cup milk

In a medium-sized bowl, beat 2 of the eggs very well. Add the matzos; set aside while preparing the remaining ingredients. In a larger bowl, beat the remaining 2 eggs; add the cottage cheese, butter, sugar, cinnamon, and raisins. Beat to blend and to distribute the raisins through the cheese mixture.

Line a buttered 9-inch square pan with some of the matzos. Spread with a portion of the cheese mixture. Continue layering, ending with matzo. Pour the milk over the top layer. Bake at 350 degrees F. for 40 minutes or until completely set and golden brown. Serves 6.

Farfel Kugel

>   2 cups matzo farfel
>   Cold water
>   3 eggs, separated
>   ⅔ cup sugar (or less, to taste)
>   ¼ cup sweet red wine
>   ¼ teaspoon salt
>   2 tablespoons grated orange rind
>   2 tablespoons oil
>   Grease for the baking dish

Place the farfel in a small bowl. Add cold water and let soak for a few minutes, then drain and crush to a paste. In a large mixing bowl, beat the egg yolks with the sugar (less if you prefer the kugel not so sweet) until thick and lemon-colored. Stir in the wine, salt, orange rind, oil, and farfel.

In separate medium-sized bowl, beat the egg whites until stiff peaks form. Fold the stiffly beaten egg whites into the yolk mixture. Transfer to a greased 1½-quart baking dish. Bake at 350 degrees F. for 30 minutes or until lightly browned. Serves 6 to 8.

Variation:

For an Apple-Farfel Kugel, alternate layers of the batter in the baking pan with 2 cups of thinly sliced apples sprinkled with a dash of cinnamon. Top the kugel with ¼ cup chopped blanched almonds.

Farfel-Vegetable Kugel

> 1 cup minced onions
> 1 cup finely diced celery
> ½ pound mushrooms, sliced, or 1 can (4 ounces) mushrooms, drained
> ⅜ cup fat of your choice
> 3½ cups matzo farfel
> 3 cups hot water seasoned with a bouillon cube
> 2 eggs
> 1 teaspoon salt
> ¼ teaspoon freshly ground black pepper
> 1 teaspoon paprika
> Grease for the pan

In a large skillet, sauté the onions, celery, and mushrooms in the fat over medium heat just until tender, not browned. Put the matzo farfel in a large bowl. Add the seasoned hot water and the sautéed vegetables. Mix well. In a small bowl, beat the eggs with the salt, pepper, and paprika. Add to the matzo farfel mixture. Blend thoroughly.

Pour the mixture into a greased 1½-quart baking pan. Bake at 375 degrees F. for 35 to 45 minutes, until firm. Serves 6 to 8.

Variation:

For *fleishig*, chicken broth may be substituted for the seasoned hot water.

Fruit Meringue Kugel

A fruit-filled kugel topped with a cloud of meringue. This may well become one of your favorites.

> 2½ matzos, broken into very small pieces,
>   or 1½ cups matzo farfel
> 2 cups apple juice
> 1 tablespoon lemon juice
> 2 tablespoons grated lemon rind
> 3 tablespoons shortening
> ¼ cup sugar
> 1 package (.43 ounces) vanilla sugar or 1
>   teaspoon vanilla flavoring
> 1 whole egg
> 2 egg yolks
> ¼ teaspoon salt
> ½ cup chopped nuts
>   Grease for the baking dish
> ½ cup sliced peeled apples or bananas
>   Pinch of salt for the meringue
> ¼ cup sugar for the meringue

In a large bowl, soak the matzos in the apple juice for 15 minutes. Add the lemon juice, lemon rind, shortening, sugar, vanilla sugar or vanilla flavoring, the whole egg, 2 egg yolks, salt, and the chopped nuts. Blend the ingredients very well. Spoon the mixture into a greased 1½-quart baking dish (6 × 10¼ inches). Top with the sliced fruit. Bake at 350 degrees F. for 25 to 30 minutes.

Now prepare the meringue. In a medium-sized bowl, beat the 2 egg whites with the salt at the low speed of an electric mixer until frothy. Increase the speed and add the sugar gradually, a tablespoon at a time, until the whites are stiff but not dry. Cover the fruit with the meringue. Return to the oven and bake for an additional 15 minutes. Serve warm. Serves 6 to 8.

Overnight Cheese Noodle Kugel

In this unusual noodle kugel, the noodles are not precooked.

Butter for the pan
1 box (8 ounces) noodles
3 eggs
½ cup sugar
2 cups milk
1 cup cottage cheese
¼ cup raisins
Cinnamon sugar (see Index for recipe)

Butter a 9 × 9-inch baking pan. Arrange the raw noodles on the bottom of the pan. In a large mixing bowl, beat the eggs and sugar until light; add the milk; beat together. Stir in the cottage cheese and raisins. Pour the mixture over the noodles, then cover and refrigerate overnight.

Before baking, sprinkle cinnamon sugar on the top. Bake for 1 hour and 15 minutes in a 350-degree F. oven, the first half of the cooking time covered and the remainder of the time uncovered. Serves 6 to 8.

Farfel Pudding

2 cups matzo farfel
Cold water
2 eggs
½ teaspoon salt
⅓ cup sugar
2 tablespoons margarine or oil
1 apple, pared and sliced or diced, or 1
banana, sliced
½ cup chopped nuts
Grease for the pan

In a small bowl, cover the farfel with cold water; drain immediately. The farfel should be moist but not soggy. In a large mixing bowl, beat the eggs with the salt, sugar, and margarine or oil. Add the farfel. Stir well. Add the apple or banana and the nuts. Gently mix. Pour the mixture into a greased 8-inch square baking pan. Bake in a 350-degree F. oven until brown, 30 to 40 minutes. Serve with a sauce if desired. Serves 6 to 8.

Farfel Casserole

1 box (8 ounces) egg farfel
2 to 3 onions, diced
Oil
¼ pound mushrooms, sliced, or 1 can (4 ounces) mushrooms, drained
½ cup chicken soup
Salt and pepper to taste
Grease for the casserole or baking pan

Cook the farfel according to package directions. In a medium-sized skillet over low heat, sauté the onions and fresh mushrooms in a small amount of oil until the onions are tender. Add the chicken soup and sautéed vegetables to the cooked farfel. Add salt and pepper. Pour the mixture into a greased 1½-quart casserole or an 8-inch baking pan. Bake at 350 degrees F. for 50 to 60 minutes, until nicely browned. Serves 6 to 8.

Variations:

• Add 2 or 3 diced broiled chicken livers to the farfel mixture before baking.

• For pareve, prepare the soup with a pareve bouillon cube.

Matzo Charlotte

4 square matzos
2 cups water
5 eggs, separated
½ cup sugar

→

   1 large apple, peeled and grated
      Juice and grated rind of 1 lemon
   ¼ cup chopped blanched almonds
   ¼ cup raisins
   ¼ teaspoon cinnamon

In a large bowl, soak the matzos in the water. Drain and squeeze dry. In a large mixing bowl, beat the egg yolks with the sugar until light; add the drained matzos, the apple, lemon juice and rind, almonds, raisins, and cinnamon.

Beat the egg whites in a large mixing bowl until stiff peaks form, then carefully fold them into the matzo mixture. Pour the mixture into a 2-quart greased casserole and bake for 30 to 35 minutes in a preheated 350-degree F. oven. Serve plain or with a wine or honey sauce (see Index for recipes). Serves 6 to 8.

10

Blintzes

It is hard to pinpoint the place of origin of the blintz. Each ethnic group has its own version: the French have the crêpe; in Sweden its the plättar; the Russians have the blini; Italians, the cannellone; Greeks, the krep; and Jews have the blintz. The blintz and crêpe are basically the same, a thin pancake, although the crêpe is usually browned on both sides.

Blintzes can be made in a variety of shapes and by various methods. The most popular blintz is the rolled blintz, which usually is filled with cheese. However, the fillings can be as varied as your imagination wills them to be.

Spread blintzes with a savory meat or vegetable filling, then cut them into wedges and serve as an appetizer. Or stack blintz leaves and fill each layer to make a splendid gâteau, a fine complement for a main dish.

In this chapter you will find a variety of new and exciting dishes that will win you laurels. Don't fail to try the extraspecial Crêpe Cups Florentine, the Apple Dumpling Crêpes, the Blintz Soufflé, and the Blintz Beignets.

Passover Blintz Leaves I

There are many blintz batter variations. This basic recipe should serve you well.

4 eggs
1¾ cups water
½ teaspoon salt
1 heaping tablespoon oil
¾ cup sifted cake meal
Oil for the skillet

Beat the eggs, water, salt, and oil in a medium-sized bowl. Gradually add the cake meal, beating continuously until the mixture is smooth. It should have the consistency of light cream. If the batter thickens as it stands, thin it with additional liquid. Stir the batter periodically.

Heat a 7 to 8-inch lightly greased skillet over moderately high heat. Ladle in sufficient batter to thinly coat the bottom of the pan. Quickly rotate the pan to distribute the batter evenly. Pour off any excess batter. Return the pan to moderate heat. Cook until the batter sets and the edge of the pancake starts to leave the sides of the pan. Invert the skillet over a clean cloth. The pancake will fall onto the cloth cooked side up. Repeat until all the batter is used up. Regulate the heat and frying time so that each pancake will cook to a uniform pale gold color. Yields 12 to 14.

Passover Blintz Leaves II

Filled with your favorite filling, blintzes may be fried in a large skillet or arranged in a greased baking pan, dotted with margarine, and baked in a 350-degree F. oven until browned.

3 eggs
1⅓ cups water
6 tablespoons potato starch
½ teaspoon salt
1 tablespoon oil
Oil for the skillet

In a medium-sized bowl, beat the eggs, water, potato starch, salt, and oil until the mixture is well blended. Stir the batter periodically because potato starch has a tendency to settle.

Lightly oil a heavy 5-inch skillet. Heat the pan over moderately high heat. Pour 3 tablespoons of batter into the skillet, then quickly rotate the pan to coat the bottom of the skillet evenly. Return the pan to moderate heat and fry the blintz leaf until it is set and the edges come away from the sides of the pan. Invert the skillet over a clean cloth. The pancake will fall onto the cloth cooked side up. Continue until all the batter is used up. Regulate the heat and frying time so each pancake will cook to a uniform pale golden color. Yields about 12 to 14.

Cheese Blintzes

Blintz Leaves:

> **3 eggs**
> **½ teaspoon salt**
> **¾ cup cake meal**
> **1½ cups water**
> **Grease for the griddle or skillet**

In a medium-sized bowl, beat the eggs with the salt. Add the cake meal and water alternately to make a thin batter. Pour about 3 tablespoons of the batter onto a well-greased griddle or into a skillet, spreading the batter as thinly as possible. Fry over medium heat until golden brown. Turn out onto a dishtowel or paper towels. Yields 8 to 10.

Cheese Filling:

> **1 pound cottage cheese**
> **1 egg**
> **½ teaspoon salt**
> **½ teaspoon sugar**
> **½ teaspoon cinnamon**
> **¼ cup raisins (optional)**
> **Butter for frying**

In a small mixing bowl, thoroughly combine the cheese, egg, and remaining ingredients. Divide the filling evenly among the blintz leaves. Fold the sides of the leaves over the cheese filling and roll up. Brown the blintzes in butter in a large skillet over medium heat. Sprinkle with additional sugar and cinnamon if desired. Serves 4 to 5.

Variation:

Spread a thin layer of preserves over each pancake, then add the cheese. Fold the sides over the filling and roll up.

Matzo-Cheese Blintzes

> 1 cup cottage cheese
> 1 egg
> ¼ teaspoon cinnamon
> 1 tablespoon sugar
> 1 teaspoon potato starch
> 2 matzos
> 1 egg
> 2 to 3 tablespoons milk
> Butter for frying

In a small mixing bowl, thoroughly blend the first 5 ingredients. Break each matzo into 4 pieces. Make sandwiches with the cottage cheese filling. Beat the egg with the milk in a shallow bowl. Dip the sandwiches into the egg mixture. In a buttered skillet over medium heat, fry on both sides until golden brown. Serves 4.

Strawberry Filling for Blintzes

> 1 pint fresh strawberries
> ⅓ cup sugar
> ⅓ cup cookie or sponge cake crumbs

Wash the strawberries and drain on a towel for at least 1 hour. Hull the strawberries. Place them in a bowl, then halve or quarter them, depending upon the size. Before placing the strawberries on the blintz leaves, add the sugar and crumbs. Makes enough filling for 12 to 16 blintzes.

Blueberry Filling for Blintzes

1 pint fresh blueberries
¼ cup sugar
¼ cup cookie crumbs

Wash the berries. Drain them on a towel for at least 1 hour. Place the berries in a small bowl. Add the sugar and the crumbs. Makes enough filling for 12 to 16 blintzes.

Apple Filling for Blintzes

4 large or 6 medium-sized Winesap or
   Jonathan apples
¼ cup margarine
⅓ cup sugar, or to taste
¼ teaspoon cinnamon
¼ teaspoon salt
2 tablespoons raisins (optional)

Peel the apples. Slice them thinly into a small bowl. In a large skillet, melt the margarine over medium heat. Add the apples and sauté for about 5 minutes, turning often. Add the sugar (more or less to taste), cinnamon, and salt. Cook for an additional 5 minutes. Remove from the heat. Stir in the raisins. Cool before using. Makes enough filling for 12 to 16 blintzes.

Cherry Filling for Blintzes

2 cups sour red cherries, drained
3 tablespoons sugar, approximately
1 tablespoon potato starch
¼ teaspoon cinnamon

Combine the cherries, sugar, potato starch, and cinnamon in a small bowl. Adjust the amount of sugar to the tartness of the cherries. Makes enough filling for 10 blintzes.

Liver Filling for Blintzes

1¼ pounds liver
2 large onions
3 tablespoons fat
1 teaspoon salt
Pinch of freshly ground black pepper
1 egg, slightly beaten

Broil and grind the liver into a bowl. Mince the onions and sauté in the fat in a medium-sized skillet over medium heat. Combine the onions with the liver. Season the liver and bind it together with the egg. Makes enough filling for 12 to 14 blintzes.

Meat Filling for Blintzes

2 cups ground cooked meat or poultry
(remove the fat and gristle from the
meat before grinding)
2 teaspoons chopped onion
2 tablespoons chopped celery
1 tablespoon oil
1½ teaspoons salt
¼ teaspoon black pepper
1 egg, well beaten
Gravy or soup stock

Put the meat in a small mixing bowl. Slowly sauté the onion and celery in the oil in a small skillet over low heat for 5 minutes. Transfer the sautéed onions and celery to the bowl with the meat. Add the salt, pepper, and well-beaten egg; add sufficient gravy or soup stock to obtain a stiff pastelike consistency. Blend thoroughly. Yields 2 cups of filling, enough for 12 to 14 blintzes.

Zucchini Egg Rolls

Green zucchini sautéed with onions, cloaked in a tender crêpe blanket. This is a distinctive way to serve zucchini squash.

Egg Roll Skins:

>   1 recipe Passover Blintz Leaves I or 10 to
>   12 prepared blintz leaves

Filling:

>   2 cups coarsely chopped zucchini
>   ¼ cup chopped onion
>   2 tablespoons margarine
>   ½ teaspoon salt
>   Dash of freshly ground black pepper
>   1 egg white
>   Oil for frying

Sauté the zucchini and onion in the margarine in a large skillet over medium heat for 3 to 4 minutes. Stir in the salt and pepper.

Take 1 blintz leaf at a time and place it on a flat dish. Carefully spread about 2 tablespoons of the filling on the leaf in an oblong mound, leaving about a half-inch border. Fold the top over the filling. Next, fold both sides over the filling. Roll up jelly roll fashion, seam side down. Seal with slightly beaten egg white brushed on the bottom.

Heat a large heavy skillet with about 1 inch of oil over medium-high heat. When the oil is hot, carefully place the egg rolls in the skillet and fry to a golden crispness. Drain on paper towels. Serves 5 to 6.

Crêpe Cups Florentine

This gourmet specialty, a crêpe (blintz) shaped unusually and with an interesting filling, is an important addition to your blintz repertoire.

>   1½ cups shredded Cheddar cheese
>   3 eggs, slightly beaten
>   ⅔ cup mayonnaise
>   1 package (10 ounces) frozen chopped
>   spinach, thawed and drained
>   1 can (4 ounces) sliced mushrooms, drained ⟶

½ teaspoon salt
Dash of freshly ground black pepper
1 recipe Passover Blintz Leaves I or 12
prepared blintz leaves
Butter or margarine for the muffin cups

Place the shredded cheese in a small bowl; set aside. In a medium-sized bowl, blend the eggs with the mayonnaise, chopped spinach, sliced mushrooms, and the pepper. Add the cheese; mix well.

Fit the blintz leaves into 12 well-greased muffin cups. Carefully spoon a portion of the spinach mixture into each lined muffin cup. Bake in a preheated 350-degree F. oven for 40 minutes or until set. Serves 6.

Apple-Filled Sour Cream Blintzes

Here, sour cream blintz leaves encase a luscious apple filling. One-half teaspoon of instant coffee added to the sugar will flavor the filling to match the topping. Consider adding ¼ cup finely chopped nuts to the filling or substituting brown sugar for the granulated sugar.

Blintz Leaves:
1 egg
½ cup milk
¾ cup sour cream
½ teaspoon salt
1 teaspoon sugar (optional)
¾ cup cake meal
Butter for the skillet

In a medium-sized bowl, beat the egg with the milk, sour cream, salt, and sugar until well blended. Stir in the cake meal, mixing until smooth. Heat a small amount of butter in a 7-inch skillet. Pour in sufficient batter to coat the skillet thinly; rotate the skillet to spread the batter evenly. Pour out the excess batter.

Cook the pancake over medium heat for about 2 minutes; turn to brown the other side. Invert the skillet and drop the pancake onto a clean dishtowel or wax paper. Repeat until all the batter is used up. It is not necessary to regrease the skillet after making each pancake. Set aside while preparing the filling.

Filling:

> 1 egg white
> 1½ cups finely chopped pared apples
> ¼ cup sugar, scant
> Butter for the baking dish plus 2
> tablespoons butter

Beat the egg white in a small mixing bowl until frothy. Set 2 tablespoons of the sugar in reserve. Gradually add the larger amount of sugar, beating until soft peaks form. Fold in the apples.

Place a heaping tablespoonful of the apple filling in the center of each blintz leaf. Fold in the sides and roll up. Arrange the rolled blintzes, seam side down, in a buttered 9 × 13-inch baking dish. Sprinkle the reserved sugar over all. Dot with the butter and bake in a 400-degree F. oven for 20 minutes or until nicely browned. Serve with Mocha Cream Topping. Serves 4 to 6.

Mocha Cream Topping:

Discover how luscious a coffee-sour cream topping can be. This Mocha Cream Topping, which tastes very much like smooth coffee ice cream, combines admirably with these apple-filled blintzes.

> ½ cup sour cream
> ½ teaspoon instant coffee
> ¼ teaspoon grated lemon rind
> 1 teaspoon sugar (optional)

Blend the ingredients in a small bowl. Refrigerate until serving time. Serve over the apple-filled blintzes or as a topping for any fruit dessert.

Apple Dumpling Crêpes

A perfect dessert, bound to please the most critical crêpe-eaters. For variety, try substituting fresh pear for the apple quarters. You will have difficulty determining which you prefer.

Lemon Crêpes:

> 4 eggs
> ¼ teaspoon salt
> 2 tablespoons sugar
> 1¾ cups water
> 2 tablespoons oil
> 1 to 2 teaspoons finely shredded lemon rind
> 1 cup cake meal
> Grease for the skillet

In a large mixing bowl, beat the eggs with the salt and sugar until thick. Add the water, oil, and lemon rind; beat until blended. Stir in the cake meal until the batter is smooth.

Pour 2 to 3 tablespoons of batter into a hot lightly greased 6-inch skillet; rotate the pan quickly to coat the bottom evenly with the batter. Pour out excess batter. Return to the heat. Brown on 1 side only. Invert the pan onto paper towels or a clean cloth. Repeat until all the batter is used up. Yields 16 crêpes.

Apple Filling:

> 4 medium-sized cooking apples, peeled, cored, and quartered
> ⅛ cup sugar
> ½ teaspoon cinnamon
> 1⅔ cups water
> ⅓ cup packed brown sugar
> ½ teaspoon cinnamon
> 2 tablespoons margarine
> 2 tablespoons lemon juice
> 1 teaspoon vanilla sugar

Place 1 apple quarter on the unbrowned side of each lemon crêpe. In a small dish, combine the ⅛ cup sugar with ½ teaspoon cinnamon. Sprinkle some of the sugar mixture over each apple quarter. Fold the sides of each crêpe over the filling, forming a square packet. Arrange the crêpes, folded side down, in an ungreased 7½ × 11-inch baking dish.

In a small saucepan, combine the water, brown sugar, and ½ teaspoon of cinnamon. Simmer uncovered for 5 minutes. Remove from the heat; stir in the margarine, lemon juice, and vanilla sugar. Stir until the margarine has melted. Pour the syrup over the crêpes in the baking dish. Bake uncovered in a 375-degree F. oven for 40 to 50 minutes, basting occasionally with the syrup. Serves 8.

Cheese Blintz Pie

The blintz leaves for this dish may be prepared slightly thicker than those prepared for conventional rolled blintzes. Lightly dust the top blintz leaf with sugar and cinnamon.

> 8 prepared blintz leaves, browned on both
> sides
> 1 pound cottage cheese
> 1 tablespoon lemon juice
> ¼ cup sugar
> ½ envelope (.43 ounces) vanilla sugar

Prepare 8 large blintz leaves, browning them on both sides. To make the filling, in a small mixing bowl thoroughly combine the remaining ingredients. Spread a thin layer of filling on 7 of the blintz leaves. Stack each leaf on top of the other to resemble a 7-layer cake. Top with the unfilled blintz leaf. Serve as a pie, cut into wedges. Serves 4 to 6.

Variation:
Add raisins or finely chopped nuts to the filling.

Blintz Kugel

This is a version of the French crêpe Suzette, which is a filled and rolled crêpe. Here, filled crêpes are stacked and baked as a kugel.

Blintz Leaves:

> 5 eggs
> Dash of salt
> ¼ cup potato starch
> ½ cup water
> Oil for the skillet

First prepare the blintz leaves. In a bowl, beat the eggs very well with the salt. Dissolve the potato starch in the water; add this to the eggs.

Pour a small amount of batter into a hot lightly greased 8-inch skillet. Immediately pour off excess batter. Cook the blintz leaf over medium heat until the edges begin to come away from the sides of the pan. Carefully turn over the blintz leaf and cook for 1 to 2 minutes. Turn out onto a clean towel. Periodically stir the batter because the potato starch has a tendency to settle. Repeat until all the batter is used up. Makes 8 to 10 blintz leaves.

Filling:

> 3 pounds apples
> Oil for the pan
> Sugar to taste
> Cinnamon to taste
> ½ cup finely ground nuts
> A handful of raisins
> ¼ to ½ cup sweet red wine

Peel and core the apples; peel 1 of the apples with a thick paring; reserve this paring. Thinly slice all of the apples into a bowl.

Place 2 blintz leaves, 1 on top of the other, in a lightly greased round baking pan comparable in size to the skillet in which the blintzes were prepared. Sprinkle the top blintz leaf with sugar, cinnamon, the ground nuts, raisins, and a layer of the thinly sliced apples. Sprinkle a few drops of the sweet red wine over all. Cover with another blintz leaf. Continue the layering process until all of the leaves are used up, ending with an unfilled leaf.

Arrange the reserved thick apple paring on the top blintz (this will prevent the top blintz from becoming too crisp during the baking). Pour the remaining wine over the kugel. Bake in a 350-

degree F. oven until the apples are tender, 45 minutes to 1 hour. Remove the top paring. Additional sugar and cinnamon may be sprinked on top. Serve hot or cold. Serves 6 to 8.

Blintz Soufflé

Luscious and lavish looking!

    1 recipe Cheese Blintzes (see recipe) or 8 cheese blintzes of your choice, filled but not browned
    ¼ pound butter or margarine, melted
    6 eggs
    1 pint sour cream
    1 envelope (.43 ounces) vanilla sugar
    ¼ cup orange juice
    2 to 4 tablespoons sugar, to taste
    ½ teaspoon salt

Roll the filled but unbrowned blintzes in the melted butter or margarine and arrange them seam side down in a 9 × 13-inch baking pan. In a large bowl, beat the remaining melted butter or margarine with the eggs, sour cream, vanilla sugar, orange juice, sugar, and salt. Pour the egg-cream mixture over the blintzes. Bake in a 350-degree F. oven for 1 hour or until nicely browned. Serve topped with sour cream or applesauce. Serves 12.

Elegant Blintz Soufflé

This is a production; it is also the ultimate in elegance! Serve plain or with a fruit sauce.

    12 Cheese Blintzes (see recipe)
    12 fruit-filled blintzes of your choice (see recipes in this chapter)
    1 pint sour cream
    1 tablespoon sugar
    4 eggs, well beaten
    ½ pound butter or margarine, melted Cinnamon

→

Sugar
Grease for the baking pan

Prepare the cheese and fruit blintzes but do not brown them. Arrange the blintzes in an 11 × 15-inch greased baking pan, alternating them, cheese and fruit. In a bowl, combine the sour cream with the 1 tablespoon of sugar, the eggs, and the melted butter or margarine. Pour the mixture over the blintzes. Sprinkle with cinnamon and sugar. Bake at 350 degrees F. for 40 to 45 minutes. Serves 16.

Blintz Beignets

These luscious dessert beignets may be served in an extremely different guise: as a crunchy snack. After frying, sprinkle with seasonings—salt, pepper, garlic and/or onion powder, etc. The selection and proportion of seasonings used are a matter of individual taste.

9 prepared blintz leaves
Oil for frying
Cinnamon sugar (see Index for recipe)

Cut the blintz leaves into 1-inch strips. Pour oil into a large deep skillet or saucepan to a depth of 1½ inches. Heat the oil to moderate (350 degrees F.). Drop a few of the blintz strips into the oil. Fry until golden and crisp, about 1 minute. Keep the strips submerged in the oil while frying, using a slotted spoon to poke them down. Remove the beignets with tongs and drain on paper towels. Dust with cinnamon sugar. Serve warm or cold with hot Brandied Raspberry Dip. Yields about 10 servings of 6 beignets each.

Brandied Raspberry Dip:
12 ounces raspberry preserves or the
preserves of your choice
¼ cup brandy
1 teaspoon lemon juice

Combine the raspberry preserves, brandy, and lemon juice in a small saucepan. Over medium heat, bring to just below boiling, stirring to blend. Serve hot. Makes about 1⅜ cups.

11
Foods With a Foreign Flavor

During Passover it is possible, with a little ingenuity, to enjoy the flavors of foreign cuisine without sacrificing the comforts or convenience of home. Our families and our guests can partake of pizza or lasagna from Italy, moussaka from Greece, wine soup from Israel, Polynesian chicken from Hawaii, Chinese egg rolls, and Japanese sukiyaki.

The recipes in this chapter, all with a foreign flavor, will add a variety to your Passover culinary repertoire that will surprise and delight those who dine with you.

Huevos Hamenadas
(Hard-cooked Eggs—Sephardi Style)

Eggs are prepared and served in countless ways, and this is the way the Sephardi prepare them most frequently. Huevos hamenadas are traditionally served at the Seder meal.

Since three to four cups of loose outer brown onion skins are used in this preparation, many homemakers start collecting the onion skins in advance of the holiday. Not only do the onion skins color the egg shells brown, they supply a flavor that permeates the eggs. The slow cooking turns the insides brown as well.

During the week of Passover these eggs are served either whole, usually warm, or mashed with a little oil and seasoned with salt and pepper.

12 eggs
Cold water
¼ cup oil
1 teaspoon salt
1 teaspoon black pepper
Outer skins from 6 to 10 brown onions

Place the eggs in a 4 to 6-quart saucepan. Add sufficient cold water to cover. Add the oil, salt, pepper, and onion skins. Bring to a boil over medium-high heat.

Reduce the heat and cook covered at a slow simmer for a minimum of 8 hours, adding more water if necessary to keep the eggs covered. Serves 6 to 12.

Persian Eggs Shabbati

Many Sephardi Jews serve these eggs on Saturday in place of the customary chopped liver. The hard-cooked egg whites have a roasted brown appearance. To prepare for Saturday, cook overnight over a covered flame (like cholent) or in the oven.

8 eggs
2 teaspoons salt
1 teaspoon black pepper
1 teaspoon cinnamon
Bones from cooked chicken or meat
Cold water

Place the eggs, salt, pepper, cinnamon, and bones in a large soup pot. Add cold water to cover. Slowly bring to a boil. Turn the heat down to just simmer. Cover the pot and cook overnight. Serves 4.

Hard-cooked Eggs—Chinese Style

2 teaspoons tea leaves
2 cups hot water
2 teaspoons salt

→

Small piece of cinnamon stick
4 hard-cooked eggs, unshelled

In a 1-quart saucepan over medium heat, prepare a tea mixture with tea leaves, hot water, salt, and cinnamon stick. With the bottom of a spoon, gently crack the hard-cooked eggs all over. Do not peel them. Immerse the eggs in the tea, bring to a boil, cover, and simmer for about 1 hour. Be sure the tea covers the eggs. Turn off the heat and let stand overnight. Peel and behold a delicate design on the eggs. Serve whole or sliced, with mayonnaise. Serve 4.

Oriental Egg Drop Soup I
(Tan Fa Tong)

This and the following soup recipe should be of special interest to those seeking alternatives to clear chicken broth.

> **6 cups chicken broth**
> **½ cup minced cooked chicken**
> **2 tablespoons potato starch**
> **3 tablespoons water**
> **3 eggs, beaten**

In a 3-quart pot, bring the broth and chicken to a boil over medium-high heat. In a measuring cup, mix the potato starch with the water. Pour the mixture into the soup, stirring constantly. Mix in the beaten eggs and cook until the eggs are set. Serves 6 to 8.

Oriental Egg Drop Soup II
(Tan Fa Tong)

A variation of the above recipe, eliminating the minced chicken and using less eggs but more potato starch. Cut scallions are used as a colorful garnish.

    5 cups clear chicken broth
    ¼ teaspoon sugar
    ¾ teaspoon salt
    1 tablespoon potato starch
    ¼ cup cold water
    2 eggs
    2 scallions (optional)

In a 3-quart pot, bring the chicken broth, sugar, and salt to a rapid boil. In a small dish, mix the potato starch with the cold water; stir this into the broth. Stir and cook until the broth is no longer cloudy. Beat the eggs until slightly foamy, then slowly swirl them into the soup. Do not stir. Turn off the heat. Cut the scallions into small pea-sized pieces. Before serving, garnish the soup with a sprinkling of the scallions. Serve hot. Serves 6.

Israeli Wine Soup

    2 cups sweet red wine
    1 cup water
    Juice of ½ lemon
    3 eggs
    2 tablespoons sugar
    ½ teaspoon salt
    2 tablespoons cold water
    1 tablespoon sugar

In a small saucepan over medium-high heat, bring the wine, cup of water, and lemon juice to a boil.

In a large bowl, put 2 eggs and 1 egg yolk, reserving the white in another small bowl. Beat together the eggs, sugar, salt, and the 2 tablespoons of cold water. Slowly add the wine mixture, stirring constantly. Refrigerate to chill thoroughly.

Before serving, beat the reserved egg white with the 1 tablespoon of sugar, using a rotary beater to form a stiff meringue. Serve the soup with swirls of the meringue on top. Serves 4.

Matzo Brei Fu Yung

This dish was inspired by such popular Chinese egg dishes as fu yung eggs and eggs fu yung.

> **2 matzos**
> **Water**
> **1 medium-sized onion, sliced**
> **2 tablespoons oil**
> **¼ green pepper, chopped**
> **2 green scallions, finely sliced or chopped**
> **¾ cup minced cooked chicken**
> **4 eggs**
> **Oil for the skillet**

Break the matzos. Soak the pieces in water in a medium-sized bowl. In a skillet over medium heat, sauté the onion in the oil until golden; add the green pepper; cook for 2 to 3 minutes, until tender. Add the scallions and chicken; cook for an additional 2 minutes.

Drain the matzos; squeeze out the excess water. Beat in the eggs. Add the vegetables and chicken. Blend thoroughly. Grease a large heavy skillet with a small amount of oil. Place the skillet over medium heat. Using a large tablespoon, spoon a portion of the mixture into the skillet to form a latke. Brown on both sides. Serve hot. Serves 4 to 5.

Dairy Italian Lasagna

> **2 eggs**
> **1 pound cottage cheese**
> **Salt and white pepper to taste**
> **1 clove garlic, minced, or ⅛ teaspoon**
> **garlic powder (optional)**
> **3 to 4 whole matzos**
> **Milk**
> **2 cans (10½ ounces each) tomato sauce**
> **½ pound Muenster cheese, shredded**

In a medium-sized mixing bowl, beat the eggs. Add the cottage cheese, salt, pepper, and garlic or garlic powder. Mix well.

Wet the whole matzos with milk until moistened, not soggy. Pour a little sauce into an 8 × 8-inch baking pan; distribute evenly. Layer the remaining ingredients, alternating matzo, cottage cheese mixture, tomato sauce, Muenster cheese. Repeat, ending with the Muenster cheese. Bake at 350 degrees F. for 45 to 50 minutes. Let the lasagna rest for 5 to 10 minutes before cutting. Serves 6.

Meat Lasagna

> **Grease for the pan**
> **3 eggs**
> **½ cup red Burgundy wine**
> **4 matzos**
> **1 recipe Meat Sauce (see Index for recipe)**

Grease a 9-inch square baking pan. Beat the eggs with the wine in a shallow pan. Dip the matzo into the egg-wine mixture; line the pan with 1 matzo. Cover the matzo with a third of the meat sauce. Place another moistened matzo on top of the meat mixture and repeat. Alternate meat and moistened matzo, ending with moistened matzo. Pour the remaining egg mixture over all. Cover with aluminum foil. Bake in a preheated 375-degree F. oven for ½ hour. Uncover and let rest before cutting. Serves 6.

Pizza I

For a different version of pizza, use a slice of breaded and baked eggplant in place of the prepared Basic Pizza Crust. Top the slice of eggplant with the tomato sauce and cheese. Before serving, slip the pizza under the broiler to brown.

This is a good company dish because it can be prepared hours in advance and be placed under the broiler immediately before serving.

Basic Pizza Crust:
>   2½ cups boiling water
>   3 cups matzo farfel
>   5 eggs, beaten
>   Salt and black pepper to taste

Place the farfel in a large bowl. Pour the boiling water over the farfel. Drain. Beat the eggs in a mixing bowl; add the salt and pepper to taste. Pour the beaten eggs over the farfel and mix well. Divide the mixture into 8 greased 5-inch (individual) pizza pans. Bake in a 350-degree F. oven for 20 minutes; or use 1 large pizza pan and bake for 30 minutes or until set.

Dairy Topping:
>   1 can (10½ ounces) tomato sauce with
>   mushrooms
>   8 slices American cheese
>   Garlic powder and onion powder to
>   taste

Spread each pizza with tomato sauce. Cut the cheese into strips and arrange evenly over the tomato sauce. Sprinkle each pizza with onion powder and garlic powder. Bake in a 350-degree F. oven just until the cheese melts, about 8 to 10 minutes. Serves 8.

Meat Topping:
>   ½ pound ground meat; or salami, grated or
>   cut into strips; or frankfurters, cut
>   crosswise into thin rounds
>   1 can (10½ ounces) tomato sauce with
>   mushrooms
>   Garlic powder and onion powder

Brown the ground meat in a small skillet over medium heat. Spread each pizza with a portion of the tomato sauce and meat; or arrange grated salami or salami strips or thin rounds of frankfurters over the tomato sauce. Sprinkle each pizza with garlic powder and onion powder to taste. Bake in a 350-degree F. oven for 10 minutes, until heated through. Optional additions to the meat topping are sautéed green pepper strips or finely minced onions. Serves 8.

Variation:

Prepare matzo meal pancakes. Cut in half horizontally. Top each half with the topping of your choice.

Pizza II

The amount of seasoning used in the sauce for this pizza may be increased or decreased to taste. This pizza serves 8.

> **1 recipe Basic Pizza Crust, baked (see recipe)**

Sauce:

> **1 can (16 ounces) tomatoes**
> **¼ teaspoon Zing flavor enhancer**
> **2 tablespoons oil**
> **2 to 3 tablespoons grated onion or a dash of onion powder**
> **1 clove garlic, minced, or a dash of garlic powder**
> **Dash of freshly ground black pepper**

Drain the tomatoes. In a small bowl, break up the tomatoes with a fork. Add the oil and the seasonings until well blended. Spread the sauce over the crust.

Mushroom Topping (dairy):

> **½ pound mushrooms sliced and sautéed, or 1 can (4 ounces) mushrooms, drained**
> **1 medium-sized onion, thinly sliced or coarsely grated**
> **Sliced mozzarella cheese**
> **¼ cup grated Muenster or Cheddar cheese**

Cover the crust with the prepared tomato sauce. Distribute the mushrooms and onions over the sauce. Cover with slices of mozzarella cheese and sprinkle the top with the grated cheese. Bake in a 350-degree F. oven until the cheeses melt. Serves 8.

Cheese Topping:
> 1 medium-sized onion, grated into the
> sauce (optional)
> ¾ pound mozzarella cheese, coarsely
> grated

Spread the cheese evenly over the crust. Top with the sauce. Bake in a 350-degree F. oven until the cheese melts.

Ground Meat Topping:
> ½ pound ground meat
> 1 onion, chopped

Brown the meat and onion in a small skillet over low heat. Distribute the mixture over the crust. Cover with the sauce. Bake in 350-degree F. oven for 10 to 15 minutes, until heated through.

Salami Topping:
> ½ pound salami

To prevent curling of the salami, grate it or slice it and score the slices. Distribute the salami over the crust. Cover with the sauce and bake at 350 degrees F. until heated through.

Mina de Espinaca

(Sephardi Matzo-Spinach Pie)

This classic Passover recipe is often served for brunch or lunch.

> 2 pounds fresh spinach
> 3 eggs, divided
> 1½ cups mashed potatoes
> ¾ cup grated Cheddar cheese
> Salt and white pepper to taste
> 4 to 5 matzos (enough to cover the
> bottom of the pan and the filling)
> Warm water
> 2 tablespoons oil

Wash the spinach very well. Drain off all excess water (a salad spinner is immensely helpful). Pat the spinach dry. Discard heavy stems. Finely chop the spinach leaves in a chopping bowl.

In a medium-sized bowl, beat 1 egg well; add half of the mashed potatoes, ½ cup of the grated cheese, and the chopped spinach. Combine well. Season with salt and pepper.

Soak the matzos in a shallow pan of warm water for about 3 minutes. Place the matzos between 2 towels to absorb excess water. Grease a 7 × 9-inch baking pan or a 9-inch pie plate with 1 tablespoon of the oil. Heat the pan in a preheated 350-degree F. oven.

Carefully line the bottom and sides of the hot pan with some of the matzo. Spread the spinach filling evenly over the matzo. Cover the filling with the remaining matzo.

In a small bowl, beat the remaining 2 eggs; add the remaining potatoes, cheese, and oil. Blend well. Spread this over the matzo. Score the top with a fork. Bake for 1 hour or until the top is lightly browned. Serves 6.

Shortcut:

Two packages of frozen chopped spinach (10½ ounces each), thawed and drained very well, may be substituted for the fresh spinach.

Pitta

(Sephardi Spinach Casserole)

> 6 matzos
> Warm water
> Butter or margarine
> 1 package (10 ounces) frozen chopped
> spinach, thawed
> ½ pound farmer cheese or dry cottage
> cheese
> 2 eggs
> 1 teaspoon salt

In a large shallow pan, soak the matzos in warm water for 5 minutes. Drain the water and place the matzos on a towel to drain.

Grease a shallow 7 × 9-inch baking pan with butter or margarine. Carefully line the bottom with half of the wet matzos.

In a mixing bowl, mix the spinach with the cheese and eggs until well blended. Add the salt. Spread the mixture over the matzos in the pan. Cover the filling with the remaining wet matzos. Cover the pan with aluminum foil and bake at 400 degrees F. for 35 to 40 minutes. Serves 4 to 6.

Variation:

To prepare an onion casserole substitute 6 sautéed onions for the spinach.

Sephardi Zucchini Pie

Hardly a pie, but this is the answer to a simple meatless dish.

    2 matzos
    Water
    4 medium-sized zucchini, approximately 2 pounds
    3 eggs
    1 teaspoon salt
    ½ pound farmer cheese
    1 tablespoon oil plus some for the baking dish

Soak the matzos in water until soft. Drain and squeeze dry. Peel and coarsely grate the zucchini into a large bowl. In a separate bowl, lightly beat the eggs with the salt. Add the matzos, farmer cheese, and the 1 tablespoon of oil. Mix well. Combine the egg mixture with the grated zucchini; mix thoroughly. Pour the mixture into a greased 2-quart baking dish. Preheat the oven to 350 degrees F. Bake uncovered for 1½ hours or until golden brown. Serves 6.

Sephardi Burmuelos de Patata

(Potato Pancakes)

The surprise ingredient in these pancakes is cheese. Serve with sour cream.

> **4 large potatoes, boiled and pared**
> **4 eggs**
> **1 teaspoon salt**
> **½ cup matzo meal**
> **½ cup grated cheese of your choice**
> **Oil for frying**

Mash the boiled potatoes in a medium-sized bowl. Add the eggs, salt, matzo meal, and grated cheese. Blend thoroughly. Do not beat. Drop by tablespoonfuls into hot oil in a large heavy skillet over medium-high heat and fry until golden brown on both sides. Drain on paper towels. Serves 6 to 8.

Burmuelos

(Sephardi Farfel Pancakes)

For a delicious variation on these pancakes, add ½ cup of the grated cheese of your choice to the farfel-egg mixture.

> **2 cups matzo farfel**
> **Water**
> **4 eggs, beaten**
> **½ teaspoon salt**
> **White pepper to taste**
> **Oil for frying**

Soak the matzo farfel in water. Drain the farfel and squeeze dry. Add the beaten eggs, salt, and pepper. Drop the mixture by the tablespoonful into hot oil in a large skillet over medium-high heat. Fry until golden brown. Drain on paper towels. May be served with honey or fruit. For dairy, serve with sour cream. Serves 4 to 6.

Sephardi Rollos

(Potato-Meat Dumplings)

Filling:

>   1 pound ground beef
>   2 tablespoons oil
>   2 hard-cooked eggs, finely chopped
>   1 teaspoon salt
>   ¼ teaspoon black pepper
>   Chopped fresh parsley (optional)
>   1 egg

Crust:

>   2½ cups mashed potatoes
>   1 egg
>   ¼ cup matzo meal
>   1 teaspoon salt
>   ¼ teaspoon black pepper
>   Oil for frying

In a large skillet over medium-high heat, sauté the ground beef in the oil. Remove from the heat. Add the finely chopped hard-cooked eggs, salt, pepper, parsley, and egg. Set aside.

Mix the potatoes with the egg, matzo meal, salt, and pepper. In the palm of the hand, form the mixture into thin cakes about 3 inches in diameter. Spread a tablespoonful of the filling on half of each cake. Fold over the other half, pinching the edges together to enclose the filling and form an oval patty. Refrigerate for 1 hour. Deep-fry in hot oil until golden brown. Drain on paper towels. Serve hot. Serves 4 to 6.

Egg Rolls

A compliment-earning dish that can be served as an appetizer as well as a main dish. For pareve, substitute canned tuna fish cut into thin slivers for the chicken.

Egg Roll Skins:

> 3 eggs
> 1 teaspoon salt
> 1 tablespoon oil
> ¼ cup potato starch
> ½ cup water
>   Oil for the skillet

In a mixing bowl, beat the eggs well. Remove and reserve 2 teaspoons of the egg in a small covered dish. Add the salt and oil. Beat together. In a measuring cup, combine the potato starch and water. Add to the egg mixture. Stir to blend well.

Grease a 7-inch skillet with oil; heat the skillet over medium heat. Pour enough batter into the skillet to make a thin pancake. Rotate the pan so the bottom is completely covered. When the edges begin to curl and the pancake looks dry, turn out onto a clean towel or paper towel. Repeat until all batter is used up. Stir the batter before making each pancake because the starch tends to settle on the bottom. It is not necessary to grease the pan before making each pancake. Yields 8 to 10 skins.

Filling:

> 1 cup thinly sliced celery
> ½ cup thinly sliced onions
> ¼ cup finely chopped scallions
> 1 cup finely shredded Chinese or green
>   cabbage
> 2 tablespoons oil
> 1 teaspoon salt
> ¼ teaspoon white pepper
> ½ cup cooked chicken or turkey, cut
>   julienne
>   Oil for frying

In a large skillet over medium heat, stir-fry the celery, onions, scallions, and cabbage in the oil for 5 minutes. Stir in the salt, pepper, and chicken or turkey. Remove from the heat. Cool. Place a heaping tablespoonful of the filling at 1 end of the pancake; fold over the top; fold over each side and roll to form an oblong egg roll. Seal with a little of the reserved egg.

Drop the egg rolls into oil heated to 375 degrees F. and deep-fry until crisp and golden. Or fry in hot oil ½ inch deep in a large heavy skillet until golden brown on both sides. Remove with a slotted spoon or with tongs. Drain on paper towels. An alternate method is to arrange the rolls seam side down on a well-oiled baking sheet. Brush the top with oil. Bake in a preheated 375-degree F. oven until golden brown. Serve hot. Serve with Sweet-and-Sour Sauce. Serves 4 to 5.

Sweet-and-Sour Sauce:

> **1 cup peach or apricot preserves**
> **1 to 2 tablespoons vinegar**
> **⅛ teaspoon ground ginger (optional)**
> **½ clove garlic, minced, or ½ teaspoon garlic powder (optional)**

Combine the jam, vinegar, ginger, and garlic in a small saucepan. Bring to a boil over medium-high heat, then simmer for 2 to 3 minutes. Stir occasionally. Cool thoroughly. Or place the ingredients in a blender container and blend at high speed for 20 seconds.

Israeli Beef Stroganoff

> **1 pound fillets of beef**
> **1 onion, sliced**
> **¼ pound fresh mushrooms, sliced**
> **3 tablespoons fat, divided**
> **Salt and black pepper to taste**
> **2 fresh tomatoes, peeled, seeded, and crushed**
> **1 tablespoon potato starch**
> **½ cup chicken broth**
> **¼ cup dry wine (preferably white)**
> **1 egg yolk, beaten**

Cut the beef into pieces 2 inches long and approximately ⅛ inch thick. Sauté the sliced onion and mushrooms in half of the fat in a large heavy skillet for 3 to 5 minutes. Sauté the beef strips in the remaining fat in another skillet; add this to the sautéed vegetables. Season with salt and pepper. Add the tomatoes. Cover and simmer over low heat for 10 minutes.

In a measuring cup, blend the potato starch with the cooled chicken broth; add the wine; pour the mixture into a small saucepan. Stir over low heat until thickened.

Blend the sautéed vegetables, the beef, and the broth; heat gently for 5 minutes. Adjust the seasoning. Spoon about ¼ cup of the sauce from the skillet into the beaten egg yolk. Blend together thoroughly, then return this mixture to the meat mixture in the skillet. Stir over low heat until thoroughly heated. Serves 4 to 5.

Israeli Mock Steak

Eggplant and salami or minced meat team to make this robust Sunday dinner special.

> 6 thick (1 inch) slices eggplant, unpeeled
> 6 thin slices salami
> 1 clove garlic
> 3 tablespoons oil for frying
> ½ tablespoon potato starch
> 1 tablespoon powdered soup mix
> 1 cup water
>   Salt and white pepper to taste
> 1 can (4 ounces) sliced mushrooms,
>   drained (optional)

Into the side of each slice of eggplant, cut a small pocket large enough to accommodate a salami slice. Insert the salami slices and set aside on a baking sheet. Put the clove of garlic into the oil in a large skillet. Heat over medium heat. With a slotted spoon, remove the garlic.

Fry the eggplant slices in the skillet until nicely browned on both sides. Remove from the pan. Set aside and keep warm. In a large measuring cup, dissolve the potato starch and powdered soup mix in the water. Carefully add to the oil in the pan. Cook until thickened. Taste and adjust the seasoning, adding salt and pepper if necessary. Add the drained mushrooms. Spoon the gravy over the mock steak. Serves 6.

Variation:

Chopped meat can be substituted, or it can be used in combination with the salami.

Israeli Moussaka

Moussaka, a casserole dish of Greek, Turkish, or Roumanian origin, can be prepared in various ways. Most frequently it consists of alternate layers of vegetables and a savory mixture of minced meat. Eggplant is the vegetable most closely associated with moussaka, but this recipe produces a dish that is equally flavorful.

> ½ pound fresh spinach or 1 package (10½ ounces) frozen chopped spinach
> 4 large potatoes
> 1 pound chopped meat
> 2 medium-sized onions, chopped
> 2 scallions, chopped
> 1 tablespoon chopped fresh parsley
> 1 medium-sized tomato, chopped
> ¼ teaspoon black pepper
> ½ teaspoon salt
> ½ teaspoon cinnamon
> 5 eggs, divided
> Pinch of salt
> Grease for the casserole

Wash the fresh spinach. In a covered 1-quart saucepan over medium heat, cook the spinach in the water that adheres to the leaves. Cook for 3 to 7 minutes or until just tender, turning often with a fork. (Or prepare the frozen spinach according to package directions.) Drain the spinach and chop.

Peel the potatoes. Cut them into thick slices. Parboil for 5 minutes in salted water (1 teaspoon of salt to 1 quart of water) in a 1-quart saucepan. Drain and cool.

In a medium-sized bowl, combine the meat with the drained spinach. Add the chopped vegetables, pepper, salt, and cinnamon. Add 2 of the eggs. Blend thoroughly.

In a lightly greased 2-quart casserole, arrange half of the potatoes in an even layer; add a layer of the meat over the potatoes; top with a layer of the remaining potatoes. Beat the remaining 3 eggs with a pinch of salt in a small bowl. Pour the eggs over the potatoes. Cover the casserole. Bake at 350 degrees F. for 30 minutes. Uncover and bake for an additional 30 minutes, until the potatoes are browned and tender. Serves 6.

Greek Moussaka

Serve this delicious meat-eggplant combination with a baked potato and tossed salad.

> 1 medium-sized eggplant, approximately
> 1½ pounds
> Oil
> 1 egg
> 1 cup tomato sauce, divided
> 1 pound ground meat of your choice
> 1 onion, finely chopped (optional)
> ½ cup water
> 1 teaspoon sugar
> Dash of black pepper
> ¼ teaspoon cinnamon
> 1 bay leaf, halved

Peel the eggplant and slice into ¼-inch-thick slices. Brush both sides lightly with oil. Arrange the slices in a large baking pan. Broil both sides until lightly browned.

In a medium-sized bowl, beat the egg with ½ cup of the tomato sauce; add the ground meat and finely chopped onion. Thoroughly blend the egg mixture with the ground meat.

Line an ungreased 7 × 11-inch baking dish with half of the eggplant slices. Spread the meat mixture over the eggplant. Top with the remaining slices of eggplant. Mix the remaining ½ cup of tomato sauce with the water, sugar, pepper, and cinnamon.

Pour the mixture over the eggplant. Place a bay leaf half in each end of the baking pan.

Bake uncovered in a preheated 350-degree F. oven for approximately 1 hour, until the top is nicely browned and most of the gravy has evaporated. Discard the bay leaf halves. Serves 4 to 6.

Stuffed Vegetable Medley

Meat-stuffed vegetables are very popular in Sephardi cuisine. There are two types: leafy stuffed vegetables—such as stuffed grape leaves and stuffed cabbage—and firm-fleshed vegetables that are hollowed out and stuffed—such as stuffed squash, peppers, tomatoes, etc.

This dish offers an interesting combination. The flavors of the various vegetables intermingle, resulting in a succulent main dish. By reducing the size of the portions served, the stuffed vegetables substitute admirably as an appetizer.

Beef Filling:

> 1½ pounds lean ground beef
> 1 small onion, grated
> 1 egg, beaten
> 1 clove garlic, minced (optional)
> Salt and black pepper to taste
> 1 tablespoon matzo meal

Vegetables:

> 2 to 3 green peppers, halved
> 3 to 4 zucchini
> 3 to 4 summer (yellow) squash, stemmed
> 3 to 4 small red tomatoes
> Salt and freshly ground black pepper, to taste
> 1 large onion
> 2 cans (10½ ounces each) tomato sauce
> 1 cup water, divided
> 1 tablespoon sugar
> Grease for the baking pan

To prepare the beef filling, combine all the ingredients in a medium-sized mixing bowl. Set aside.

Now prepare the vegetables. Remove the seeds and inner membranes from the peppers; parboil them in a small saucepan for approximately 5 minutes. With a slotted spoon remove the peppers from the water; drain well. Stem and halve the zucchini lengthwise; scoop out the center seed section, forming long narrow hollows. Scoop out the centers of the stemmed summer squash and the tomatoes. Season all the vegetables with the salt and pepper, reserving the scooped-out portions of the vegetables. Stuff the vegetables with portions of the prepared meat filling.

In a chopping bowl, chop the onion and the scooped out portions of the assorted vegetables into small pieces. Spread the mixture on the bottom of a large (9 × 13-inch) greased baking pan.

Arrange the stuffed vegetables over the mixture; spoon portions of tomato sauce from 1 can of undiluted tomato sauce on top of each vegetable. Pour the second can of tomato sauce over the vegetable pulp. Rinse each can with ½ cup of water. Pour into the pan to dilute the sauce. Add the sugar.

Bake covered in a 350-degree F. oven for 20 minutes. Uncover the pan; adjust the seasoning. Add additional boiling water if necessary. Continue baking for an additional 20 to 25 minutes, until the meat is crusty and golden brown. Serves 12 to 15 as an appetizer; 6 to 7 as a main dish.

Sukiyaki

Sukiyaki, a dish of Japanese origin, offers an excellent opportunity to use up many *Yom Tov* leftovers—cooked beef, chicken broth, mushrooms, etc. What makes this dish extra special is its comparatively low caloric value.

To make one generous serving, you will need:

**½ pound cooked beef, cut diagonally into
 thin slices
 ¼ cup sliced mushrooms**

➡️

½ cup sliced celery, cut diagonally into 1-
inch strips
1 medium-sized onion, thinly sliced
¼ pound fresh spinach, washed, drained,
and torn into pieces
½ small green pepper, seeded and cut into
thin strips
4 scallions, cut into 1-inch lengths
1 teaspoon salt
⅛ teaspoon black pepper
⅛ teaspoon ground ginger
1 clove garlic, halved (optional)
½ cup chicken broth

Combine the meat and vegetables in a medium-sized saucepan. In a small bowl, mix the salt, pepper, ginger, and garlic with the chicken broth. Pour the mixture over the meat and vegetables in the pan. Bring to a boil over medium heat, then simmer until the celery is barely tender, about 7 to 10 minutes. Do not overcook: the vegetables should be tender but crisp. Adjust the seasoning. Serve hot. Serves 1.

Polynesian Chicken

This ready-cooked barbecued chicken, enhanced with an exotic blend of canned fruits and vegetables, can be prepared in no time. Luscious party fare with a touch of Hawaiian flavor.

1 ready-cooked barbecued chicken (3½ to
4 pounds), cut up
1 can (23 ounces) sweet potatoes
1 can (16 ounces) sliced peaches
½ cup lemon juice
1 jar (12 ounces) apricot jam or preserves
1 can (8¼ ounces) sliced pineapple

Place the chicken pieces in a single layer in a 9 × 13-inch baking pan. Arrange the drained potatoes and peaches around the chicken. In a small bowl, combine the lemon juice with the preserves and pour over the chicken. Top the chicken pieces with the sliced pineapple. Cover the pan with aluminum foil and bake at 350 degrees F. for 30 minutes. Remove the foil and return to the oven. Baste frequently until the fruit is nicely browned. Serves 4 to 5.

Chicken Chow Mein

A Passover version of the classic Chinese dish. Serve spooned over cooked farfel or spooned over Chinese noodles (recipe below) and garnished with shreds of egg.

> ¼ cup oil
> 3 ribs celery, thinly sliced
> 3 medium-sized onions, shredded
> ¼ to ½ pound mushrooms, sliced
> 2 to 3 cups diced or coarsely shredded
> cooked chicken
> 1 tablespoon potato starch
> ½ teaspoon salt
> ½ teaspoon black pepper
> 1½ cups water or chicken soup
> 1 beaten egg, fried and cut into thin
> shreds

Heat the oil in a large skillet. Sauté the celery and onions over medium heat until transparent, not browned. Add the mushrooms and sauté for an additional 2 to 3 minutes. Add the chicken to brown lightly.

In a large measuring cup, mix the potato starch, salt, and pepper with the water or chicken soup. Add to the skillet. Cook uncovered over low heat, stirring constantly until the sauce thickens. Garnish each serving with a portion of the shredded egg and top with Chinese noodles. Serves 4 to 5.

Variation:

Drained canned tuna fish can be substituted for the chicken, in which case chicken soup is not used in making the sauce. Put the drained tuna fish in a colander. Carefully pour boiling water over it. Drain well before shredding coarsely.

Chinese Noodles

1 package (8 ounces) noodles
Oil for frying
Salt and pepper

Heat the oil in a deep saucepan over medium-high heat. Drop in about 2 ounces of noodles at a time and fry until golden. Remove the noodles with a slotted spoon and drain on paper towels. Season to taste. Yields ½ pound noodles.

Variation:

The noodles may be precooked and drained thoroughly before frying. However, because they tend to stick together, the noodles must be separated with 2 forks while frying.

Hawaiian French Toast

3 eggs
½ cup pineapple juice
2 tablespoons sugar
⅛ teaspoon salt
6 to 8 slices stale sponge cake
Butter or margarine for the griddle
Sliced pineapple

In a medium-sized bowl, beat the eggs with the pineapple juice. Add the sugar and salt. Dip the sponge cake into the egg mixture.

Brown on a hot, well-greased griddle or in a skillet. Turn and brown the other side. Serve the toast on a slice of heated sliced pineapple. Serves 3 to 4.

12

Fruit Desserts, Puddings, and Other Sweet Finales

A dessert should complement and enhance that which has preceded it. Whereas a delectable light dessert should follow a hearty main course, a hearty pie or sumptuous cake makes a fitting conclusion to a light meal.

The dessert recipes in this chapter vary greatly, from nature's natural desserts—fruit and nuts—to recipes which rely on your refrigerator or freezer for their preparation. Select the dessert best suited to the meal prepared, whether that be the light, colorful, zestful Banana-Strawberry Sherbet or the substantial and majestic Fruit-Nut Chocolate Bonbons.

The apple, a fruit readily available, is a perfect base for desserts. You will note that in this chapter there are many succulent and unusual recipes using this fruit. But you are not limited to the recipes in this chapter, for there are recipes in this book for many dishes that are often overlooked as dessert possibilities. Consider a baked kugel that tastes so tantalizing served warm (see Chapter Nine). Do not overlook blintzes (see Chapter Ten), the most elegant in the pancake family; they make many lavish desserts—the Blintz Soufflé, for example.

If you prefer cakes and pastries—cream puffs or éclairs or meringue shells with marvelous fillings—see Chapter Fourteen (Cakes) and Chapter Sixteen (Pies and Pastries). Be sure to check the Index for other possibilities.

233

Stuffed Apples

6 large baking apples
¼ cup ground blanched almonds
   Sugar to taste
   Cinnamon to taste
   A few raisins (optional)
½ cup water or ¼ cup water and ¼ cup
   wine
   Grease for the pan

Peel the baking apples. Slice off the top of each apple, which will be used later as a cover. Carefully remove the greater part of the pulp from the inside of each apple. In a large mixing bowl, chop the apple pulp with the ground nuts; add the sugar and cinnamon. Chop in a few raisins if desired. Fill the apple cases with the apple mixture. Put an apple lid on each apple. Place the filled apples in a greased stewing pan. Add the water or water and wine. Cover and stew slowly over low heat for 10 to 15 minutes, until the apples are soft but not broken. Carefully remove the apples from the pan. Serves 6.

Stuffed Baked Apples

Filling:

6 macaroons
1 teaspoon grated orange or lemon rind
¾ cup brown sugar
¼ cup raisins (optional)

Apples:

6 large baking apples
¾ cup wine (Muscatel)
⅓ cup honey
½ teaspoon cinnamon
   Dash of ginger (optional)

To prepare the filling, crumble the macaroons into a small bowl; add the remaining ingredients and blend well. Set aside.

Core the apples and peel the top to about 1 inch down from the stem. Place the apples in a 7 × 11-inch baking dish. With a fork, prick the sides in 2 or 3 places. Fill the cavity of each apple with filling. In a small bowl, combine the wine, honey, cinnamon, and ginger; pour over the apples. Cover the pan and bake in a 350-degree F. oven for 30 minutes or longer, basting frequently, until the apples are tender. Serves 6.

Baked Stuffed-Apple Pudding

Apples:

> 6 medium-sized apples
> ½ cup sugar
> ½ teaspoon cinnamon
> ¼ cup raisins
> ¼ cup chopped nuts
> Grated rind of 1 lemon
> 2 tablespoons white wine
> Grease for the baking dish

Batter:

> 4 eggs, separated
> ½ cup sugar, divided
> 5 tablespoons cake meal
> 2½ tablespoons potato starch
> ½ teaspoon vanilla flavoring or 1 teaspoon
> vanilla sugar
> 2 tablespoons margarine, melted

Peel the apples. Cut ½ inch off the top of each apple and reserve for later use. Remove the cores. Carefully scrape out the insides of the apples, leaving a wall ¼ inch thick. Chop the pulp in a medium-sized mixing bowl. Add the sugar, cinnamon, raisins, nuts, lemon rind, and wine. Fill the apple cavities with this mixture. Top each apple with the reserved apple slices. Place the stuffed apples in a greased baking dish large enough to accommodate the apples comfortably. Bake for about 10 minutes in a preheated 350-degree F. oven. In the meantime, prepare the batter.

In a medium-sized mixing bowl, beat the egg whites until foamy. Gradually beat in ¼ cup of the sugar, 1 tablespoon at a time, until the whites are stiff but still shiny. In a separate medium-sized bowl, beat the egg yolks until thick; beat in the remaining ¼ cup of sugar until light. Carefully combine the egg yolk mixture with the beaten egg whites. Add the cake meal to the potato starch; carefully fold these dry ingredients into the egg mixture. Add the vanilla flavoring or vanilla sugar. Gently stir in the melted margarine.

Pour the batter over the partially baked apples. Return the apples to the oven and continue to bake for another 30 minutes, until the pudding is set and the apples are tender. Serve warm or cold, plain or with a fruit or wine sauce (see Index for recipes). Serves 6.

Apple Brown Betty

⅓ cup sugar
½ teaspoon cinnamon
¼ teaspoon salt
   Grease for the baking dish
2 cups fine dry sponge cake crumbs or egg
   kichel crumbs
4 apples, peeled and diced
3 tablespoons melted fat

In a small mixing bowl, mix the sugar, cinnamon, and salt. Set aside. In a greased 1½-quart baking dish, put a layer of crumbs; cover with a layer of apples; sprinkle with a portion of the sugar mixture. Continue layering the ingredients until all are used up, ending with a layer of crumbs. Pour the melted fat over the crumbs. Cover the dish and bake in a 375-degree F. oven for 40 minutes. Remove the cover for the last 10 minutes to brown the top. Serve warm. Serves 4.

Apple Shalet

½ cup raisins
1 cup water
1 cup finely crushed matzo
4 eggs, separated
1 tablespoon oil
½ cup sugar
½ teaspoon salt
¼ teaspoon cinnamon
1½ cups grated tart apples
½ cup chopped walnuts or pecans
1 teaspoon grated lemon rind
1 tablespoon grated orange rind
Grease for the baking dish

In a small saucepan, simmer the raisins in the water until softened. Cool slightly. Add the crushed matzo and toss until moist. In a medium-sized mixing bowl, beat the egg yolks well; add the oil, sugar, salt, cinnamon, grated apples, nuts, rinds, and raisin-matzo mixture. Blend well.

In a clean mixing bowl, beat the egg whites until stiff but not dry. Fold the beaten egg whites into the egg yolk mixture. Turn the mixture into a greased 8½-inch baking dish. Bake in a preheated 350-degree F. oven for about 40 minutes, until a knife blade inserted into the center comes out clean. Serve hot, with a wine sauce if desired (see Index for recipe). Serves 6.

Apple Crisp

For a luscious dairy dessert, spoon warm into dessert dishes and top with whipped cream or ice cream.

½ cup packed brown sugar
½ cup fine mandelbread crumbs or toasted
    sponge cake crumbs
½ teaspoon cinnamon
¼ cup soft margarine or butter

———▶

Grease for the baking dish
2½ cups peeled and thinly sliced apples
1 tablespoon lemon juice

In a small mixing bowl, combine the brown sugar, crumbs, cinnamon, and the margarine or butter. Mix until crumbly. Grease a 6 × 10-inch baking dish. Arrange the apples in the baking dish. Sprinkle with the lemon juice. Spread the crumbly mixture over the apples. Bake in a preheated 375-degree F. oven for 25 to 30 minutes, until the apples are tender.

Variation:

For additional flavor, increase the brown sugar to ¾ cup, the crumbs to 1½ cups, the thinly sliced apples to 4 cups; add 3 cups of drained diced canned pineapple slices. Arrange alternate layers of apples and pineapple in a 1½-quart casserole. Proceed with the lemon juice and crumb mixture. Cover the casserole and bake for 30 minutes. Uncover and bake for an additional 15 minutes or until the apples are tender.

Pesach Fludent

Fludent, a layered pastry, is comparable to baklava. This beautiful, wonderfully satisfying dessert should be served in wedges.

Crêpe Batter:

10 eggs
Pinch of salt
3 tablespoons potato starch
½ cup water
Oil for the skillet

Filling:

4 egg whites
¼ to ½ cup sugar
½ pound nuts, ground fine
Juice of 1 lemon
¼ to ½ cup cherry jelly

Topping:

2 egg whites
4 tablespoons sugar

To prepare the crêpes, beat the eggs with the salt in a large mixing bowl. Mix the potato starch with the water to dissolve well. Add to the beaten eggs; continue beating until well blended.

Heat a heavy 8-inch skillet that has been lightly greased. Into the hot skillet pour enough batter to form a very thin pancake, tilting the pan from side to side so that the batter covers the entire bottom surface and spreads evenly. Cook over low heat until the batter in the skillet looks dry and the edges begin to brown. Carefully turn over the crêpe and cook a bit longer. (Regulate the heat so that all of the pancakes will be pale gold.) Invert the skillet onto a clean dishtowel. The crêpe will fall out. Repeat the procedure until all the batter is used up. Stir the batter frequently because potato starch has a tendency to settle.

Prepare the filling by beating the egg whites at low speed in a medium-sized mixing bowl. Increase the speed to high as the egg whites form soft peaks; gradually add the sugar, 2 tablespoons at a time. When the egg whites form stiff shiny peaks, add the juice of the lemon; beat in the finely ground nuts.

To assemble the fludent for baking, place 1 crêpe in the bottom of a very lightly greased large round baking pan. Cover the center of the pancake with a portion of the meringue filling; dab small amounts of jelly near the edges. Cover the filling with a second crêpe. Now reverse the way the filling is placed, that is, dab the jelly in the center and place the meringue towards the edges. Use up all the crêpes, alternating the placing of the filling on each crêpe.

Prepare the topping by beating the 2 egg whites at low speed in a medium-sized mixing bowl. Increase the speed to high as the egg whites form soft peaks. Gradually add the sugar; continue beating until the egg whites are stiff but not dry. Spread the stiffly beaten egg whites over the top crepe. Bake in a preheated 350-degree F. oven for 15 minutes or until the meringue is golden brown. Serves 6 to 8.

Apple Fludent

This is similar to a layer cake or pancake pie, with an apple filling between the layers.

Crêpe Batter:

> 8 eggs
> ¼ cup potato starch
> 1 cup water
> Dash of salt

Filling:

> 3 to 4 apples, peeled, cored, and thinly sliced
> ¼ pound nuts, finely ground
> Sugar to taste
> Cinnamon to taste

First, prepare the crêpes as outlined in the Pesach Fludent above. To assemble the fludent, place a crêpe leaf in the bottom of a greased round pan. Sprinkle the crêpe leaf with sugar (amount depending upon the tartness of the apples and personal taste), cinnamon, and a portion of the ground nuts. Arrange some of the thinly sliced apples over the sugar-cinnamon-nut mixture. Cover with another crêpe leaf. Repeat the layering until there are 8 layers, ending with a crêpe. Lightly sprinkle the top with sugar and cinnamon. Bake in a 350-degree F. oven for 1 hour. Serve hot or cold. Cut into wedges. Serves 6 to 8.

Grated-Apple Pudding

More an apple cake than a pudding, this dessert may be served hot with a lemon or orange sauce, or with applesauce or whipped cream.

> 8 eggs, separated
> ½ cup sugar
> Juice and grated rind of 1 lemon

➡

6 apples, peeled and cored
½ cup matzo meal
½ cup slivered almonds or coarsely
chopped walnuts

In a large mixing bowl, beat the egg yolks at medium speed; add the sugar, lemon juice, and grated rind. Coarsely grate the apples into a small bowl. Stir the apples into the egg yolk mixture; add the matzo meal and nuts.

In a clean large bowl, beat the egg whites at high speed until stiff but not dry. Gently fold the beaten egg whites into the egg yolk mixture. Pour the batter into a 9 × 13 × 2-inch baking pan. Bake in a preheated 350-degree F. oven for 30 to 40 minutes, until golden brown. Serves 8.

Lemon Sponge Pudding

This bakes into a luscious lemon filling with its own baked-on sponge cake topping.

1 cup sugar
¼ cup cake meal
½ tablespoon potato starch
⅛ teaspoon salt
2 tablespoons melted shortening or oil
4 to 5 tablespoons lemon juice
1 teaspoon grated lemon rind
2 eggs, separated
1 cup water

In a large mixing bowl, combine the dry ingredients. Stir in the oil, lemon juice, and lemon rind. In a small bowl, beat the egg yolks with the water; add to the lemon mixture and mix well.

In a clean small bowl, at high speed, beat the egg whites until stiff but not dry; fold them into the egg yolk-flour mixture. Pour the batter into a 1½-quart casserole or 6 custard cups. Set the casserole or custard cups into a pan containing 1 inch of hot water. Bake in a preheated 350-degree F. oven for 40 to 50 minutes. Serve warm or cold. Serves 6 to 8.

Coconut Surprise

In *Don Quixote,* Cervantes wrote, "The proof of the pudding is in the eating." You will certainly approve of this one, for it is a combination of cake and pudding.

For pareve, substitute water or juice for the milk, and margarine for the butter.

> 2 tablespoons butter
> 1 cup sugar
> 4 eggs, separated
> ⅓ cup lemon juice
> 1 teaspoon grated lemon rind
> ¼ teaspoon salt
> ¾ to 1 cup freshly grated coconut
> 1 tablespoon potato starch
> 1 cup milk

In a large mixing bowl, cream the butter; gradually add the sugar and cream together until light and fluffy. Add the egg yolks; beat well. Add the lemon juice, lemon rind, and salt; blend well. Fold in the coconut and potato starch. Stir in the milk.

In a clean medium-sized mixing bowl, beat the egg whites until stiff but not dry; fold them into the lemon-coconut mixture. Pour the batter into a greased 6 × 10-inch baking dish or a 1½-quart casserole. Set the dish into a pan containing 1 inch of hot water and bake in a preheated 375-degree F. oven for 35 to 40 minutes. Chill if desired. Garnish servings with toasted coconut. Serves 6 to 8.

Date Pudding

> 3 eggs
> ¾ teaspoon salt
> ¾ cup sugar
> 1 cup cake meal
> ½ cup chopped walnuts or pecans
> 1 cup chopped pitted dates
> Grease for the mold

In a medium-sized mixing bowl, beat the eggs with the salt. Gradually add the sugar and continue beating until thick and light. Blend the cake meal into the egg mixture; add the nuts and dates. Mix just until blended. Turn the mixture into a 1-quart greased mold; cover. Steam on a rack in a deep pan in 2 inches of boiling water for about 2 hours. Add additional boiling water as necessary. Remove from the water. Unmold onto a serving dish, and serve at once. Serves 8.

Fruit Pudding Meringue

> 3 eggs, separated
> ⅜ cup sugar
> Juice and grated rind of 1 lemon
> ¾ to 1 pound apples, peeled and grated
> ½ cup matzo meal
> ¼ cup sugar
> 2 bananas, peeled and thinly sliced

In a medium-sized mixing bowl, beat the egg yolks with the ⅜ cup sugar at high speed until light. Add the lemon juice, grated lemon rind, and grated apples. Stir in the matzo meal; mix well. Pour the batter into an 8 or 9-inch baking dish. Bake in a 350-degree F. oven for about 40 minutes.

While the pudding is baking, prepare a meringue by beating the egg whites in a clean medium-sized bowl at slow speed for almost 1 minute, until the egg whites foam and begin to take shape. Increase the speed to high and gradually add the ¼ cup of sugar, 2 tablespoonfuls at a time so it dissolves completely, until stiff peaks form.

At the end of the 40 minutes of baking time, remove the pudding from the oven. Arrange the sliced bananas on top of the pudding. Gently spread the meringue over the bananas. Return the pudding to a cooler oven, 300 degrees F., and bake until delicately browned, 8 to 10 minutes. Serves 6 to 8.

Meringue Peaches

Dress up a canned peach half by wrapping it in a cloak of meringue then baking it until golden.

> **6 canned peach halves, well drained**
> **Strawberry or cherry preserves**
> **3 egg whites**
> **Pinch of salt**
> **¾ cup sugar**
> **1 tablespoon lemon juice**
> **1 teaspoon grated lemon rind**
> **¼ cup chopped nuts**

Place the drained peaches, hollow side up, in an 8 × 8-inch baking dish. Fill each peach cavity with a teaspoonful of strawberry or cherry preserves.

Prepare the meringue by beating the egg whites at low speed in a medium-sized mixing bowl for 1 minute, until the egg whites begin to foam and take shape. Add the salt. Increase to high speed and gradually beat in the sugar, a few tablespoonfuls at a time so it dissolves completely. When the whites form stiff peaks, beat in the lemon juice and grated lemon rind.

Spread a cloak of meringue over each peach half. Sprinkle each with a portion of the chopped nuts. Bake in a preheated 300-degree F. oven until the meringue is delicately browned, 45 minutes or longer. Remove to individual dessert dishes or to a large serving dish. Serve hot or cold. Serves 6.

Peachy Cheese Puff

An elegant-looking dessert for a special dairy dinner.

Filling:

> **1 cup creamed cottage cheese**
> **¼ cup sugar**
> **1 tablespoon potato starch**

➡

1 tablespoon sour cream (optional)
1 teaspoon vanilla sugar or ½ teaspoon
   lemon juice
1 teaspoon butter or margarine
1 egg, separated
½ teaspoon grated lemon rind

Dough:

½ cup butter, margarine, or oil
1 cup water
1 cup cake meal
¼ teaspoon salt
4 eggs
   Grease for the cookie sheet
8 canned peach slices, well drained
1 tablespoon sugar mixed with ⅛
   teaspoon ground cinnamon
   Blanched sliced almonds

To prepare the filling, in a medium-sized mixing bowl beat the cheese, sugar, potato starch, sour cream, vanilla sugar or lemon juice, butter or margarine, and the egg yolk (reserve the white) until well mixed; stir in the grated lemon rind. Set aside.

In a medium-sized saucepan over medium heat, cook the butter, margarine, or oil in the water until the mixture comes to a boil. Turn the heat down to low. Combine the cake meal and salt and add the mixture to the saucepan all at once; stir vigorously over medium heat until the dough leaves the sides of the pan in a smooth compact ball. Transfer the dough to a large bowl, and with an electric mixer at medium speed beat in the eggs, 1 at a time, beating well after each addition. Continue beating the batter until it is thick and has a satiny sheen.

On a greased cookie sheet spread enough batter to make a 7-inch circle ¼ inch thick (use a plate or pan cover as a guide). Then, using rounded measuring tablespoonfuls of the same batter, make a ring of cream puffs around the circle, touching the circumference.

In a small clean bowl, beat the egg white until stiff but not dry.

Brush each cream puff with the beaten egg white; sprinkle with sliced almonds. Pour the cheese filling into the shell; arrange the 8 peach slices, petal fashion, in the center of the cheese mixture; sprinkle the top of the peaches with the tablespoon of sugar mixed with the cinnamon. Bake in a preheated 375-degree F. oven for 35 to 45 minutes, until the border is high and brown and the filling is golden.

With a broad spatula, slide the puff onto a wire rack to cool. The filling will fall as soon as the puff is removed from the oven. Serves 8

Fruit Tzimmes-Compote

There are many variations on the tzimmes theme (see Carrot, Sweet Potato, and Apple Tzimmes in Chapter Eight, Side Dishes). In Roumania and the Balkan countries, a compote, a dessert made of fresh or dried fruits to which sugar or honey is added, is referred to as a tzimmes. In this recipe a vegetable is added, making it resemble a traditional tzimmes, hence the name "tzimmes-compote." It makes a wonderful ending for a meal.

> 1 pound prunes
> ½ pound dried apricots
> ½ pound dried pears or apples
> 2 cups water
> 2 tablespoons honey
> 3 tablespoons brown sugar
> ¼ teaspoon salt
> ½ teaspoon cinnamon
> ½ pound sweet potatoes, peeled and sliced

In a large mixing bowl, presoak all the fruit overnight. Drain the water. Pit the prunes. In a medium-sized saucepan, combine all the ingredients and bring to a boil. Cook over very low heat for 25 minutes or until the liquid is absorbed. Stir occasionally. Serves 8 or more.

Spiked Fruits

An unusual fruit dessert and an excellent cake topping. For a dairy meal, top the fruits with whipped cream.

2 cups dried fruits of your choice
2 cups medium-sweet or sweet Sherry
wine or brandy

One week before Passover, put 2 cups of dried fruits into a screw-top quart jar. Add the 2 cups of wine or brandy. Cover the jar and let the fruit macerate at room temperature for a week, then refrigerate. Serve chilled as a compote. Replenish the jar with dried fruits and wine or brandy as the fruits are used, and you will be assured of having an unusual dessert on hand at all times. Two cups of dried fruits serves 6 or more.

Note: For a topping, the fruits should be coarsely chopped.

Prunes in Wine

1 pound prunes
1 cup sweet grape wine
1 cup water
¼ cup sugar
3 slices lemon
¼ teaspoon cinnamon

In a large mixing bowl, place the prunes, the wine, and water. Let soak overnight in the refrigerator. Add the sugar, lemon slices, and cinnamon to the prunes; place the mixture in a large saucepan. Simmer over low heat until tender. For a more concentrated juice, remove the prunes and continue to simmer the liquid until slightly syrupy. Pour over the prunes. Chill before serving. Yields about 4 cups.

Variation:

Soak the prunes overnight in 2½ cups of apple juice. Transfer to a saucepan. Cook over medium heat until it comes to a boil; lower the heat and simmer for 20 minutes. Add the sugar, cover, and simmer 10 minutes longer. Chill before serving.

Wine Custard

6 egg yolks
3 tablespoons sugar
6 tablespoons Sherry-type wine

In a large mixing bowl, beat the egg yolks until light and lemon-colored. Gradually add the sugar, beating until fluffy. Add the wine and continue to beat until thoroughly blended. Transfer the egg yolk mixture to the top of a double boiler and cook over hot, not boiling, water until thick, beating continuously. Pour the mixture into sherbet glasses and chill in the refrigerator for at least 2 hours. Serves 3.

Pareve Ice Cream

Serve pie à la mode after a meat meal with this pareve ice cream.

3 eggs
½ cup margarine
½ cup sugar
¼ cup hot water

Put the eggs into a blender container. Add the margarine, sugar, and hot water. Cover and blend at high speed for 20 seconds. Remove the cover and add any of the flavors below. Replace the cover and blend for an additional 10 seconds. Pour into a freezer container. Cover and freeze overnight. Serves 6 or more.

Ice Cream Flavors:
Cocoa: 2 teaspoons unsweetened cocoa
Coffee: 1 teaspoon instant coffee
Mocha: 2 teaspoons unsweetened cocoa and 1 teaspoon instant coffee
Orange: 2 teaspoons grated orange rind
Vanilla: 1 teaspoon vanilla sugar

Israeli Wine Float

> 2 cups red wine
> ¾ cup water
> 1 stick cinnamon
> ½ cup sugar
> 3 tablespoons potato starch
> Juice of 1 lemon
> 3 egg whites

In a medium-sized saucepan, bring to a boil the wine, water, and stick of cinnamon. Mix together the sugar, potato starch, and lemon juice until the potato starch is dissolved. Stir the potato starch mixture into the wine; continue to cook over low heat, stirring constantly until thick and clear. Discard the cinnamon stick. Remove the saucepan from the heat.

In a clean small mixing bowl, beat the egg whites until stiff. Fold the stiffly beaten egg whites into a third of the warm, not hot, wine mixture. Divide the remaining wine mixture into 4 individual sherbet glasses or 1 large bowl. Top each glass with the fluff mixture or place large dollops of the fluff on the wine mixture in the large bowl. Chill before serving. Serves 4 to 6.

Stuffed Knaidlach in Honey

> 4 eggs, separated
> 1 teaspoon salt
> Dash of white pepper
> 3 tablespoons margarine, divided
> ½ cup cold water
> 1 cup matzo meal
> Pitted prunes
> ½ cup honey
> Ground nuts (optional)

In a medium-sized mixing bowl, beat the egg whites with the salt and pepper until stiff. In a separate medium-sized bowl, cream the egg yolks with 1 tablespoon of the margarine. Add the cold water, then the matzo meal; blend well. Fold in the stiffly beaten egg whites. Shape the mixture into balls; stuff each ball with a pitted prune.

In a medium-sized saucepan, cook the knaidlach in boiling water for 20 minutes. Remove the knaidlach with a slotted spoon and place on a platter. In a deep casserole, boil the honey with the remaining margarine. Gently drop the knaidlach into the boiling honey. Cover and bake in a 350-degree F. oven for 30 minutes or until golden brown. Sprinkle with ground nuts. Serves 6 to 8.

Fruit Parfait

A regal-looking dessert that is easily prepared. The sponge cake need not be fresh.

> **4 cups diced sponge cake**
> **1½ cups fruit cocktail, drained and chilled**
> **1 cup Apple Fluff (recipe below)**
> **¼ cup sweet grape wine**
> **Ground nuts (optional)**

In parfait glasses, arrange alternate layers of small cubes of sponge cake, fruit cocktail, and fluff. Sprinkle each layer with wine. Decorate the top with nuts if desired. Serves 6.

Apple Fluff
Use as a filling or as a topping.

> **1 apple**
> **1 egg white**
> **1 cup sugar**
> **1½ tablespoons lemon juice**

Peel, core, and thinly slice or grate the apple into a medium-sized mixing bowl. Add the remaining ingredients. With an electric mixer at low speed, begin to beat the mixture; gradually increase the speed. Continue to beat until the apple mixture is smooth and thick enough to hold its shape. Makes a generous 1 cup.

Chocolate Charlotte Russe

A Passover version of the charlotte russe that used to be sold in individual paper cups. Chocolate whipped cream corseted with strips of sponge cake, crowned with a dollop of whipped cream, and topped with a walnut is served in individual serving dishes. Your meal may be best remembered for this majestic dessert.

> 4 ounces bittersweet chocolate
> 1 cup whipping cream
> ¼ cup sugar
> 2 tablespoons cold brewed coffee
> 20 strips sponge cake (approximately 4 inches long, 1½ inch wide, and ⅜ inch thick)
> Walnuts

In the top of a double boiler over hot water, melt the chocolate. In a medium-sized mixing bowl, whip the cream until thick; remove and reserve ½ cup. Fold the melted chocolate, sugar, and coffee into the remaining cream. Spoon into individual sherbet glasses lined with 4 strips of sponge cake. Chill. Garnish with a dollop of the reserved whipped cream. Top with a walnut. Serves 5.

Strawberry Ice Cream

> 1 cup strawberries, hulled
> 1½ cups orange juice, divided
> 1½ cups dry skim milk
> 6 tablespoons lemon juice

In a blender cup, place the strawberries and ½ cup of the orange juice. Blend until smooth; set aside. In a large mixing bowl, combine the remaining orange juice with the milk powder. Beat with an electric mixer until very fluffy, approximately 5 minutes. Add the lemon juice gradually; continue beating until the mixture holds soft peaks. Fold in the puréed strawberries. Pour the mixture into a freezer container and freeze overnight. If the strawberries are tart, sugar to taste may be blended with the strawberries and orange juice in the blender cup. Serves 6 to 8.

Pineapple Sherbet

> 1 package lemon-flavored gelatin
> 1 cup boiling water
> 1 can (20 ounces) crushed pineapple
> 2 tablespoons lemon juice
> 2 egg whites, stiffly beaten

In a small bowl, dissolve the gelatin in the boiling water. Add the crushed pineapple and lemon juice; blend well. Pour the mixture into a plastic container and freeze partially. Remove from the freezer and place in a medium-sized mixing bowl that has been chilled in the refrigerator. Beat with an electric mixer until light. Gently fold in the stiffly beaten egg whites. Return to the freezer container and freeze overnight. Serves 6.

Banana-Strawberry Sherbet

> 4 egg whites
> 1 cup sugar
> 2 bananas, mashed
> 1 pint strawberries, hulled and sliced

In a large mixing bowl, beat the egg whites with an electric mixer until frothy; gradually add the sugar, mashed bananas, and sliced strawberries. Beat at the highest speed until thickened. Transfer to a covered container and freeze overnight. Serves 8 or more.

Three-Fruit Ice

This frozen dessert can be made well in advance. The blending of the three flavors—banana, lemon, grape—results in an irresistible combination.

½ cup sugar
1 cup water
2 bananas, mashed
    Juice of 2 lemons
1 cup grape juice

In a medium-sized saucepan over low heat, cook the sugar and water together for 5 minutes. Remove from the heat. Add the mashed bananas, lemon juice, and grape juice. Cool. Pour into a plastic container or freezer tray; freeze partially. Remove the mixture from the freezer and place in a medium-sized bowl that has been chilled in the refrigerator. Beat with an electric mixer until light. Return to the plastic container, cover, and freeze overnight. Serves 6.

13
Confections

Homemade confections will make a wonderful addition to your holiday repertoire. Serve the goodies in this chapter as desserts, as between meal snacks, or present a platter to company.

Passover confections are often made distinctive by the fruits and nuts used. Chocolate is frequently featured as well. You will be delighted to find that the sugar, honey, cake meal, and matzo farfel used in many of the confections produce superb results.

Fruit-Nut Chocolate Bonbons

To add zest to these luscious bonbons, replace one to two tablespoons of the water with one to two tablespoons of brandy.

>   1 cup sugar
>   1 teaspoon ground ginger
>   2 teaspoons cinnamon
>   ½ cup honey
>   ½ cup hot water
>   6 ounces bittersweet chocolate, chopped
>   2 tablespoons oil
>   ¾ cup seedless raisins
>   ⅔ cup finely chopped walnuts
>   2½ cups cake meal
>   Sugar or finely chopped nutmeats for garnish

Combine the sugar, spices, honey, and water in a 1-quart saucepan. Cook over low heat until the syrup forms a thread (232 degrees F. on a candy thermometer). Remove from the heat and stir in the chocolate and oil. Add the raisins, walnuts, and cake meal. Blend thoroughly and quickly. Form into 1-inch balls. Roll each in sugar or in more finely chopped nutmeats. Place the bonbons into individual tea-sized paper cups and chill until firm. Makes approximately 24.

Brandied Bonbons

A brandy-laced bonbon that adds real spirit to your holiday celebration.

> 3 ounces bittersweet chocolate
> 3 tablespoons honey
> ½ cup brandy or Slivovitz
> 2½ cups matzo farfel
> ¾ cup sugar
> 1 cup finely chopped walnuts

Melt the chocolate in the top of a double boiler over hot water; stir in the honey and the brandy. Remove from the heat. Put the farfel through a food mill or crush with a rolling pin; the crumbs should be slightly coarser than matzo meal.

Add the sugar, finely chopped walnuts, and the crushed farfel to the chocolate mixture; blend thoroughly. Shape into bonbons and set them individually into small petit four cases. Let mellow for a day or 2 in a cool dry place. Makes approximately 18 to 20.

Banana Bonbons

> 1 teaspoon water
> 1 tablespoon carob powder
> 2 teaspoons honey
> 1 large ripe banana
> ½ cup finely chopped blanched almonds

In a small dish, blend the water with the carob powder to make a paste. Stir in the honey; mix well.

Cut the banana into 8 pieces. Using a spoon, coat each banana piece with a portion of the carob mixture, then dip into the chopped nuts.

Place a piece of plastic wrap over a dish and arrange the bonbons on the plastic wrap. Freeze until firm, then wrap in aluminum foil or place in a container with a tight-fitting lid. Return to the freezer. Serve frozen, 2 bonbons per person. Serves 4.

Note: A peeled ripe banana can be successfully frozen. Merely rub the banana with lemon juice, wrap in plastic, and store in the freezer.

Chocolate-Glazed Prunes

> 1 package (12 ounces) ready-to-eat pitted
>   prunes
> 36 whole blanched almonds or filberts
> 2 ounces semisweet chocolate
> ¼ to ½ cup finely grated nuts

Stuff each of the individual prunes with a whole nut. Put each prune into a bonbon-sized paper cup. Melt the semisweet chocolate over hot water. Drizzle about 1 teaspoon of chocolate over each prune. Sprinkle with chopped nuts. Chill before serving. Yields 36.

Honey Candy

As a variation, drizzle some slightly cooled, melted chocolate over each piece of this honey candy.

> ¾ cup honey
> 1 cup sugar
> ½ cup water
>   Dash of salt
> ¼ to ½ teaspoon ground cinnamon

    1 cup chopped nutmeats
    2 cups matzo farfel
      Grease for the cookie sheet
      Cold sweet wine

Place the honey, sugar, and water in a medium-sized saucepan. Cook over medium heat, stirring continuously until the sugar has completely dissolved. Lower the heat and cook for 30 to 40 minutes or until a drop of syrup forms a firm ball when dropped into cold water. Stir only as necessary to prevent scorching. Remove from the heat. Add the salt, ginger, cinnamon, chopped nuts, and farfel. Stir quickly. Pour out onto a lightly greased cookie sheet. With the back of a tablespoon moistened with cold wine, flatten out to the desired thickness, about ½ inch. When lukewarm, cut into squares or diamonds. Separate when cold. Yields about 20 squares or diamonds.

Honey Balls

    ½ cup honey
    ⅓ cup sugar
    1¼ cups chopped walnuts
    ¼ cup matzo farfel
    2 teaspoons grated orange or lemon rind

In a medium-sized saucepan over low heat, heat the honey and sugar to boiling. Stir constantly. Add the nuts and the farfel; stir until the mixture is thick. Add the grated rind. Remove from the heat. Drop by the teaspoonful onto a wet cookie sheet or wax paper, forming small balls. Cool. Yields 18 to 24 balls.

Variation:
Roll the balls in finely grated nuts or coconut.

Apple Candy

A candy that looks like Turkish delight. Makes an excellent lunchbox snack.

2 cups sweetened applesauce
1 tablespoon lemon juice
2 packages cherry-flavored gelatin dessert
1 cup chopped walnuts
Superfine sugar

In a medium-sized saucepan over medium heat, heat the applesauce to boiling. Add the lemon juice and simmer gently for 10 to 15 minutes, until the sauce is very thick. Add the cherry gel powder and stir until it is dissolved. Remove from the heat and stir in the chopped nuts. Pour into an 8 × 8-inch pan that has been rinsed with cold water. Cool, then refrigerate until set. Cut into 1-inch squares. Remove from the pan with a spatula and roll each square in superfine sugar. Makes 64 pieces.

Apricot Pletzlach

Pletzl (plural, *pletzlach*) connotes the form in which this confection is prepared. The word *pletzl*, in Yiddish, refers to something that is "flat as a board." Here, the cooked apricot mixture is turned out onto a wet board or cookie sheet and is flattened before being cut.

1 pound dried apricots
1 cup hot water
1 small orange
1 pound sugar
½ cup coarsely chopped blanched almonds
Additional sugar (optional)

Place the apricots in a medium-sized bowl. Add the cup of hot (not boiling) water and soak overnight. Finely mince the apricots and the whole orange, removing the pits. In a heavy saucepan over medium-high heat, combine the apricots and orange with the sugar. Bring to a boil, then turn the heat down and simmer, stirring continuously for 20 to 25 minutes. Just before finishing the cooking, add the almonds. Turn out onto a wet board or cookie sheet; flatten the mixture with the back of a tablespoon. Cut when cool. Roll each piece in additional sugar if desired. Yields 24 pieces.

Mehren Pletzlach

(Carrot Candy)

Traditionally, Passover candies and preserves are made from vegetables, which are usually sweetened with honey and flavored with the permissible spices. This fine example is a variation on the Apricot Pletzlach above.

> **1 pound large carrots, peeled**
> **2 cups sugar**
> **1 tablespoon water**
> **1 cup finely chopped nuts**
> **¼ to ½ teaspoon sugar**

Wash and grate the carrots into a bowl on the finest side of the grater. Transfer to a medium-sized saucepan; add the sugar and tablespoon of water and mix thoroughly. Simmer over low heat, stirring constantly until the mixture is thick and syrupy (about 1 hour). Add the nuts and ginger about 5 minutes before removing the pan from the heat. Pour the mixture onto a cookie sheet rinsed with cold water. Flatten with the back of a spoon. Cool for 1 hour and cut into diamonds or any desired shape. Yields about 36 pieces.

Variation:
Substitute beets for the carrots.

Ingber

A traditional holiday favorite. The intensity of flavor varies with the amount of ginger used.

> **2 cups finely grated raw carrots**
> **2 cups honey**
> **½ cup sugar**
> **2 to 2½ teaspoons ginger (or less, to taste)**
> **Sugar for sprinkling**

In a large saucepan, blend the grated carrots, honey, and sugar very well. Cook over medium heat. When the mixture begins to boil, turn the heat down and cook until all liquid is absorbed; stir frequently. Remove from the heat; add the ginger and cook 5 minutes longer. Pat out to ½ inch thickness on a sugared board or cookie sheet. Sprinkle sugar on top and cut into diamonds or squares. Let dry for 30 minutes to 1 hour. Remove with a spatula. Yields approximately seventy-two 1-inch to 1½-inch diamonds.

Noent

This Passover nut confection is also a favorite Purim delicacy. Another popular Passover noent recipe includes matzo farfel as an ingredient.

> **1 pound honey**
> **1 cup sugar**
> **Juice of ½ lemon**
> **2 pounds nuts, grated very fine**

Combine the honey, sugar, and lemon juice in a large saucepan. Bring to a boil over medium heat. Add the nuts and cook over low heat until very thick, stirring every few minutes. Pour the mixture onto a moistened cookie sheet and flatten with the back of a wet spoon. Cut into desired shapes. Yields about 40 to 48 pieces.

Almond Crunch Candy

A delectably crunchy candy.

> **Margarine or butter for the pan**
> **⅓ cup margarine or butter**
> **¼ cup honey**
> **¾ cup slivered blanched almonds**

Grease an 8 × 8-inch baking pan with margarine or butter. Melt the margarine in a small heavy skillet over medium heat. Stir in the honey and almonds. Cook over medium heat, stirring constantly until the mixture turns golden brown, approximately 5 minutes.

Working quickly, spread the mixture into the prepared pan and cut into squares with a greased sharp knife. Cool. Store covered in the refrigerator. Yields sixteen 2-inch squares.

Sugared Walnuts or Almonds

    1½ cups sugar
       Dash of salt
     ½ cup water
     ¼ cup honey
     3 cups chopped walnuts or walnut halves;
       or blanched almonds, whole or chopped
     ½ teaspoon vanilla flavoring or 1 teaspoon
       vanilla sugar
     1 teaspoon grated orange rind

Mix the sugar, salt, water, and honey in a medium-sized saucepan. Cook over medium heat to the soft ball stage (242 degrees F. on a candy thermometer, or when drops of the syrup will form a soft ball when dropped into cold water). Remove from the heat. Add the nuts, vanilla flavoring or vanilla sugar, and the grated orange rind. Stir until thick and creamy. Turn out onto wax paper; separate with 2 forks. Yields 1½ pounds.

Variation:

Flavor with 1 teaspoon lemon juice and 1 teaspoon grated lemon rind.

14
Cakes

Even though the use of flour during Passover is prohibited, there is no reason why delicious holiday cakes cannot be prepared. The recipes that follow will attest to that.

There are billowy sponge cakes that will be applauded served au naturel, straight from the pan, or with a delectable sauce spooned over each serving. And there are fruit cakes, honey cakes, nut cakes, and more. The choice is yours.

Please note. In some of the recipes that follow, baking powder is required. Kosher for Passover baking powder is available in markets that carry a wide selection of Passover foods. Note also that baking soda (sodium bicarbonate) is kosher for Passover use.

Angel Food Cake

This cake does not have the same appearance or consistency as 'year-round angel food cake, but it is very good nonetheless. Do not be alarmed: the cake may fall out of the baking pan when it is inverted to cool.

> 1¼ cups egg whites (about 10 whites)
> 1 teaspoon cream of tartar
> 1½ cups sugar, divided
> 1 envelope (.43 ounces) vanilla sugar
> ½ teaspoon lemon juice
> 1 cup potato starch
> ½ teaspoon salt

In the large bowl of an electric mixer, beat the egg whites until frothy. Add the cream of tartar and beat until stiff peaks form. Gradually add 1 cup of the sugar, 1 tablespoon at a time, beating well after each addition. Add the vanilla sugar and lemon juice.

Sift together the potato starch, salt, and the remaining ½ cup of sugar. Slowly fold the dry mixture into the beaten egg white mixture. Pour the batter into an ungreased 9-inch tube pan and bake in a preheated 350-degree F. oven for 45 minutes. Remove from the oven and invert immediately onto a cake rack to cool. Serves 10 or more.

One-Bowl Sponge Cake

A high-rise sponge cake beaten in only one bowl. The addition of one-quarter teaspoon ground ginger to the ingredients will give an unusual aroma to this cake. Serve plain, frosted, or with a sauce.

If this or any other sponge cake should get stale, use it for Passover French Toast (see Index for recipe). Or cut it into one-inch-thick slices, toast until golden brown, and serve hot with chocolate sauce or ice cream. An elegant dessert can be made by sandwiching two slices of the toasted cake with ice cream; serve with a bowl of piping hot sauce.

> 9 eggs, separated
> 1½ cups sugar
> 2 tablespoons lemon juice
> ½ cup cake meal
> ¼ cup potato starch

In a large mixing bowl, beat the egg whites at low speed for about 1 minute, until the whites are loose and have begun to foam. Increase the speed of the mixer to high; gradually add the sugar and continue to beat for at least 5 minutes. Add the yolks and lemon juice; continue beating. Sift the cake meal with the potato starch; add to the mixing bowl. Beat until thoroughly blended. Turn the batter into an ungreased 10-inch tube pan and bake in a preheated 350-degree F. oven for 1 hour and 10 minutes. Invert to cool for at least 1 hour. Serves 10 to 12.

Variety Sponge Cake

7 eggs, separated
1 cup sugar
Juice of ½ lemon
½ cup potato starch
¼ cup cake meal

In a large mixing bowl, beat the egg yolks until light. Add the sugar and lemon juice; continue beating until very fluffy. Combine the dry ingredients and stir into the batter. In a separate mixing bowl, beat the egg whites until stiff; fold them into the egg batter. Bake in an ungreased 10-inch tube pan in a preheated 300-degree F. oven for 30 minutes. Increase the temperature to 325 degrees F. and bake for an additional 15 minutes. Invert to cool. Serves 10 or more.

Variations:

Carrot Cake: Fold 1 cup grated carrots and ½ cup chopped walnuts into the batter before folding in the stiffly beaten egg whites.

Chocolate Chip Cake: Fold 2 ounces grated or finely chopped bittersweet chocolate into the batter before folding in the stiffly beaten egg whites.

Marble Cake: Pour ⅔ of the batter in the pan. Add 1 to 2 tablespoons unsweetened cocoa to the remaining batter. Cut in the cocoa to blend. Using a tablespoon, evenly distribute the chocolate batter over the white batter. Cut through the batter several times with a spatula or knife to create a marble effect.

Mocha Cake: Add 3 tablespoons of instant coffee, or 2 tablespoons instant coffee and 1 tablespoon unsweetened cocoa, to the dry ingredients.

Date-Nut Cake: Add 2 cups finely cut dates, ½ cup chopped nuts, and 1 teaspoon cinnamon to the batter before folding in the stiffly beaten egg whites.

Strawberry Shortcake: Split the sponge cake in half; spread sweetened whipped cream and sliced strawberries on the bottom half. Place the second half of cake on top; top with whipped cream and whole berries.

Versatile Sponge Cake

Here is a sponge cake deliciously flavored with two fruit juices: orange and lemon. Note that it contains no matzo meal.

9 eggs
1¼ cups sugar
1 cup potato starch
Juice of 1 orange
Juice of 1 lemon

Using 2 large mixing bowls, separate 7 of the 9 eggs. Add the remaining 2 whole eggs to the bowl with the yolks and beat until foamy. Gradually add the sugar; beat until light and lemon-colored. Add the potato starch alternately with the juices. With an electric mixer, beat the egg whites until stiff and dry. Carefully fold the yolk mixture into the stiffly beaten egg whites. Pour into an ungreased 10-inch tube pan and bake in a preheated 325-degree F. oven for 1 hour and 10 minutes. Invert and cool for at least 1 hour. Serves 10 or more.

Variations:

Banana-Nut Cake: Omit the orange juice. Increase the lemon juice to the juice of 2 lemons. Add 2 ripe bananas, mashed, along with ½ cup chopped nuts.

Chocolate Cake: Substitute 3 tablespoons of unsweetened cocoa for 3 tablespoons of the potato starch. Add ½ cup chopped nuts if desired.

Wine Cake: Substitute ½ cup sweet wine for the juices. Add ½ cup chopped nuts.

Chocolate-Wine Sponge Cake

8 eggs, separated
1½ cups, sugar
¾ cup cake meal
2 tablespoons unsweetened cocoa
1 tablespoon potato starch
Juice and grated rind of 1 orange
¼ cup sweet red wine

In a large mixing bowl, beat the yolks with the sugar until thick and creamy. Sift the cake meal with the cocoa and potato starch; stir into the egg yolk mixture. Add the orange juice, grated rind, and wine. Mix well. In another large bowl, beat the egg whites until stiff; fold them into the egg yolk mixture. Pour the batter into an ungreased 9 or 10-inch tube pan and bake in a preheated 325-degree F. oven for 50 minutes. Invert and cool. Serves 10 or more.

Chocolate Cake

    7 ounces semisweet chocolate
      Scant ½ cup (1 stick) butter or
      margarine
    ⅔ cup sugar, divided
    6 eggs, separated
    ¾ cup (4 ounces) blanched almonds, finely
      chopped

In the top of a double boiler, melt the chocolate over hot water. In a medium-sized mixing bowl, cream the butter or margarine with ⅓ cup of the sugar. Add the egg yolks and beat at high speed until very light. Add the melted chocolate and almonds. Mix well.

In a separate bowl, beat the egg whites stiff with the remaining ⅓ cup of sugar. With a rubber spatula, fold the stiffly beaten egg whites into the chocolate batter.

Reserve ½ cup of the batter. Pour the remaining batter into an ungreased 8-inch spring-form pan and bake in a preheated 325-degree F. oven for 30 minutes. The cake is done when a toothpick inserted into the center comes out dry. When cool, run a knife around the edge and remove the frame. Pour the reserved uncooked batter over the top of the cake and chill. Garnish with chocolate shavings. Top with whipped cream for a dairy meal. Serves 6 to 8.

Chocolate Torte

        4 eggs, separated
        ½ cup sugar
        ¼ pound almonds, blanched and ground
        ¼ pound raisins
        ⅓ cup cake meal
        ¼ pound semisweet chocolate, grated, or ½
            cup unsweetened cocoa
        ¼ cup sweet red wine
            Juice of 1 orange
            Cake meal for the pan

In a medium-sized mixing bowl, beat the egg yolks and sugar
until very light. Add the ground almonds, raisins, cake meal,
chocolate or cocoa, wine, and orange juice. In a separate mixing
bowl, beat the egg whites until stiff but not dry. Carefully fold
the egg whites into the batter. Grease an 8-inch spring-form
pan; dust with cake meal. Transfer the batter to the pan and bake
in a preheated 350-degree F. oven for 1 hour. Invert and cool.
Serves 8 to 10.

Simple Honey Cake

   A slight variation may be made in the texture and taste of this
cake by adding the juice and rind of one-half lemon to the yolk
mixture and one-half cup finely ground nuts seasoned with one
to two teaspoons cinnamon to the dry ingredients. Chopped
nuts are a welcome addition to any honey cake.

        6 eggs, separated
        ½ cup sugar
        ½ cup honey
        ½ cup cake meal
        2 tablespoons potato starch

In a large mixing bowl, with an electric mixer, beat the egg
whites at low speed until frothy; slowly increase to the highest
speed. Gradually add the sugar, 2 tablespoons at a time, and
continue to beat the egg whites until stiff. Set aside.

In a separate, medium-sized mixing bowl, beat the egg yolks with the same beaters until light. Gradually add the honey; continue beating until very well blended.

Fold the stiffly beaten egg whites into the yolk mixture. Sift the dry ingredients together; carefully fold them into the egg yolk mixture. Transfer the batter to an ungreased 9-inch angel cake pan. Bake in a preheated 325-degree F. oven for 50 minutes. Invert the cake onto a cake rack to cool. Serves 8 or more.

Honey Cake

A "heavier" cake than the Simple Honey Cake above.

> **1 cup honey**
> **1 cup sugar**
> **1 cup fresh-brewed strong coffee**
> **4 eggs, separated**
> **Juice and grated rind of ½ orange**
> **1 cup cake meal**
> **1 tablespoon potato starch**
> **½ teaspoon cinnamon**
> **¼ teaspoon ground ginger (optional)**
> **½ cup ground walnuts**

In a large mixing bowl, beat the honey, sugar, coffee, egg yolks, orange juice, and orange rind until well blended. In a small bowl, sift together the cake meal, potato starch, cinnamon, and ginger. Mix well. Fold in the nuts. Combine the dry ingredients with the egg yolk mixture.

In a clean bowl, beat the egg whites until stiff but not dry; gently fold them into the batter. Pour the batter into a well-greased 5 × 9-inch loaf pan. Bake in a 350-degree F. oven for about 1 hour. Serves 10.

Honey Sponge Cake

> **6 eggs, separated**
> **1 cup sugar**

⟶

¼ cup orange juice
1 tablespoon lemon juice
  Grated rind of 1 lemon
⅓ cup honey
½ cup cake meal, sifted
½ cup potato starch
1 teaspoon salt

In a large bowl, beat the egg yolks for 4 to 5 minutes, until light. Gradually beat in the sugar. Stir in the juices, rind, and honey; blend well. Sift the cake meal with the potato starch; stir into the egg yolk mixture.

In a large bowl, beat the egg whites with the salt until stiff but not dry. Gently fold the egg whites into the egg yolk mixture. Pour the batter into an ungreased 9-inch tube pan. Bake in a preheated 325-degree F. oven for 55 to 60 minutes. Invert and cool. Serves 10 or more.

Jelly Roll

3 eggs, separated
1 whole egg
¾ cup sugar
2 teaspoons lemon juice
  Grated rind of ½ lemon
¼ cup plus 1 tablespoon potato starch
  Dash of salt
  Confectioners' sugar (see Index for
  recipe)

In a medium-sized mixing bowl, beat the 3 egg yolks with the whole egg until light. Gradually add the sugar, lemon juice, and lemon rind; continue beating for 2 minutes. Sift the potato starch; gradually stir it into the egg yolk mixture.

In a separate medium-sized bowl, beat the egg whites with the salt until stiff but not dry; gently fold the egg whites into the egg yolk mixture.

Line a greased jelly roll pan with wax paper; grease the wax paper. Distribute the batter evenly in the pan. Bake in a pre-heated 350-degree F. oven for 25 minutes or until the cake springs back when lightly touched.

Turn out the cake onto a towel that has been dusted with confectioners' sugar. Remove the wax paper. Roll up the cake together with the towel. When cool, unroll, spread with 1 or more cups of the filling of your choice (see Index for possibilities) and reroll. Serves 6 to 8.

Variations:

• To make an ice cream roll, after cooling the baked rolled cake, unroll and spread with slightly softened ice cream. Roll up the cake lengthwise. Wrap airtight in foil and freeze. Thirty minutes before serving, put the roll in the refrigerator to thaw some-what. Cut into 2-inch diagonal slices and serve at once.
• For a festive party treat, do not roll this jelly roll. When cool, cut into squares and drizzle with brandy. Then use the squares to make sandwiches, filling them with jelly, sweetened whipped cream, or your favorite filling. They will be as luscious as French pastry.

Lemon Meringue Cake Roll

This roll may be filled with a lemon filling or with a jelly, chocolate, or mocha filling. The choice is yours, but sans me-ringue it will lack a glamorous finishing touch. When you have cloaked the cake roll with meringue, witness the glow of excite-ment as it is served.

> **4 eggs, separated**
> **½ cup sugar**
> **Juice and grated rind of ½ lemon**
> **¼ cup potato starch**
> **Additional potato starch**

In a medium-sized bowl, beat the egg yolks at high speed until thick and lemon-colored. Gradually add the sugar, beating con-stantly. Add the lemon juice, rind, and ¼ cup of potato starch.

In a clean bowl, beat the egg whites until stiff but not dry. Gently fold the egg yolk mixture into the stiffly beaten egg whites, just until blended. Distribute the batter evenly in a wax paper-lined and greased 10 × 15 × 1-inch jelly roll pan. Bake in a preheated 325-degree F. oven for 10 to 12 minutes, until the surface springs back when lightly touched.

Sprinkle a dishtowel with potato starch. Invert the hot cake onto the towel. Immediately peel off the wax paper and cut off the edges of crust. Starting at the narrower edge, roll up the cake and towel together. Let cool completely. While the cake is cooling, prepare the filling (see recipe below). Unroll; spread the filling evenly over the cake. Reroll the cake. Place the rolled cake seam side down on an ungreased baking sheet. Prepare the meringue (see recipe below). Spread it over the top and sides of the cake. Bake in a 350-degree F. oven for 10 to 15 minutes, until the meringue is golden brown. Serves 6 to 8.

Lemon Filling:

> 1 cup sugar
> 3 tablespoons potato starch
> Pinch of salt
> 1 cup water
> 3 egg yolks
> 1 to 2 teaspoons finely shredded lemon rind
> ¼ cup lemon juice
> 1 tablespoon margarine

To prepare the filling, combine the sugar, potato starch, and salt in a medium-sized saucepan; gradually add the water; stir well to dissolve the potato starch. In a small bowl, beat the egg yolks until light and creamy; stir into the saucepan along with the lemon rind and juice. Cook over medium heat. stirring constantly until the mixture begins to bubble. Boil and stir for 1 minute; remove from the heat. Stir in the margarine and blend well. Cool. Makes about 1⅓ cups of filling.

Meringue:

> 3 egg whites
> ¼ teaspoon cream of tartar
> 6 tablespoons sugar

In a medium-sized mixing bowl, at low speed, beat the egg whites with the cream of tartar until frothy. Increase the speed to high. Gradually beat in the sugar, 1 tablespoon at a time, beating well after each addition. Beat until stiff peaks form when the beater is slowly raised.

Apple Cake I

Cake:

> 3 eggs
> ¾ cup sugar
> ⅓ cup oil
> ¾ cup cake meal
> 5 apples, peeled and sliced

Topping:

> ⅓ cup chopped walnuts
> ½ cup sugar
> 2 teaspoons cinnamon

In a medium-sized mixing bowl, beat the eggs with the sugar and oil until the mixture is light. Add the cake meal and mix well. Pour half of the mixture into a lightly greased 8 or 9-inch square baking pan. Distribute half of the apples over the batter. Pour the remaining batter over the apples and cover with the remaining apples.

Combine the topping ingredients in a small bowl; sprinkle over the apples. Bake in a preheated 350-degree F. oven for approximately 1½ hours. Serves 8 or 9.

Note: Double the recipe and you will have a 9 × 13-inch cake.

Apple Cake II

> 4 apples
> 6 tablespoons cake meal, divided

→

¾ cup sugar, divided
8 eggs, separated
½ teaspoon salt
1 teaspoon lemon juice

Peel and core the apples; slice them thinly into a bowl. Mix the apples with 2 tablespoons of the cake meal and ¼ cup of the sugar. Prepare the sponge cake mixture with the rest of the ingredients by beating the egg yolks in a large mixing bowl until light; gradually add the remaining ½ cup of sugar. Add the remaining cake meal, salt, and lemon juice; continue to beat until well blended. In a clean large mixing bowl, beat the egg whites until stiff but not dry. Fold the egg whites into the egg yolk mixture. Pour half of the sponge cake mixture into an ungreased 9-inch spring-form pan. Distribute the apple mixture over the batter. Top with the remainder of the cake batter. Bake in a preheated 325-degree F. oven for 40 to 50 minutes. Cool. Serves 10.

Apple Cake III

To make this apple cake more festive, fold in one cup of chopped walnuts and one-half cup of raisins when you fold in the cubed apples. When the cake has cooled completely, spoon a lemon glaze over the cake.

4 to 5 apples, preferably Granny-Smith
5 tablespoons cake meal
2 teaspoons cinnamon
4 eggs
2 cups sugar
1 cup oil
¼ cup water, lemon juice, orange juice or
   a combination
2 cups cake meal
1 cup potato starch
3 teaspoons Passover baking powder
¼ to ½ teaspoon salt
Grease and potato starch for the pan

Peel, core, and dice the apples into 1-inch cubes. Set aside in a medium-sized bowl. Combine the 5 tablespoons of cake meal with the cinnamon; sprinkle the mixture over the apples. Toss the apples to coat them. Set aside.

In a large mixing bowl, beat the eggs and sugar until light; add the oil; continue beating for an additional 10 minutes. Add the water, juice, or combination liquid mix.

Into a separate bowl, sift the cake meal with the potato starch, baking powder, and salt. Add the sifted dry ingredients to the beaten egg mixture. Beat at low speed until blended. Fold in the diced apples. Grease and dust with potato starch a 9-inch tube pan or bundt pan. Pour the batter into the pan and bake in a preheated 350-degree F. oven for 1 hour and 15 minutes or until a cake tester inserted comes out clean. Set the pan on a wire rack to cool for 10 minutes. Remove the cake from the pan and continue to cool completely. Serves 10.

Apple Cake Roll

A change of pace from the popular apple cake. Here, the dough is a little unusual: a cake mix is used as one of the ingredients.

Dough:

> 1 box (12 ounces) yellow cake mix
> 2 eggs
> Water
> ¾ cup cake meal
> ⅛ cup cake meal, approximately, as needed

Filling:

> 3 to 4 apples, peeled and cored
> 1 to 2 tablespoons sugar
> ½ teaspoon cinnamon
> Jelly, variety of your choice
> ¼ cup chopped nuts or grated coconut
> ⅛ teaspoon sugar and cinnamon mixture,
> proportions to taste

Empty the cake mix into a large mixing bowl. Break the eggs into a measuring cup and add water to make a total of ¾ cup liquid. Add the water and eggs to the mix; beat for about 4 minutes. Add the ¾ cup cake meal; continue beating until well blended. Turn the dough out onto a work surface. Knead the dough together, adding additional cake meal if necessary to make a soft, pliable dough.

To prepare the filling, coarsely chop the peeled and cored apples. Sprinkle them with the 1 to 2 tablespoons sugar (quantity depending on the sweetness of the apples) and the ½ teaspoon cinnamon.

Divide the dough in half. Roll out each half between 2 pieces of wax paper, lightly dusting the bottom piece of wax paper with cake meal.

Spread the jelly very lightly over the dough. Sprinkle the nuts or coconut over the jelly. Spread half of the apple filling over three-fourths of the dough. Roll up the dough jelly roll fashion, making sure the unfilled portion is the last to be rolled up. Carefully place the roll on a lightly greased baking sheet. Repeat with the other half of dough. Slice the dough, but not completely through. Sprinkle the top with the sugar and cinnamon mixture. Bake in a preheated 350-degree F. oven for 25 to 30 minutes. Remove from the oven and cut the slices through. Serve warm or at room temperature. Serves 10.

Israeli Upside-Down Apple Cake

Here, whole apples are sugared and enclosed in a sponge cake batter. The result is an upside-down cake.

Apples:

 ¼ cup margarine
 ½ cup brown sugar
 ½ cup white sugar
 7 or 8 apples, peeled and cored
 Walnuts
 Raisins
 Juice of 1 lemon

Batter:

> 5 eggs, separated
> 5 tablespoons sugar
> 1 teaspoon lemon juice
> 4 tablespoons potato starch, sifted

To prepare the apples, melt the margarine and the sugars in the bottom of a deep round pan large enough to hold the apples comfortably. Arrange the apples over the sugar. Fill the core openings with walnuts and raisins. Pour the lemon juice over the apples. Bake in a preheated 375-degree F. oven for 30 to 35 minutes, until the apples are tender.

To prepare the batter, in a large mixing bowl beat the egg yolks with the sugar until very light. Add the lemon juice and sifted potato starch. In a clean bowl, with clean beaters, beat the egg whites until stiff but not dry; carefully fold the beaten egg whites into the egg yolk mixture. Pour the batter over the hot apples and bake for an additional 30 minutes or until the cake tests done. Let the cake rest on a cake rack for 10 minutes before turning it out, upside down, onto a large cake plate. Serve cold. Serves 8 or more.

Pineapple or Peach Upside-Down Cake

> 1 tablespoon margarine
> ½ cup brown sugar
> 4 pineapple slices or 4 peach halves, sliced
> 4 egg yolks
> ¾ cup sugar
>   Juice and grated rind of ½ lemon
> 4 egg whites
> ¾ cup potato starch
> 1 teaspoon Passover baking powder

Melt the margarine and sugar in a 9-inch square baking pan. Arrange the pineapple or peach slices over the melted sugar. Set aside.

In a large mixing bowl, beat the egg yolks until light. Gradually add the sugar, lemon juice, and grated rind; continue beating until creamy. In a clean bowl, with clean beaters, beat the egg whites until stiff but not dry. Gently fold the stiffly beaten egg whites into the egg yolk mixture.

Combine the potato starch and baking powder; fold into the batter. Carefully pour the batter over the fruit. Bake in a preheated 350-degree F. oven for 30 minutes. Invert the cake onto a serving platter and let cool. Serves 6 to 8.

Banana Cake

It is not mandatory that this cake be frosted. The bananas provide sufficient moisture to prevent the cake from drying out.

Note that the cake can be made successfully without cake meal. Simply increase the potato starch to three-fourths cup.

> **7 eggs, separated**
> **1 cup sugar**
> **1 cup mashed ripe bananas**
> **¼ teaspoon salt**
> **¾ cup cake meal**
> **¼ cup potato starch**
> **½ cup chopped nuts**
> **Grease for the pan**

In a large mixing bowl, beat the egg yolks with the sugar at medium speed until light and creamy. In a separate bowl, combine the mashed bananas with the salt, cake meal, and potato starch. Blend well; add to the egg yolk mixture.

In a large mixing bowl, with clean beaters, beat the egg whites slowly for about 1 minute, until the whites are loose and have begun to foam. Gradually increase the speed of the mixer to high and continue beating the egg whites until stiff but not dry. Fold the beaten egg whites into the egg yolk batter. Lightly fold in the ½ cup nuts.

Turn the batter into a lightly greased 10-inch spring-form cake pan or a 10-inch tube pan. Bake in a preheated 325-degree F. oven for 45 minutes to 1 hour, until golden brown on top. Test for doneness with a toothpick after 45 minutes of baking. Invert onto a cake rack to cool. Turn out onto a serving plate. Frost if desired. Serves 8 to 10.

Frosting:

> 1 egg white
> ⅞ cup sugar
> Pinch of salt
> 3 tablespoons cold water
> 1 tablespoon orange or lemon juice (optional)
> ¼ cup chopped nuts

Combine the egg white, sugar, salt, and water in the top of a double boiler. Place over boiling water and low heat. Beat for 7 minutes or until thick enough to spread. Remove from the heat. Beat in the juice. Quickly spread the frosting over the cake. Sprinkle with the ¼ cup of chopped nuts.

Variations:

Strawberry Cake: Substitute strawberries for the bananas and use a strawberry frosting.

Chocolate Banana Cake: Add ¼ cup unsweetened cocoa to the dry ingredients.

Banana-Cherry Cake: Cut the cake into 2 layers when cool and spread with cooled Cherry Filling. Glaze with the Wine Glaze.

Cherry Filling:

> 1 cup finely cut dates
> 1 cup cherry preserves
> ¾ cup semisweet wine
> 1 tablespoon lemon juice

Combine the ingredients in a small saucepan. Cook over low heat, stirring constantly until thoroughly blended. Cool.

Wine Glaze:

> ½ cup sweet wine
> ½ cup water
> 1 tablespoon potato starch
> 2 tablespoons sugar

Combine the ingredients in a saucepan. Stir to dissolve the potato starch. Cook over low heat until thick and clear. Pour over the filled cake.

Banana Chiffon Cake

In preparing the bananas for this cake, gently press the peeled fruit with a fork. This will help the bananas retain their consistency.

> 5 eggs, separated
> 1 cup sugar, divided
> ¾ cup sifted cake meal
> ¼ cup sifted potato starch
> ¼ cup oil
> ½ cup mashed ripe bananas
> 1 teaspoon grated lemon rind

In a large mixing bowl, beat the egg whites at low speed for about 1 minute, then increase the speed to high and continue beating until soft peaks form. Gradually add ½ cup of sugar, 2 tablespoons at a time, and continue beating the egg whites until stiff peaks form.

In a separate mixing bowl, mix the dry ingredients, including the remaining sugar. Make a well in the dry ingredients and add the egg yolks, oil, mashed bananas, and grated lemon rind. Beat until smooth. Fold the egg yolk mixture into the stiffly beaten egg whites. Transfer the mixture to a 10-inch ungreased tube pan. Bake in a preheated 325-degree F. oven for 50 to 60 minutes or until a cake tester inserted in the center of the cake comes out clean. Remove the cake from the oven; invert the pan. Let cool completely before removing the cake from the pan. Serves 8 to 10.

Carrot Torte

> 5 eggs, separated
> 1 cup sugar

→

> 1 cup grated raw carrots
> ½ pound almonds, blanched and grated
> 1 teaspoon cinnamon
> ½ cup matzo meal

In a large mixing bowl, beat the egg yolks and sugar until thick and lemon-colored. Add the grated carrots and almonds. Sift together the dry ingredients and add to the egg yolk mixture; blend well. In a clean large bowl, beat the egg whites until stiff but not dry; gently fold them into the egg yolk mixture. Turn the batter into an 8-inch spring-form or tube pan with a removable bottom. Bake in a preheated 325-degree F. oven for about 1 hour. Let cool before removing from the pan. Serves 8 to 10.

Carrot Cake

Here, the versatile carrot appears in a cake studded with raisins and chopped nuts.

> 2 cups sugar
> 1½ cups oil
> 4 eggs
> 1 cup potato starch
> 2 cups cake meal
> 2 teaspoons Passover baking powder
> 2 teaspoons baking soda
> 1 teaspoon salt
> 1 teaspoon cinnamon
> 3 cups grated carrots
> 1 cup chopped nuts
> ½ cup raisins
> Grease and potato starch for the pan

Combine the sugar, oil, and eggs in a large mixing bowl. Beat with an electric mixer at medium speed until well blended. The mixture should be light and creamy.

Into a separate clean bowl, sift the dry ingredients. Add the sifted dry ingredients to the egg yolk mixture; continue beating at low speed for an additional 2 minutes. Add the grated carrots, nuts, and raisins. Mix well.

Grease and lightly dust with potato starch a 10-inch tube pan. Transfer the batter to the pan. Bake for 1 hour in a preheated 350-degree F. oven. Cool in the pan. Serves 10 to 12.

Epicurean Carrot Cake

As good a reason as any for gathering at coffee time.

    1 cup applesauce
    Juice and grated rind of 1 large lemon
    1 cup shredded carrots
    ½ cup ground or finely chopped almonds
    ½ cup finely chopped golden raisins
    ¾ cup cake meal
    ¾ cup potato starch
    ½ teaspoon salt
    2 teaspoons cinnamon
    9 eggs, separated
    1½ cups sugar, divided

In a medium-sized bowl, combine the applesauce, lemon juice and rind, carrots, almonds, and raisins; set aside. In a second medium-sized bowl, sift together the cake meal, potato starch, salt, and cinnamon; set aside.

In a large bowl, beat the egg whites with an electric mixer at high speed until foamy. Gradually beat in ½ cup of the sugar. Continue beating until soft peaks form; set aside.

In another large bowl, beat the egg yolks at high speed until thick. Gradually beat in the remaining cup of sugar. Continue beating until well blended. At low speed on the electric mixer, gradually beat the sifted dry mixture into the egg yolk mixture. Add the applesauce mixture and continue to beat just until well mixed.

With a spatula, gradually and gently fold the egg yolk mixture into the stiffly beaten egg whites. Turn the batter into a 10-inch ungreased tube pan. Bake in a preheated 325-degree F. oven for 1 hour and 20 minutes or until a cake tester comes out clean. Invert the pan to cool. With a spatula, carefully loosen the cake;

remove onto a cake plate. Serve plain, with an apple-lemon sauce, or with the sauce of your choice. Serves 10 or more.

Prune Compote Seder Cake

Cake:

12 ounces pitted prunes
2 cups boiling water
7 large eggs, separated
1⅓ cups sugar, divided
1 teaspoon salt
1 teaspoon grated lemon rind
3 tablespoons lemon juice
1 cup cake meal
1 cup finely chopped nuts

Compote:

12 ounces pitted prunes
1 cup of the reserved prune juice or water
(see method)
2½ teaspoons potato starch
1 tablespoon lemon juice
¼ cup sugar
1 teaspoon grated lemon rind

In a small saucepan, place the pitted prunes; cover with the boiling water. Simmer for 5 minutes. Drain and reserve the juice. Purée the drained prunes. Measure 1 cup of the purée, reserving the remainder for the compote.

In a large mixing bowl, beat the egg yolks until very thick and light. Gradually add 1 cup of sugar and the salt, beating continuously. Stir in the lemon rind, lemon juice, and cooled prune purée. Lightly but thoroughly fold in the cake meal and nuts.

In a clean large bowl, beat the egg whites until soft peaks form. Gradually add the remaining ⅓ cup of sugar. Continue beating until the egg whites are very stiff. Gently fold the beaten egg whites into the batter. Pour the batter into an ungreased 10-inch tube pan. Bake in a preheated 350-degree F. oven for 45 minutes or until brown. Invert to cool.

To prepare the prune compote, put the prunes and the reserved juice or water in a small saucepan. Cook for about 3 minutes. With a slotted spoon, remove the fruit and set aside. Dissolve the potato starch in the lemon juice; add to the pan; stir in the sugar and lemon rind. Cook over low heat until the sauce is smooth and thickened. Remove from the heat. Return the prunes and the reserved prune purée to the pan. Stir to blend.

Prick the cake with a toothpick and gently spoon some of the prune sauce over the cake. Pour the remainder into a dish set in the center of the cake plate. Serves 10 to 12.

Cream Cheese Cake

Crust:

> 1 large package (1¾ ounces) soup nuts,
>   crushed fine
> 1 tablespoon sugar
> ¼ teaspoon cinnamon
> ⅓ cup softened butter

Filling:

> 4 eggs
> 1½ pounds cream cheese, at room
>   temperature
>   Juice of ½ orange
> 1 cup sugar
>   Strawberry preserves for topping
>   (optional)

In a medium-sized mixing bowl, mix the dry ingredients; add the softened butter. Blend well with a pastry blender. Pat the mixture firmly into a 9-inch spring-form pan. Chill thoroughly. While the crust is chilling, prepare the filling.

To prepare the filling, in a large bowl beat the eggs until light and fluffy. Add the remaining ingredients and continue beating until thoroughly blended. Pour the cheese mixture into the lined cake pan and bake in a 350-degree F. oven for 50 minutes. When cool, top with strawberry preserves if desired. Serves 8.

Variation:

Mix 1 pint sour cream with 2 tablespoons sugar and 1 teaspoon vanilla flavoring or vanilla sugar. Pour the sour cream mixture over the cake and bake for an additional 10 minutes.

Two-Cheese Cheesecake

With cream cheese, cottage cheese, and sour cream, how could this be anything but a deliciously rich cake?

Crust:

> ½ cup butter or margarine
> 1¼ cups matzo meal
> 3 tablespoons sugar
> ¼ teaspoon salt
> 2 tablespoons water

Filling:

> ½ pound cream cheese
> 1 cup creamed cottage cheese
> 3 eggs, separated
> ¾ cup sugar
> 1 tablespoon potato starch
> 1 cup sour cream
> 1½ tablespoons grated lemon rind

To prepare the crust, cream the butter or margarine in a medium-sized mixing bowl until fluffy. Add the matzo meal, sugar, and salt; mix until crumbly. Stir in the water. With the fingertips, press the mixture around the sides and bottom of an 8-inch spring-form pan. Set aside.

To prepare the filling, in a large mixing bowl beat the cream cheese with the cottage cheese until almost smooth. Add the egg yolks and sugar; beat until blended. Add the potato starch, sour cream, and lemon rind. Mix well. In a clean mixing bowl, beat the egg whites until stiff but not dry. Gently fold the stiffly beaten egg whites into the cheese mixture. Pour the batter into the prepared crust. Bake in a preheated 325-degree F. oven for 1 hour or until set. Turn off the heat. Leave the cake in the oven, with the door partially open, for another 30 minutes. Remove from the oven. Cool completely. Serves 8 to 10.

Almond Torte

The combination of finely grated almonds and mashed potatoes gives this torte an unusual texture and makes the use of cake meal or potato starch unnecessary.

6 eggs, separated
1 cup sugar, divided
1½ cups grated almonds
Juice and grated rind of 1 lemon
1 cup cold mashed potatoes, sieved
Grease and potato starch for the pan

In a large mixing bowl, beat the egg yolks until light and lemon-colored. Gradually add ½ cup of the sugar, a small amount at a time; continue beating for approximately 10 minutes. Add the grated almonds, lemon juice, lemon rind, and the mashed potatoes. Beat until well blended.

In a separate medium-sized mixing bowl, beat the egg whites until stiff; gradually add the remaining ½ cup of sugar; continue beating until the egg whites are stiff but not dry. Fold the stiffly beaten egg whites into the egg yolk mixture.

Grease well and dust with potato starch a 10-inch tube pan. Pour the batter into the pan. Bake in a 325-degree F. oven for 45 to 60 minutes. Serves 10.

Almond Cake

3 eggs, separated
⅔ cup sugar

→

¼ cup potato starch, sifted
½ cup orange juice
1¾ cups ground blanched almonds
½ teaspoon cinnamon
Grease and potato starch for the pan

In a medium-sized bowl, with an electric mixer, beat the egg yolks and sugar until the mixture is thick and fluffy, at least 7 to 10 minutes. Reduce the electric mixer speed to low; beat in alternately the potato starch and orange juice. Add the almonds and cinnamon; mix well.

In a clean small bowl, beat the egg whites until stiff but not dry; fold the beaten egg whites into the egg yolk mixture.

Grease and dust with potato starch an 8-inch spring-form pan. Bake in a preheated 325-degree F. oven for 35 to 40 minutes, until the cake tests clean. Serve with a fruit salad. Serves 8.

Walnut Cake

The nuts used in this cake should be grated on a nut grater or chopped fine. They should not be ground in a grinder because too much oil is released.

9 eggs, separated
1⅓ cups sugar
1 cup potato starch
1½ cups grated or finely chopped nuts
⅓ cup sweet wine

In a large bowl, with an electric mixer, beat the egg yolks well at high speed. Reduce the speed and gradually add the sugar; beat until thick and lemon-colored. Beat in half of the potato starch. Fold in alternately the rest of the potato starch and walnuts; stir in the wine.

In a clean large bowl, beat the egg whites at low speed until frothy; increase to the highest speed and continue beating until the egg whites are stiff but not dry. Gently fold the beaten egg whites into the egg yolk-nut mixture.

Line the bottom (only) of a 9-inch spring-form pan with brown paper. Turn the batter into the pan and bake in a preheated 350-degree F. oven for 50 minutes. Allow the cake to cool completely in the pan. Serves 10 to 12.

Walnut-Brandy Cake

4 eggs, separated
⅔ cup sugar
2 tablespoons brandy
1⅓ cups finely chopped walnuts
⅛ teaspoon cinnamon
⅓ cup matzo meal
¼ cup melted margarine or oil
Grease for the pan

In a medium-sized mixing bowl, beat the egg yolks well; gradually add the sugar. Continue to beat until light and lemon-colored. Add the brandy, chopped walnuts, cinnamon, matzo meal, and melted margarine or oil; continue beating until well blended.

In a clean mixing bowl, beat the egg whites until stiff but not dry. Gently fold the beaten egg whites into the egg yolk mixture.

Grease a 9 × 9-inch pan; line with wax paper; grease the wax paper. Pour the batter into the pan. Bake in a preheated 375-degree F. oven for 35 minutes or until firm. Let the cake stand in the pan for 5 minutes before removing. When the cake is cool, cut into diamonds, squares, or rectangles. Yields 24 to 32 pieces.

Walnut Roll

The quantity of sugar, cinnamon, and nuts to be sprinkled on the towel before rolling the cake has deliberately been omitted. This depends upon the amount of sweetness, spice, and crunchiness you desire.

6 eggs, separated
½ cup sugar

➤

> 1 cup finely chopped walnuts
> Grease for the pan
> Sugar, cinnamon, and chopped nuts for
> rolling

In a medium-sized mixing bowl, beat the egg yolks until thick and lemon-colored. Gradually add the sugar and continue beating. Add the cup of nuts. In a clean mixing bowl, beat the egg whites until stiff but not dry; gently fold them into the egg yolk mixture. Spread the batter in a well-greased 10 × 15 × 1-inch jelly roll pan. Bake in a 325-degree F. oven for 15 to 20 minutes, until lightly browned on top.

Turn out the cake onto a towel that has been sprinkled with sugar, cinnamon, and chopped nuts. While the cake is still hot, roll up cake and towel together. When the roll has cooled, unroll and spread with your favorite filling or with whipped cream and berries; reroll, placing the seam side down. For miniature rolls, cut the cake in half lengthwise while hot and roll from each side towards the center. Serves 10.

Nut Torte

When served warm, the texture of this torte resembles that of a soufflé.

> 1¼ cups ground walnuts
> ¾ cup sugar
> ⅓ cup unsweetened cocoa
> 4 eggs, separated
> 1 teaspoon lemon juice
> 1 teaspoon grated lemon rind
> 2 tablespoons matzo meal

Combine the walnuts, sugar, and cocoa in a medium-sized bowl. Set aside. In a small bowl, beat the egg yolks with the lemon juice and rind until light. Add the beaten egg yolk mixture to the dry ingredients; beat well. In a clean bowl, beat the egg whites until stiff but not dry. Carefully fold the beaten egg whites into the egg yolk batter.

Grease a 9-inch baking dish and dust with the matzo meal.

Pour the batter into the baking dish and bake in a 350-degree F. oven for 30 minutes or until a cake tester comes out clean. Serve warm or cold. Serves 8.

Mocha-Nut Cake

This is a delightfully delicious chocolate-nut torte subtly flavored with instant coffee. It is advisable to prepare two cakes at the same time, one for immediate use, the other for the freezer. The cake freezes very well and can be served without hesitation in a semifrozen state.

> **12 eggs, separated**
> **2 cups sugar, divided**
> **Juice and grated rind of 1 lemon**
> **½ pound walnuts, finely ground**
> **1 heaping tablespoon unsweetened cocoa**
> **1 heaping tablespoon instant coffee**
> **½ cup grated semisweet chocolate**
> **½ cup cake meal**
> **1 tablespoon potato starch**

In a large mixing bowl, with an electric mixer, beat the egg yolks with 1 cup of sugar until very thick and light. Add the lemon juice and rind; continue to beat at high speed until thick and light, about 3 minutes.

In a clean large bowl, beat the egg whites at a low speed for about 1 minute; increase the speed to high and beat until the whites stand in peaks but are not dry. Beating continuously, make a meringue by beating the remaining cup of sugar into the whites, 1 tablespoon at a time.

In a medium-sized bowl, stir together the dry ingredients. Into the egg yolk mixture alternately fold a small amount of the beaten egg whites and the dry ingredient mixture.

Turn the batter into 2 ungreased 10-inch tube pans. Bake in a 325-degree F. oven for 1 hour or until the cake springs back when lightly touched. Invert the pans over cake racks. Cool for at least 45 minutes. When still slightly warm, remove the cakes from their pans by running a sharp thin-bladed knife around the side of each pan in a long steady stroke. Ice with Mocha Frosting (see Index for recipe). Each cake serves 10 to 12.

Mocha Cream Torte

In this airy sponge-type cake, ground nuts take the place of the matzo meal, cake meal, or potato starch usually found. It is very important that the maximum amount of air be incorporated into the egg whites to insure the lightness of the cake. Start beating the egg whites at low speed, gradually increasing to the highest speed until the egg whites are stiff but not dry.

This is a very rich torte. A thin slice makes an adequate serving.

Cake:

> ¾ cup sugar, sifted
> 1 cup finely ground blanched almonds
> 6 egg whites
>   Grease for the pans
> 2 tablespoons potato starch for the pan

Mocha Cream Filling:

> ½ cup sugar
> ⅓ cup brewed coffee
> 4 egg yolks
> ¼ pound sweet butter
> ½ cup heavy cream, whipped

In a small mixing bowl, mix the sugar with the almonds. In a large mixing bowl, with an electric mixer at low speed, beat the egg whites for 1 minute. Increase the speed to high and continue beating until the whites are stiff but not dry. Gently fold in the sugar-nut mixture.

Grease two 9-inch layer cake pans and dust with the potato starch. Divide the mixture into the pans; smooth off the tops.

Bake in a preheated 300-degree F. oven for 40 minutes. Cool in the pans before removing.

To prepare the filling, first make a coffee syrup by boiling the sugar with the coffee in a small saucepan for 5 minutes. In the top of a double boiler, beat the egg yolks until frothy; gradually add the coffee syrup, stirring constantly. Place the top pot over hot water and continue stirring until the mixture thickens and is smooth. Cool.

In a large bowl, cream the butter; gradually add the egg yolk mixture. Mix well. Fold in the whipped cream. Spread the filling between the layers and over the top of the cake. Serves 10 to 12.

Ice Box Cake
With
Lemon Fluff Filling and Coconut

>   4 eggs, separated
>   Pinch of salt
>   5 tablespoons potato starch
>   2 cups water or water and wine mixed
>   Juice and grated rind of 1 lemon
>   1 cup sugar
>   1 cup freshly grated coconut
>   1 sponge cake (your favorite recipe),
>   prepared

To prepare the filling, put the egg yolks in the top of a double boiler; add the salt and beat well. Dilute the potato starch with a few tablespoons of the water; add to the egg yolks along with the remainder of the water, the lemon juice, lemon rind, and sugar. Stir over boiling water until thick and smooth. Cool.

In a clean medium-sized bowl, beat the egg whites until stiff but not dry. Gently fold the whites into the cooled lemon mixture; fold in the freshly grated coconut.

Slice the sponge cake into thin slices. Line a deep 8 or 9-inch pan with the thin slices of sponge cake. Cover the cake slices with some of the filling. Top the filling with more slices of the cake. Continue to alternate layers until all the filling has been used up. The top layer should be cake. Chill in the refrigerator for about 12 hours. Serves 10 to 12.

No-Bake Seven-Layer Cake

To make fine sugar, put one cup of regular sugar into a blender jar. Blend at high speed for a few seconds, until powdered.

> 3½ ounces bittersweet chocolate
> ¼ pound margarine
> 1 cup fine sugar
> 3 eggs, separated
> 1 cup sweet wine
> 8 whole matzos
> ½ cup chopped walnuts
> 1½ ounces bittersweet chocolate for
> chocolate curls

Melt the chocolate over warm water in a double boiler; allow to cool. In a medium-sized mixing bowl, cream the margarine with the sugar until the margarine is fluffy and the sugar dissolved. Add the egg yolks, 1 at a time; beat well.

In a clean medium-sized bowl, beat the egg whites until stiff. Fold the cooled melted chocolate into the egg yolk mixture; fold in the stiffly beaten egg whites.

Pour the wine into a large shallow pan. Dip each matzo, 1 at a time, into the wine, just enough to moisten but not soak. Place 1 moistened matzo on a serving plate. Cover with 1½ tablespoons of the chocolate filling. Top with another moistened matzo and more filling. Continue this process until the eighth matzo is on the top. Cover the top and sides with the remainder of the filling. Decorate the top with chopped walnuts and chocolate curls. Cover the cake loosely with plastic wrap and let the cake mellow for 24 hours in the refrigerator. Cut into thin slices or into small squares. Serves 8 or more.

Pesachdig Savarin aux Fraises
(Savarin With Strawberries)

This is baked as a génoise (a sponge cake into which melted butter or margarine is beaten to make a particularly light cake) but is treated as a regular savarin cake. After the cake is baked, it is soaked with a syrup, glazed with melted jam, and the center is filled with fruit, a soft custard, or whipped cream.

>   6 eggs, separated
>   1 cup sugar, divided
>   ½ cup cake meal
>   ¼ cup potato starch
>   1 teaspoon vanilla flavoring or lemon
>   juice
>   ¼ cup melted margarine
>   Grease for the pan
>   Wine Sauce (see recipe below)
>   1 pint fresh strawberries, washed and
>   hulled
>   ½ cup apricot preserves
>   2 tablespoons lemon juice

In a large mixing bowl, beat the egg whites until foamy; slowly beat in ½ cup sugar, 1 tablespoon at a time. Beat until stiff but not dry.

In a clean large mixing bowl, beat the egg yolks with the same beaters until thick; gradually beat in the remaining ½ cup of sugar.

Combine the cake meal and potato starch. Fold the egg yolk mixture into the egg white mixture, then gradually fold in the dry ingredients. Add the vanilla flavoring or lemon juice. Drizzle the melted margarine into the mixture very slowly; continue folding until blended.

Grease well and line the bottom of a 10-inch tube pan. Pour in the batter and bake in a preheated 350-degree F. oven for about 40 minutes, until the cake springs back when lightly touched. Let cool in the pan.

When the cake is completely cool, slide a knife around the edges of the pan to loosen; remove the cake from the pan onto a platter. Baste the cake with Wine Sauce. Fill the center of the cake with the berries and their juice. Mix the apricot preserves with the lemon juice. Brush this carefully over the top and sides of the cake. Chill until serving time.

Wine Sauce:
> ½ cup sugar
> Juice of 1 lemon
> ¼ cup water
> ½ cup sweet wine

Combine the sugar, lemon juice, and water in a small saucepan. Cook over medium heat until boiling. Reduce the heat and simmer 1 to 2 minutes longer. Add the wine; stir. Remove from the heat. Makes approximately 1 cup.

Scripture Fruit Cake

A variety of cakes was baked in Biblical times. Cake is first mentioned in the Bible when Father Abraham instructs Mother Sarah to "make cakes" (Genesis 18:6). In Exodus 16:31 we read of manna that "the taste of it was like wafers made with honey." Biscuits are mentioned in I Kings 14:3: "Take with thee ten loaves, and biscuits."

On Passover, prepare and serve your family a Scripture Fruit Cake, "a piece of cake of figs and two clusters of raisins" (I Samuel 30:12). The recipe uses ingredients that are mentioned in the Bible to make a deliciously fragrant and appetizing treat.

To prepare the cake follow the directions in Exodus 30:36: "Thou shalt beat . . . it very small."

2 cups I Samuel 25:18 *"a hundred clusters of raisins"* **(raisins)**
2 cups Isaiah 34:4 *"fig from the fig tree"* **(figs)**
2 cups Numbers 17:23 *"bore ripe almonds"* **(almonds)**
2 cups Exodus 12:39 *"they baked unleavened cakes"* **(matzo cake meal)**
1 cup Leviticus 2:5 *"fine flour, unleavened"* **(potato starch)**

→

Pinch Leviticus 2:13 *"season with salt"* **(salt)**
1 tablespoon Exodus 30:23 *"of sweet cinnamon"* **(cinnamon)**
¼ teaspoon Song of Songs 4:10 *"all manner of spices"* **(ginger)**
2 teaspoons Amos 4:5 *"of that which is leavened"* **(baking powder)**
6 Isaiah 10:14 *"one gathereth eggs"* **(eggs)**
2 cups Jeremiah 6:20 *"and the sweet cane"* **(sugar)**
1 cup Numbers 11:8 *"cake baked with oil"* **(oil)**
½ cup Exodus 4:9 *"take of the water"* **(water)**
2 tablespoons Judges 14:18 *"what is sweeter than honey?"* **(honey)**

In a medium-sized bowl, combine the raisins, figs (chopped), and the almonds (slivered or chopped). Set aside. In another medium-sized bowl, sift together the matzo cake meal, potato starch, salt, cinnamon, ginger, and baking powder.

In a large bowl, beat the eggs for at least 5 minutes, until very light. Gradually add the sugar and continue beating for an additional 10 minutes. Add the oil as you continue beating for a few more (4 to 5) minutes. Add the dry ingredients, alternating with the water. Stir in the honey; stir the mixture until well blended. Lastly, fold in the fruit and the nuts.

Spoon the batter into a large greased tube pan, or into 2 greased 5 × 9½ × 3-inch loaf pans. Bake in a preheated 325-degree F. oven for about 1 hour, until it tests done. Turn the cake out onto a cake rack. Let cool completely. Slices best after a few hours. The cake keeps well in the refrigerator or freezer. Serves 16 or more.

Note: Using a lesser amount of nuts, figs, or raisins will not significantly alter the taste of the cake.

Passover Bobka

Today, there is a large variety of kosher for Passover cake mixes available. To use these mixes most successfully, one must add "a generous pinch of imagination." The addition of one or two flavorful ingredients can transform these mixes into elegant cakes or pastries. Here, a yellow cake mix is used to prepare a pâte à choux (cream puff batter), while the packaged chocolate fudge frosting becomes the streusel filling and topping.

> 1 box (12 ounces) yellow cake mix with fudge frosting
> Cake meal
> ½ cup oil
> 1 cup boiling water
> 2 whole eggs
> 4 eggs, separated
> 2 tablespoons cake meal
> 1 tablespoon margarine
> ¼ to ½ cup chopped nuts

Measure the yellow cake mix into a small bowl, adding sufficient cake meal to make 2 cups. In a medium-sized saucepan, bring the oil and water to a boil over high heat. Remove the pan from the heat; stir in the cake mix and cake meal. Beat vigorously. Return to low heat; cook, stirring constantly until the mixture forms a compact ball that no longer adheres to the sides of the pan. Transfer the batter to a large mixing bowl. Let cool.

While the batter is cooling, prepare the streusel by emptying the envelope of fudge frosting mix into a small bowl. Add the cake meal. Cut in the margarine; stir in the chopped nuts.

With an electric mixer at medium speed, beat the 2 whole eggs and 4 egg yolks into the batter, 1 at a time, beating well after each addition. Beat until the batter is thick and has a satinlike sheen.

In a clean medium-sized mixing bowl, beat the egg whites until stiff. Gently fold the stiffly beaten egg whites into the yolk batter until well blended.

Very lightly grease an angel cake pan. Spoon portions of the batter into the pan, sprinkling each portion with some of the streusel, leaving a generous amount to sprinkle on the top.

Place the cake pan in the center of the oven rack in a preheated 450-degree F. oven for 10 minutes; turn the heat down to 350 degrees F. and continue baking for an additional 30 to 40 minutes, until the cake tests dones. Invert the cake and let it cool thoroughly before removing it from the pan. Serves 10 or more.

Note: I would not recommend that a novice make this Passover Bobka. Folding the stiffly beaten egg whites into the egg yolk batter requires patience and experience. However, the end result is well worth the effort.

15

Frostings and Fillings

A frosting, also called an icing, is used either to coat a cake or to fill it. As a coating, the frosting complements and enhances the flavoring of the cake while it helps keep the cake fresh by sealing out air.

During Passover ingenuity must be used in planning our frostings and fillings. Substitutions must be made for basic ingredients used throughout the year. Instead of using commercial confectioner's sugar, we make our own at home (see recipe). Flavoring extracts, which contain alcohol, are replaced with grated citrus fruit rind or fruit juices. Sugar syrup takes the place of corn syrup. For eye appeal, we rely on the natural colors of such items as strawberries, cocoa, and the like.

Explore this section to find recipes that will add a festive look to your baked goods. The recipes range from a simple uncooked cake glaze to the ever-popular cooked Seven-Minute Icing with its many variations. You will also find luscious fillings for cakes and prepared pie shells, as well as recipes for flavored sugars.

Basic Cake or Doughnut Glaze

Starting with a basic cake glaze, you can create variations to please all tastes. Experiment to arrive at the special flavor you desire. If the glaze is too thick to drizzle, stir in a little water, a drop at a time. For extra appeal, sprinkle snowy shreds of coconut or finely chopped nuts over the glaze.

Confectioner's Sugar:

The basic glaze requires confectioner s sugar. To prepare this sugar, you will need:

1 cup less ½ tablespoon granulated sugar
1½ teaspoons potato starch

Pulverize the sugar in an electric blender or food processor, then sift it together with the 1½ teaspoons of potato starch.

Basic Icing Glaze:

To prepare the basic glaze, you will need:

1 cup confectioner's sugar
2 to 3 tablespoons hot water

Place the sugar in a small bowl. Gradually add the hot water, stirring well after each addition, until the consistency is such that the mixture will coat the back of a spoon. Yields about 1 cup of glaze, enough to glaze an 8 or 9-inch cake.

To Flavor:

Vanilla: Add 1 teaspoon of vanilla sugar.

Lemon: Combine the sugar with 1 teaspoon of lemon juice and ½ teaspoon grated lemon rind. Add 1 to 2 tablespoons of water. Mix until smooth and thin enough to coat the back of a spoon.

Orange: Combine the confectioner's sugar with 1 teaspoon of grated orange rind and 2 to 3 tablespoons of orange juice. Mix until smooth.

Coffee: Combine the confectioner's sugar with 1 to 2 tablespoons of coffee essence and mix until smooth.

Pineapple Glaze

3 tablespoons sugar
1 tablespoon potato starch
1 cup unsweetened pineapple juice
¼ teaspoon grated lemon rind

In a small saucepan, mix the sugar with the potato starch. Stir in the pineapple juice and grated lemon rind. Bring to a boil over medium-high heat and cook, stirring all the while, for 1 minute or until clear and slightly thickened. Cool. Will glaze an 8 or 9-inch cake.

Seven-Minute Icing

Actually, this popular icing may take as few as five or as many as ten minutes to form firm peaks when the beaters are lifted.

For a less crusty surface when the icing hardens, increase the water to one-half cup. And by substituting or adding ingredients, the flavor of the frosting can be easily adjusted to suit personal taste.

> **2 egg whites**
> **1½ cups sugar**
> **⅛ teaspoon salt**
> **¼ teaspoon cream of tartar**
> **⅓ cup water**
> **1 teaspoon lemon juice**

Combine the egg whites, sugar, salt, cream of tartar, and water in the top pot of a double boiler. Beat with a rotary beater until well mixed. Place the pot over but not touching boiling water; beat constantly with a rotary beater for 7 minutes or until the icing stands in firm peaks. Remove from the water. Cool. Add the lemon juice. Spread on cooled cake. Makes sufficient icing for the top and sides of two 9-inch layers or 24 cupcakes.

Variations:

Coffee Icing: Substitute brewed coffee for the water.

Coconut Icing: Sprinkle snowy shreds of toasted coconut over the frosting immediately after icing the cake, before it has hardened.

Chocolate Icing: When the icing stands in firm peaks, gently fold in (don't beat) 2 or 3 squares (2 or 3 ounces) of melted semisweet chocolate.

Harvest Moon Icing: Substitute 1½ cups packed brown sugar for the granulated sugar.

Lemon Icing: Substitute 2 tablespoons lemon juice and the grated rind of ½ to 1 lemon (no pith) for 2 tablespoons of the water called for.

Orange Icing: Substitute 3 tablespoons orange juice and the grated rind of ½ to 1 orange (no pith) for 3 tablespoons of the water called for.

Two-Fruit Icing: Substitute ⅜ cup (6 tablespoons) orange juice and 1½ teaspoons lemon juice for the water. Fold in ½ teaspoon grated orange rind or ¼ teaspoon grated lemon rind when the icing stands in firm peaks.

Boiled Frosting for Cakes

> 1 cup sugar
> ½ cup water
> 2 egg whites, stiffly beaten
> 1 apple, grated (optional)

Boil the sugar and water together in a 1-quart saucepan until the mixture forms a thread. Remove the saucepan from the heat. In a medium-sized mixing bowl, beat the egg whites until stiff. Slowly pour the syrup into the egg whites. While continuing beating, add the grated apple and beat until stiff. Ample frosting for an 8 or 9-inch cake.

Variation:

In place of the grated apple, substitute mashed strawberries, cooked mashed pineapple, or mashed cooked prunes.

Chocolate Frosting

> 2 eggs
> ¾ cup sugar
> 4 tablespoons water
> 1 teaspoon instant coffee (optional)

⅓ cup unsweetened cocoa
2 heaping tablespoons margarine

In a small saucepan, beat the eggs with the sugar and water until light and thick. Add the coffee and cocoa. Place the saucepan over low heat and cook until the sugar is dissolved. Remove from the heat and pour the mixture into a medium-sized mixing bowl. Add the margarine and beat with an electric mixer until very light and fluffy. Yields adequate frosting for the top and sides of a 9-inch layer cake.

Mocha Frosting

To add character to a plain sponge cake, decorate it with this frosting and garnish with chopped nuts.

⅓ cup unsweetened cocoa
⅔ cup sugar
1 egg
2 tablespoons cold water or brewed coffee
2 heaping tablespoons margarine or
Nutola
1 teaspoon instant coffee

Mix the cocoa, sugar, egg, and water or coffee in a 1-quart saucepan. Place over low heat and cook, but do not bring to a boil. Remove from the heat. Cool. Add the margarine or Nutola and the instant coffee; beat with an electric mixer until very light and fluffy. Yields sufficient frosting for one 9-inch cake or two 9-inch layers.

Honey Fluff Frosting

A light-as-a-feather cake garnished with swirls of this frosting will be a sweet treat for anyone.

½ teaspoon salt
2 egg whites
¼ cup sugar
¼ cup honey
1 teaspoon grated lemon rind

In a medium-sized bowl, combine the salt with the egg whites. Beat with an electric mixer at low speed until frothy. Increase the speed to high, gradually add the sugar, and beat until the sugar has dissolved. Slowly add the honey and continue beating until the frosting stands in stiff peaks. Fold in the lemon rind. Makes enough frosting for two 9-inch layers.

Chocolate Meringue

Here, the cake comes out of the oven deliciously frosted.

> ¼ cup firmly packed brown sugar
> 2 tablespoons unsweetened cocoa
> 1 egg white
> ⅛ teaspoon salt
> ¼ cup chopped walnuts

Mix the sugar and cocoa in a small bowl. In the small bowl of an electric mixer, whip the egg white with the salt until stiff. Gradually add the cocoa mixture to the egg white, 2 tablespoons at a time, beating thoroughly after each addition. Continue beating for 2 to 3 minutes.

Pile the mixture over cake batter in a shallow 8-inch baking pan; or spread the meringue over 8 to 12 cupcakes. Sprinkle with nuts. Bake in a preheated 350-degree F. oven for 20 to 25 minutes.

Variation:

To make a coconut meringue, substitute ½ cup granulated sugar for the brown sugar and omit the nuts. Sprinkle the meringue with ½ cup shredded coconut before baking.

Jelly Meringue

A very simple meringue to make. Excellent filling for a jelly roll.

> 1 egg white
> ½ cup jelly

Put the egg white and jelly together in a small mixing bowl. Beat with an electric mixer at high speed until stiff. Spread over the cake or between layers. Sufficient to frost one 9-inch cake.

Strawberry Meringue

This fluffy frosting is luscious and lavish-looking.

> 1 egg white
> 1 cup sliced strawberries
> 1 cup sugar

Put the egg white into the medium-sized bowl of an electric mixer. Add the strawberries to the egg white and beat until the berries are mashed. Add the sugar gradually. Beat until very thick. Spread over the cake. Will frost one 9-inch cake.

Pineapple Meringue

After spreading this meringue over a pie, return the pie to a preheated 350-degree F. oven for 12 to 15 minutes, until the meringue peaks are golden brown.

> ½ cup unsweetened juice from canned
>   pineapple
> 1 tablespoon potato starch
> 3 egg whites
>   Dash of salt
> 6 tablespoons sugar

In a small saucepan, mix together the pineapple juice and potato starch. Cook over low heat, stirring constantly until thick and clear. Cool. In a clean medium-sized bowl, beat the egg whites with salt until soft peaks form. Gradually beat in the sugar. Then, slowly beat in the syrup mixture, beating constantly until a stiff meringue is formed. Adequate for an 8 or 9-inch pie.

Mocha Topping

¼ pint sweet cream
1 teaspoon sugar
1 teaspoon instant coffee
Bittersweet chocolate for garnish

In a chilled bowl, whip the cream until thick. Do not overbeat. Add the sugar and the instant coffee. Spread over the pie or cake. Decorate with shaved bittersweet chocolate. Will frost a 9-inch cake.

Cherry Topping

A sparkly sweet glaze highlights the cherries.

2 cups canned pitted sour cherries
1 cup cherry juice, divided
1 cup sugar
2 tablespoons potato starch
½ teaspoon lemon juice

Drain the cherries and set aside in a bowl. Heat ¾ cup of cherry juice and the sugar in a small saucepan over medium heat. Bring to a boil and boil for 3 minutes.

Combine the potato starch with the remaining ¼ cup juice (add water if necessary); blend well. Remove the saucepan from the heat. Stir about 3 tablespoons of hot cherry juice into the potato starch mixture. Return the combined mixture to the saucepan; blend together. Cook over simmering water or over very low heat for 3 to 5 minutes, then add the cherries and the lemon juice. Stir to blend. Cool before spreading over the cake. Sufficient for an 8-inch cake or pie.

Meringue Pie Shell Fillings

A meringue pie shell (see next chapter for recipe) filled with a luscious filling will make a party out of any occasion. These fillings are luscious, rich, unforgettable.

Fruit Whip:

> ½ pint whipping cream
> 1 cup sliced strawberries or blueberries

In a chilled bowl, whip the cream until soft peaks form and hold their shape. Do not overbeat. Fold in the sliced strawberries or blueberries. Fills an 8 or 9-inch meringue pie shell.

Mocha Chocolate Filling:

> ½ pint whipping cream
> 6 ounces semisweet chocolate
> 3 tablespoons hot water
> 1 teaspoon instant coffee
> 1 tablespoon brandy (optional)

In a chilled bowl, whip the cream until it stands in soft peaks that hold their shape. Do not overbeat. Set into the refrigerator.

Melt the chocolate in the top of a double boiler over hot water. Add the hot water and coffee. Stir until smooth. Add the brandy. Cool.

Gently fold the chocolate mixture into the whipped cream. Transfer to a 9-inch meringue shell. If desired, decorate the pie with chocolate shavings prepared by sliding a slightly heated vegetable peeler along the side of a chocolate bar.

Chocolate Filling:

Omit the instant coffee from the Mocha Chocolate Filling.

Lemon Cream Filling:

> 4 egg yolks
> 4 tablespoons sugar
> 4 tablespoons lemon juice
> ½ pint whipping cream
> ¼ teaspoon grated lemon rind

In the top pot of a double boiler, beat the yolks, sugar, and lemon juice with a rotary beater until light. Cook over hot water until the mixture is thick. Cool. In a chilled bowl, beat the cream. Do not overbeat. Add the lemon rind. Fold in the cooled lemon filling and pile it into a 9-inch meringue shell.

Lemon Meringue Pie Filling

Lemon pie piled high with meringue is a refreshing tart/sweet way to end a meal. When spooning meringue over a pie, care must be exercised to seal the meringue to the edge of the crust. This will prevent shrinkage and "weeping."

> 5 tablespoons potato starch
> ¼ teaspoon salt
> 1 cup sugar, divided
> 2 cups water
> 3 eggs, separated
> 2 tablespoons shortening
> 5 tablespoons lemon juice
> 1 tablespoon grated lemon rind
>   Dash of salt
> 6 tablespoons sugar

Combine the potato starch, salt, and ½ cup of sugar in the top pot of a double boiler. Gradually add the water, mixing until smooth. Place the top pot over boiling water. Cook, stirring constantly until the mixture thickens. Cover and cook for 10 minutes, stirring occasionally.

In a small bowl, beat the egg yolks with the remaining ½ cup of sugar. Spoon a little of the hot cooked mixture into the egg yolks. Stir rapidly (to prevent curdling) until smooth. Immediately pour the mixture back into remaining hot mixture. Blend thoroughly. Cook 2 minutes longer, stirring constantly. Remove from the heat. Stir in the shortening, lemon juice, and grated rind. Cool to room temperature without stirring (do not refrigerate). Pour into a baked pie shell.

In the small bowl of an electric mixer, beat the egg whites with the salt at low speed until frothy; increase the speed to high and add the sugar, 1 tablespoon at a time, until the mixture is stiff, smooth, and glossy. Top the lemon filling with the meringue, sealing well at the edges of the pie. Bake in a preheated 325-degree F. oven for about 15 minutes, until the meringue is golden brown. Chill before serving. Serves 8.

Lemon Filling for Cream Puffs

2 eggs
¾ cup sugar
1 tablespoon potato starch
1 cup water
1 teaspoon oil
Juice of 1 lemon

In a small mixing bowl, beat the eggs well. Mix together the sugar and the potato starch; slowly add this to the beaten eggs. In another small bowl, combine the water, oil, and lemon juice; add to the egg mixture. Cook the egg mixture in the top of a double boiler until thick. Cool and insert into the puffs. Adequate filling for 10 to 12 puffs.

Mocha Pie Filling

1 tablespoon instant coffee
½ cup boiling water
2½ cups milk
¼ cup potato starch
⅔ cup sugar
⅛ teaspoon salt
3½ ounces bittersweet chocolate

In a medium-sized bowl, dissolve the coffee in the boiling water. Add the milk. Mix the potato starch with the sugar and salt in the top of a double boiler. Gradually stir in the milk mixture. Add the chocolate and place over boiling water; stir until blended, 3 to 5 minutes. Cover and cook 5 minutes longer, stirring occasionally. Cool and pour into a baked pie shell. Top with whipped cream. Adequate filling for a 9-inch pie shell.

Grape Filling

½ cup grape juice
½ cup water

⟶

> 1 tablespoon lemon juice
> 1¼ tablespoons potato starch
> 2½ tablespoons sugar

Combine the grape juice, water, and lemon juice in a small saucepan. Mix together the potato starch and sugar; dissolve the mixture in the liquid ingredients in the saucepan. Cook over low heat, stirring constantly until the mixture boils and thickens slightly. Cool before spreading between cake layers. Fills a 10-inch 2-layer cake.

Wine Filling

This filling sandwiched between two small squares of sponge cake will substitute admirably for petits fours.

> ½ cup sugar
> 2 tablespoons potato starch
> Dash of salt
> 1¼ cups Concord grape wine
> 1 teaspoon lemon juice

Mix the sugar, potato starch, and salt in a small saucepan. Gradually add the wine and stir to make a smooth mixture. Over medium heat, heat the mixture to boiling, stirring constantly. Cook for 5 minutes or until the filling is thick and smooth. Add the lemon juice. Mix well and remove from the heat. Cool. Yields approximately 1½ cups of filling.

Syrup for Pancakes

This pancake syrup is certain to stimulate appetites. For a milder syrup, substitute one and one-half cups of granulated sugar for the brown sugar; increase the cinnamon to one and one-half teaspooons. Simmer over medium heat for about eight minutes, stirring occasionally.

> 2 cups firmly packed brown sugar
> 1 cup water
> 1 teaspoon cinnamon

Combine the ingredients in a 1-quart saucepan; bring to a boil. Turn the heat down and simmer for 10 minutes, stirring occasionally. Cool and serve with pancakes. Yields approximately 1½ cups of syrup.

Vanilla Sugar

Flavored sugars are excellent for quick flavoring. Vanilla sugar merits a place in your kitchen during Passover, as it is a superb substitute for vanilla extract.

1 cup sugar
1 vanilla bean

Place a cup of sugar in a container. Cut the vanilla bean crosswise into 2 or 3-inch lengths; cut over the container to salvage the entire contents of the pod. Cover the container tightly. Vanilla fragrance intensifies on standing. Let stand for at least 24 hours before using.

The sugar used can be replaced with additional sugar and the bean pieces reused until they lose their flavoring power.

Variation:
Crush the bean pieces with a few tablespoons of sugar before adding it to the sugar in the jar. Sift the sugar before using.

Note: Vanilla sugar is sold commercially in .43-ounce packets, the equivalent of 2½ teaspoons. Each packet has the flavoring strength of 1 teaspoon of vanilla extract.

Cinnamon Sugar

Try over pancakes.

1 cup sugar
2 tablespoons cinnamon

Place the sugar in a bowl. Blend the cinnamon with the sugar. Transfer the mixture into a shaker or use directly from the bowl.

Fruit Sugars

Orange Sugar:

1 cup sugar
1 tablespoon grated orange rind (see method)

Place the sugar in a bowl. Grate a tablespoon's worth of zest of an orange (the outermost deep orange part; do not include any white pith). Mix the grated rind together with the sugar. Place the mixture into a covered container and let stand for at least 2 hours for the flavors to blend.

Lemon Sugar:

Substitute grated lemon rind for the orange rind.

Tangerine Sugar:

Substitute tangerine rind for the orange rind.

16

Pies and Pastries

Other than the conventional matzo meal crust, a wide variety of kosher for Passover pie crusts can be prepared. Cake, cookie, and soup nut crumbs make marvelous crusts, as do meringue, coconut, and chopped nuts. Select the crust that will best suit the filling. And remember that the texture contrast of pie crust and filling can add distinction to the pie. A crunchy nut crust, for example, when mated with a smooth and creamy cheese filling, will surely evoke compliments.

An exciting collection of baked goods is contained in this chapter. Many are the Passover counterparts of pies and pastries so popular during the year, such as cream puffs, doughnuts, and éclairs. You will find new recipes adapted for Passover, such as napoleons, strudel, and tarts. All rank high in flavor appeal.

Matzo Meal Pie Shell I

¼ cup margarine or oil
2 tablespoons sugar
⅛ teaspoon salt
¼ teaspoon cinnamon (optional)
1 cup matzo meal or cake meal
2 tablespoons water, approximately

In a small mixing bowl, cream the margarine or oil with the sugar, salt, and cinnamon. Gradually add the matzo or cake meal. Add water if necessary, just enough to bind the mixture together. With the back of a tablespoon, press the mixture into a 9 or 10-inch pie plate. Bake in a preheated 350-degree F. oven until lightly browned, 10 to 15 minutes. Cool and fill as desired.

Matzo Meal Pie Shell II

This crust is recommended for fruit pies.

1½ matzos
1 tablespoon melted shortening or oil
¼ cup matzo meal
2 tablespoons sugar mixed with ½
teaspoon cinnamon
2 eggs, well beaten

Soak the matzos in a bowl of water; drain and squeeze dry; set aside. In a small bowl, combine the melted shortening, matzo meal, sugar-cinnamon mixture, and the beaten eggs. Add the drained matzos. Mix well and press the mixture into a 9-inch pie plate. Fill with a fruit filling and bake in a 375-degree F. oven until the fruit is cooked.

Matzo Meal Pie Shell III

This pie shell should be chilled thoroughly in the refrigerator before filling and baking. After chilling, it may be prebaked in a preheated 375-degree F. oven for 15 to 20 minutes, until golden brown. Cool before adding the filling and returning to the oven to bake.

⅓ to ½ cup softened butter or margarine
1 cup matzo meal
2 to 3 tablespoons sugar
¼ teaspoon cinnamon (optional)

In a small mixing bowl, work the softened butter or margarine into a mixture of the matzo meal, sugar, and cinnamon until the mixture can be pressed out with a spoon to line a 9-inch pie plate. Refrigerate to chill thoroughly.

Cake Crumb Pie Shell

Sponge cake crumbs used to form a pie shell should be as fine as matzo meal. To prepare them, dry sponge cake slices on a cookie sheet in a 300-degree F. oven for fifteen minutes or until the slices are as dry as toast, then pulverize. Mandelbread or macaroon crumbs may be substituted for the sponge cake crumbs. Remember to adjust the amount of sugar in this pie shell according to the sweetness of the cake crumbs being used.

¼ cup shortening or margarine
¼ cup sugar
¼ teaspoon cinnamon (optional)
1⅓ cups sponge cake crumbs

In a small bowl, cream the shortening or margarine with the sugar and cinnamon. Add the cake crumbs; mix well. Press the mixture evenly onto the bottom and sides of a 9-inch pie plate. Bake in a 375-degree F. oven for 7 minutes or until golden brown. Cool before filling.

Almond-Matzo Crust

½ cup ground blanched almonds
½ cup matzo meal
2 tablespoons sugar
⅛ teaspoon salt
¼ cup oil
1 egg white

In a small bowl, combine the ground blanched almonds, matzo meal, sugar, and salt; set aside. In a second small bowl, combine the oil and egg white; beat slightly; stir into the almond mixture. Turn the combined mixture into a 9-inch pie plate. Using a tablespoon, press the mixture firmly and evenly against the sides and bottom of the pie plate. Bake in a preheated 375-degree F.

oven for 15 to 20 minutes, until golden brown. Cool thoroughly before filling.

Walnut Crust

Use your favorite kind of nuts to make this delightfully crunchy crust. The crust is perfect for a smooth cream cheese filling.

1¼ cups finely chopped walnuts
3 tablespoons sugar
2 tablespoons margarine, softened
¼ cup cake meal
Grease for the pie plate

In a medium-sized bowl, combine all the ingredients; mix well. Using the back of a tablespoon, press the mixture onto the bottom and sides of a greased 9-inch pie plate, making sure to make a small rim around the top of the pie plate. Bake in a preheated 400-degree F. oven for 8 to 10 minutes. Cool completely before filling.

Chocolate-Nut Crust

3 ounces semisweet chocolate
2 tablespoons margarine
1¼ cups whole blanched almonds, toasted
and finely chopped
Grease for the pie plate

In a small saucepan, melt the chocolate and margarine over low heat. Add the finely chopped almonds; stir until well mixed. Refrigerate for 30 minutes.

Spoon the chocolate mixture into a greased 9-inch pie plate. Using the back of a tablespoon, press the mixture firmly and evenly onto the bottom and sides of the pie plate. Refrigerate for 2 hours before filling. Spoon in the filling of your choice.

Toasted Coconut Crust

½ cup margarine or butter, melted
2 cups freshly grated coconut
Grease for the pie plate

In a medium-sized bowl, combine the melted margarine or butter with the freshly grated coconut; toss lightly with a fork until well mixed. Using the back of a tablespoon, press the coconut mixture firmly and evenly onto the bottom and sides of a greased 9-inch pie plate. Bake in a preheated 325-degree F. oven for 20 minutes or until lightly browned. Cool completely before filling.

Meringue Pie Shell

A meringue shell looks so very fragile and difficult to make, but one can be prepared successfully even by the novice. Before adding the sugar, make sure the egg whites have been beaten until soft peaks are formed, or you will have a marshmallow sauce.

1 cup sugar
½ teaspoon cream of tartar
4 egg whites
½ teaspoon salt
Grease for the pie plate

In a small bowl, sift the sugar with the cream of tartar. Set aside. In a large mixing bowl, beat the egg whites with the salt until soft peaks form. Gradually add the sugar-cream of tartar mixture, 2 tablespoons at a time; beat after each addition until the sugar dissolves before adding the next 2 tablespoons. When all the sugar has been added, beat at high speed for an additional 10 minutes. The meringue should be stiff and glossy. Be sure not to underbeat.

Spoon the meringue into a greased 9-inch pie plate. With a tablespoon, build up the sides to form a pie shell; smooth out the meringue.

Preheat the oven to 275 degrees F. Place the pie shell in the oven and turn the heat down to 250 degrees F. Bake for 1¼ hours. Turn the heat off, set the door ajar, and let the shell dry out in the oven for 1 hour. Remove the shell from the oven and set to cool in a draft-free place. When cool, fill with your favorite filling.

Variation:

When the meringue is stiff and glossy, gently fold in ¼ cup finely chopped nuts.

Cream Puffs, Doughnuts, and Éclairs

Cream puff dough is very versatile. From the basic cream puff paste (pâte à choux) you can prepare a myriad of toothsome delicacies that will be very gratifying to serve. Consider all that can be prepared with this dough:

Deep-fried puff shells are excellent croustades. They add elegance and distinction to the filling served in them. In fact, they are used to make the ever-popular jelly doughnut.

And there are cream puffs and éclairs, elegant pastries that are tender on the outside with luscious filling within.

Miniature cream puff cases parade as profiteroles, impressive party morsels. Filled with a sweet filling, they are served as dessert; with a savory filling, they are marvelous hors d'oeuvres requiring no other embellishment. Tiny baked profiteroles may be used as a soup garnish.

There are innumerable cream puff fillings, but the dough used to make the puffs is usually the same. However, if you wish to add a new dimension to dessert cream puff shells, add one-third cup chopped walnuts to the batter once it is smooth and satiny. The result will be "nutty" cream puff cases.

> 1 cup water
> ½ cup oil
> ½ teaspoon salt
> (1 tablespoon sugar for doughnuts only)
> 1 cup matzo meal
> 4 eggs
> Grease for the baking sheet

In a 2-quart saucepan, bring the water, oil, and salt to a slow boil. (**Note:** For doughnuts add 1 tablespoon of sugar to the water and oil.) Remove the pan from the heat and immediately pour in all of the matzo meal. Stir briskly at once. When the mixture is smoothly blended, return the saucepan to low heat to evaporate the excess water. Cook and beat vigorously until the mixture forms a ball that leaves the sides of the saucepan. Remove from the heat.

Add the eggs, 1 at a time, beating well after each addition until the egg is well absorbed. Mix until the dough is smooth and glossy (a portable electric beater will serve you well).

The next step is to form the dough into the desired shape.

Fried Puff Shells:

For appetizer or main dish. Spoon 1 rounded tablespoonful of dough per puff into a deep saucepan of hot fat (370 degrees F.). Fry for about 12 minutes, turning often. Remove with a slotted spoon; drain well on paper towels or unglazed paper. Yields 12 puffs.

Cream Puff Shells:

For dessert. Spoon rounded tablespoonfuls of dough onto a lightly greased baking sheet. Place about 2 inches apart. Bake in a preheated 450-degree F. oven for 10 minutes; then lower the temperature to 400 degrees F. and bake for 15 to 20 minutes, until the puffs are well puffed and browned. Let cool. Yields 10 to 12 puffs.

Doughnuts:

Shape the dough as for cream puffs, then dip the forefinger in water and make a hole in the center of each puff on the baking sheet. Bake as for cream puffs. Yields 10 to 12 large doughnuts.

Jelly Doughnuts:

Drop the dough by the level teaspoonful or rounded tablespoonful (depending on the size doughnut desired) into a deep saucepan of hot fat (370 degrees F.). Fry until delicately browned on all sides. With a slotted spoon, remove the doughnuts from the oil. Drain on paper towels or unglazed paper.

Vary the flavor of the jelly or jam used as the doughnut filling. Doughnuts are best eaten fresh. They may be shaken in a paper bag containing confectioner's sugar or a flavored sugar. Yields 12 large or 32 small doughnuts.

Éclair Shells:

For dessert. Force the puff paste through a pastry bag with a large round tube or no tube at all. Pipe éclairs about 1 inch wide and 4 inches long; or drop the dough by the rounded tablespoonful onto a lightly greased cookie sheet; place 3 inches apart. With a spatula, shape the dough into 4-inch-long, 1-inch-wide strips; slightly round the ends. Bake as for cream puffs. Yields 12 to 18.

Miniature Puff Shells:

For hors d'oeuvres. Spoon about 1 teaspoonful of the batter onto the greased baking sheet. Bake until puffed and brown, as for cream puffs. Yields 36 to 48.

Filling Puff Dough

To fill the shells, cut a hole in the side of the shell and use a pastry bag and tube to insert the filling. Or cut off a portion of the top and spoon in the filling. Press the top back in place. Fill all puff dough shells as near to serving time as possible. Refrigerate until needed.

French Crullers

> 1 cup water
> ½ cup oil or margarine
> ¼ cup sugar
> ¼ teaspoon salt
> 1 cup matzo meal
> 4 eggs
> Oil for frying

Combine the water, oil or margarine, sugar, and salt in a large saucepan. Bring to a boil. Remove the pan from the heat; add the matzo meal; beat at once. When smoothly blended, return the pan to low heat to evaporate the excess liquid. Cook and beat vigorously until the mixture forms a ball that leaves the sides of the saucepan. Remove from the heat. Add the eggs, 1 at a time, beating well after each addition until the egg is absorbed. Refrigerate the dough for 15 minutes.

Cut out twelve 3-inch squares of aluminum foil; oil each square. Put the dough through a pastry bag with a ½-inch star tube, or form a 3-inch ring of dough on each square.

Pour the oil into a large saucepan. Heat the oil over medium-high heat to 370 degrees F. Carefully slip a ring of dough from the foil into the oil. Fry 3 rings at a time, turning once, until golden brown and puffed. With a slotted spoon, remove the crullers from the oil. Drain on paper towels. Cool. Glaze as desired. Yields 12.

Orange Beignets

For a spectacular dessert, prepare the very light fritters known as beignets, which are made with pâte à choux (cream puff paste). Serve plain, sugared, or with a sauce.

**1 recipe French Crullers batter
1 teaspoon grated orange rind**

Prepare the batter as directed; stir the orange rind into the batter. Drop the batter by teaspoonfuls into a deep skillet with hot oil (370 degrees F.). Fry 6 at a time until golden and puffed, about 5 minutes. Drain on paper towels. If desired, toss with superfine sugar in a plastic or paper bag. A dash of cinnamon may be added to the sugar. Yields about 30 beignets.

Glazed Strawberry Pie

A sparkly sweet glaze coats the strawberries.

**1½ cups sugar
2 tablespoons potato starch**

→

⅛ teaspoon salt
1½ cups cold water
1 teaspoon lemon juice
1 quart strawberries, washed and hulled
1 9-inch pie shell, prebaked

Combine the sugar, potato starch, and salt in a medium-sized saucepan. Gradually add the water and blend well. Cook over low heat, stirring until the mixture is clear, about 10 minutes. Blend in the lemon juice. Pour the mixture over the strawberries that have been placed in a medium-sized mixing bowl. Toss gently. Cool. Pour the strawberries into the pie shell. Let set before serving. Serves 6 to 8.

Strawberry Custard Pie

1 pint strawberries, washed and hulled
1 Matzo Meal Pie Shell III, prepared (see recipe)
2 tablespoons potato starch
½ cup sugar
2 eggs, well beaten
1 cup sour cream

Arrange the fairly dried strawberries in the prepared matzo meal pie shell. Mix the potato starch with the sugar in a small mixing bowl. Add the well-beaten eggs and sour cream; blend together very well. Pour the batter over the berries in the pie shell. Bake in a preheated 300-degree F. oven for 1 hour or until the custard is set. Cool to serve. Serves 6 to 8.

Applesauce Crumb Pie

The flavor of the pie shell greatly enhances the applesauce filling.

2 cups thick applesauce
1 Matzo Meal Pie Shell II, unbaked (see recipe)

———→

½ cup sugar
1 teaspoon cinnamon
½ cup matzo meal
¼ cup chopped nuts

Pour the applesauce into the prepared but unbaked pie shell.

In a small mixing bowl, combine the sugar, cinnamon, matzo meal, and chopped nuts. Mix thoroughly. Sprinkle the mixture over the applesauce. Bake in a preheated 375-degree F. oven until the crust is brown, about 20 to 30 minutes. Serves 6 to 8.

Crazy-Crust Apple Pie

A pie so easy to prepare! And it makes its own crust as it bakes!

2½ cups sliced peeled apples
1 tablespoon lemon juice
⅓ cup sugar
1 tablespoon potato starch
½ teaspoon cinnamon
⅝ cup potato starch
¼ cup cake meal
1 teaspoon Passover baking powder
½ teaspoon salt
1 tablespoon sugar
1 egg
½ cup shortening
½ cup water
1 to 2 tablespoons brown sugar

To make the filling, in a small bowl combine the apples, lemon juice, sugar, potato starch, and cinnamon. Stir carefully to coat the apples evenly with the seasoning. Set aside.

Sift together the potato starch, cake meal, baking powder, salt, and sugar into a small mixing bowl. Add the egg, shortening, and water. Blend well; beat for 2 minutes with an electric mixer at medium speed.

Transfer the batter to a deep 9-inch pie pan. Pour the pie filling into the center of the batter. Do not stir. Sprinkle the filling with

1 to 2 tablespoons of brown sugar. Bake in a preheated 425-degree F. oven for 35 to 40 minutes. Serves 6 to 8.

Prune-Apple Deep Dish Pie

Layers of juicy, lightly spiced apples and stewed prunes, topped with a matzo crust. A luscious dessert for a robust dinner.

> **1 cup pitted stewed prunes**
> **1 cup peeled and sliced apples**
> **½ cup prune juice**
> **½ cup water**
> **1 tablespoon oil or margarine**
> **½ cup sugar**
> **1 teaspoon cinnamon**
> **1 whole matzo**
> **Grease for the casserole**

Drain the prunes thoroughly before measuring. Cut them into small pieces. Place alternate layers of prunes and apples in a 1-quart greased casserole. Bring the remaining ingredients, except the matzo, to the boiling point in a small saucepan; pour half of the mixture over the fruit.

Crumble the matzo coarsely and soak it in the remaining syrup until softened. Spread the matzo over the fruit. Bake in a 350-degree F. oven for about 40 minutes, until the apples are tender. Serve hot or cold. Serves 6.

Variation:

Substitute ¾ cup matzo farfel for the whole matzo. Add ¼ cup coarsely chopped walnuts to the topping.

Peach Sponge

This delectable dessert sits in a hot water bath as it bakes. The juicy peaches and cheese combine in a custard that is graced with a light, feathery, spongelike topping. Equally delicious served warm or cold.

1 can (16 ounces) sliced peaches
⅔ cup creamed cottage cheese
1 cup sugar
⅛ cup potato starch
¼ teaspoon salt
1 teaspoon grated lemon rind
2 tablespoons butter or margarine,
    melted, or oil
1 cup milk
3 eggs, separated
¼ cup lemon juice

Drain the peaches very well; arrange them in an 8-inch square baking pan. Spread the cheese over the peaches. In a small bowl, combine the sugar with the potato starch, salt, grated lemon rind, and melted butter, margarine, or oil. Add the milk. Blend the ingredients thoroughly.

In a medium-sized mixing bowl, beat the egg yolks until thick and lemon-colored. Add the lemon juice; blend well. Stir the egg yolk mixture into the milk mixture.

With clean beaters, beat the egg whites in a medium-sized bowl until stiff but not dry; fold the whites into the milk-yolk mixture. Pour the batter over the peaches and cheese. Set the pan into a larger pan with 1 inch of hot water. Bake in a preheated 325-degree F. oven for about 1¼ hours. Serves 6 to 8.

Cream Pie

½ cup plus 4 tablespoons sugar
2 tablespoons potato starch
½ teaspoon salt, divided
2 cups milk
2 eggs, separated
2 tablespoons fat
1 teaspoon lemon juice
1 9-inch pie shell, prebaked

In the top part of a double boiler, mix ½ cup sugar, the potato starch, and ¼ teaspoon salt with a little of the milk; mix until the potato starch is dissolved. Add the rest of the milk; mix well. Cook over hot water, stirring until thick. Cover and cook 15 minutes longer, stirring occasionally.

In a small mixing bowl, beat the egg yolks slightly. Add a little of the hot mixture to the egg yolks; blend well. Pour the egg yolk mixture into the pot. Stir. Cook a few minutes longer. Add the fat and lemon juice. Pour the filling into the pie shell. Cool slightly.

Prepare a meringue by beating the egg whites with the remaining ¼ teaspoon of salt until stiff. Gradually beat in the 4 tablespoons of sugar, 1 spoonful at a time, beating until smooth and glossy. Gently spread the meringue over the pie filling. Bake in a preheated 325-degree F. oven for 10 to 15 minutes, until the meringue is lightly browned.

Variations:

Banana Cream Pie: Slice 2 bananas into the pie shell before adding the filling.

Coconut Cream Pie: Add ½ cup shredded coconut to the cream filling. Pour into the pie shell. Sprinkle coconut over the meringue. Bake as for Cream Pie.

Fruit Cocktail Pie

1 can (28 ounces) fruit cocktail, drained
1 pint sour cream
2 tablespoons sugar
1 teaspoon vanilla or almond flavoring
1 9-inch pie shell, prebaked for 10 minutes

Place the drained fruit cocktail in a medium-sized mixing bowl. Add the sour cream, sugar, and vanilla or almond flavoring. Blend the ingredients together well. Pour the mixture into the pie shell. Bake in a preheated 250-degree F. oven for 20 to 30 minutes, until set. Chill overnight in the refrigerator. Garnish with crushed nuts if desired. Serves 6 to 8.

Cheeseless Cheese Pie

A memorable, fine-textured pie that tastes like cheesecake but contains no cheese.

Crust:

> 1 package (1¾ ounces) soup nuts, finely crushed
> 1 tablespoon sugar
> ¼ teaspoon cinnamon
> ⅓ cup softened butter

Filling:

> 3 eggs, separated
> ¾ cup sugar
> 1 pint sour cream

For the crust, in a medium-sized mixing bowl combine the dry ingredients; add the softened butter and blend well with a pastry blender. Pat the mixture firmly onto the bottom and sides of a 9-inch pie plate. Chill while preparing the filling.

In a medium-sized mixing bowl, beat the egg yolks with the sugar; blend in the sour cream.

In a clean small mixing bowl, beat the egg whites until stiff but not dry. Fold the beaten egg whites into the cream mixture. Pour the mixture into the chilled pie shell. Bake in a preheated 350-degree F. oven for 30 minutes. Turn off the heat but let the pie remain in the oven for an additional 15 minutes. Cool thoroughly, then refrigerate to chill completely. Serves 6 to 8.

Variations:

Pat only half of the crumbs into the pie plate. Make the filling, pour into the pie crust, and top with the remaining pie crust crumbs. Top the pie with a fruit glaze.

Crustless Cheesecake Pie

If you do not have the time to prepare a pie shell, try this crustless cheesecake.

> 1 pound cream cheese, softened
> 2/3 cup sugar
> 1/4 teaspoon almond flavoring or 1
>   teaspoon lemon juice
> 3 eggs
> 1 cup sour cream
> 3 tablespoons sugar
> 1 teaspoon vanilla sugar
> 1 bar bittersweet chocolate

In a medium-sized mixing bowl, beat together the cream cheese, 3/8 cup sugar, and the almond flavoring or lemon juice until very fluffy. Add the eggs, 1 at a time, beating with an electric mixer at low speed after each addition, just until blended.

Pour the batter into an ungreased 9-inch pie plate. Bake in a preheated 350-degree F. oven for 35 minutes or until set. Test by inserting a knife just off-center; it should come out clean.

In a small mixing bowl, stir together the sour cream, the 3 tablespoons sugar, and the teaspoon of vanilla sugar. Carefully spread the cream over the hot pie. Cool. Using a vegetable peeler, shave thin curls of chocolate over the top of the pie. Refrigerate to chill thoroughly. Serves 6 to 8.

Cheese Torte

Whereas a cheese pie is baked or chilled in a pie pan and is served like any other pie (in wedges), a cheese torte or cheese-cake is baked or chilled in a spring-form pan. The sides of the pan can be removed, leaving the cake to stand alone.

Crust:

> Butter for the pan
> 2 cups macaroon crumbs
> Chopped nuts (optional)

Filling:

> 5 eggs, separated
> 1¼ pounds cottage cheese

→

   3 tablespoons potato starch
   Pinch of salt
1 cup sugar
   Juice of ½ lemon
1 pint sour cream

Generously butter a 9-inch spring-form pan. Set aside ⅓ cup of the macaroon crumbs. Transfer the remaining crumbs to the baking pan. Press the crumbs firmly onto the bottom and sides of the pan.

In a medium-sized mixing bowl, beat the egg yolks until thick and light. Sieve the cheese into a large bowl. Add the potato starch and blend well. Add the salt, beaten egg yolks, and sugar. Stir thoroughly. Gradually add the lemon juice and sour cream; stir well to maintain a smooth consistency.

In a clean medium-sized bowl, with clean beaters, beat the egg whites until very stiff. Carefully fold the stiffly beaten egg whites into the cheese mixture. Pour the cheese batter into the crumb-lined pan. Sprinkle the reserved crumbs over the top. (Chopped nuts may be added to the crumbs.)

Bake in a preheated 325-degree F. oven for 1 hour or longer, until the filling is firm. Test by inserting a knife into the torte; it should come out clean. Turn off the heat and let the torte remain in the oven, with the door open, for 30 minutes. Remove from the oven. Cool before serving. Serves 10 or more.

Pineapple Cheese Pie

For variety, instead of using the pineappple mixture as a filling for this pie, use it as a topping. Try eliminating a few calories by using skim milk in place of the whole milk in the cheese filling.

Crust:

   1 large package (1¾ ounces) soup nuts,
      crushed fine
   2 tablespoons brown sugar
   2 tablespoons margarine

Pineapple Filling:

⅓ cup sugar
1 tablespoon potato starch
1 cup crushed pineapple with juice

Cheese Filling:

½ pound cream cheese
½ cup sugar
½ teaspoon salt
2 eggs
½ cup milk
½ teaspoon vanilla flavoring
¼ cup chopped pecans

To prepare the crust, in a medium-sized mixing bowl combine and thoroughly mix all of the crust ingredients. Firmly pat the crumbs into a 9-inch pie plate. Set aside.

Prepare the pineapple filling next. In a small saucepan, blend the sugar and potato starch. Add the crushed pineapple and cook over low heat, stirring constantly until the mixture is thick and clear. Cool.

Prepare the cheese filling while the pineapple mixture cools. In a medium-sized mixing bowl, combine the cheese with the sugar and salt; blend until smooth. Add the eggs, 1 at a time, stirring well after each addition. Blend in the milk and vanilla flavoring.

Spread the cooled pineapple filling in the prepared pie shell. Pour the cream cheese mixture over the pineapple mixture. Sprinkle with the chopped nuts. Bake in a preheated 400-degree F. oven for 5 minutes; reduce the heat to 325 degrees F. and continue to bake for an additional 55 minutes. Serves 6 to 8.

Fruit-Topped Cheese Pastry

The preparation of this pastry is not as difficult as it might seem. The pastry itself is rich and satisfying, an epicurean delight. It freezes very well, and it will feel good knowing that you have this cheese pastry on hand to serve when needed.

Pastry:

    ½ cup finely chopped nuts
    ½ cup brown sugar
    ½ cup shortening or ¼ pound (1 stick)
       margarine, at room temperature
    1½ cups cake meal

Filling:

    1 pound cream cheese, at room
      temperature
    1 teaspoon lemon juice or 1 teaspoon
      vanilla flavoring
    ½ cup sugar
    3 eggs

Topping:

    Fruit topping of your choice
    ½ cup freshly grated coconut
    ½ cup coarsely chopped walnuts
    ¾ cup reserved crust crumbs

To prepare the pastry, in a small mixing bowl blend the pastry ingredients together with a pastry blender or a fork until the mixture resembles matzo meal. Set aside ¾ cup for the topping. Turn the remaining mixture into a 9 × 13-inch pan. Press firmly onto the bottom and sides of the pan. Use the back of a tablespoon to facilitate packing the mixture firmly into the corners of the pan. Bake in a preheated 350-degree F. oven for 12 minutes or until the edges are light brown.

To prepare the filling, in a medium-sized mixing bowl beat the filling ingredients together until very light and creamy, at least 5 minutes. Pour the batter onto the hot crust. Bake for 10 minutes.

Pour your favorite fruit topping over the hot cheese filling. Add the ½ cup freshly grated coconut and ½ cup chopped walnuts to the reserved crumb mixture. Sprinkle this over the fruit. Return the cake to the oven and bake for an additional 15 to 20 minutes. Cool thoroughly before serving. Serves 12 or more.

Basic Viennese Pastry

⅓ cup sugar
⅔ cup finely ground blanched almonds
⅔ cup cake meal
1 cup margarine or butter
Matzo meal
Preserves of your choice
Grease for the cookie sheet

In a medium-sized mixing bowl, combine the first 3 ingredients.
Cut in the margarine or butter with a pastry blender or fork;
knead until well blended.

Fruit Bars:

Form the pastry into logs about 2 inches in diameter; place on a
very lightly greased cookie sheet. With the back of a knife dipped
in matzo meal, make a depression down the center of the log. Fill
the depression with your favorite preserves. Bake in a preheated
325-degree F. oven for 20 to 25 minutes. If desired, sprinkle with
shredded coconut 5 minutes before removing from the oven.
Cut diagonally into bars. Serves 10 to 14.

Cookies:

Form the pastry into a roll; cut the roll into slices ½ inch thick.
Place the cookies on a lightly greased cookie sheet. Bake in a
preheated 350-degree F. oven for 10 to 15 minutes. Remove from
the oven and drizzle the cookies with chocolate icing. Or put 2
cookies together, sandwich-fashion, with jam as a filling.

Jelly Tarts

Dough:

¾ cup oil
¼ cup apple juice
3 tablespoons sugar
1 large egg, well beaten

2 cups cake meal
Grease for the muffin cups

Filling:

1½ cups strawberry jam
½ cup chopped blanched almonds

In a medium-sized mixing bowl, mix the oil, apple juice, and sugar. Add the well-beaten egg; stir in the cake meal and blend thoroughly. Divide the dough into 24 greased muffin pan cups. Press the dough gently onto the bottom and sides of the muffin cups.

In a small bowl, mix the jam and the nuts until well combined. Divide the mixture among the muffin pan cups. Bake in a preheated 400-degree F. oven for 10 minutes or until the cakes are golden. Cool before removing from the pan. Serve plain or topped with whipped cream. Makes 24 tarts.

Miniature Cheese Tarts

For a more elegant and richer "finishing touch," mix 1 pint of sour cream with 2 teaspoons of sugar. Spread the cream mixture over each tart and return to a 425-degree F. oven for 5 minutes. Remove from the oven and cap each tart with a large strawberry, a spoonful of jelly, or a sprinkling of chopped nuts.

Dough:

½ pound (2 sticks) margarine
6 ounces cream cheese
2 cups sifted cake meal

Filling:

½ cup sugar
12 ounces cream cheese
½ teaspoon lemon juice
2 eggs

Place the margarine and cream cheese in a medium-sized mixing bowl. Let stand until they reach room temperature, then combine and beat until creamy. Add the cake meal; knead until smooth.

Divide the dough into 48 small ungreased tea muffin cups. With the thumb, pat the dough onto the bottom and sides of the muffin cups. Refrigerate while making the filling.

Prepare the filling by creaming the sugar with the cheese in a medium-sized mixing bowl. Add the remaining ingredients and beat until very creamy.

Divide the filling into the 48 small tart shells. Bake in a preheated 425-degree F. oven for 5 minutes. Turn down the heat and continue to bake at 350 degrees F. for 15 minutes. Makes 48 small tarts.

Variations:

Orange Flavor: Add 1 teaspoon orange rind and ¼ teaspoon lemon rind to the well-creamed cream cheese and margarine.

Bit o' Spice Flavor: Add ½ teaspoon cinnamon and 2 tablespoons sugar to the well-creamed cream cheese and margarine.

Pecan Tassies

These tiny delights provide a mouthwatering dessert for a festive dairy meal. Garnish each with a dollop of whipped cream and top with a pecan half.

Dough:

> ½ pound cream cheese
> ½ pound margarine
> 2 cups sifted cake meal

Filling:

> 2½ cups brown sugar
> 3 eggs
> 1 tablespoon melted butter
> 2 teaspoons vanilla sugar
> Dash of salt
> 1½ cups coarsely chopped pecans

Place the cream cheese and margarine in a medium-sized mixing bowl. Let stand until they reach room temperature, then combine, beating until creamy. Add the cake meal; knead together until smooth.

Divide the dough into 48 ungreased small tea muffin cups. With the thumb, pat the dough onto the bottom and sides of the muffin cups. Refrigerate while preparing the filling.

To prepare the filling, in a medium-sized mixing bowl beat together the sugar, eggs, melted butter, vanilla sugar, and salt until very creamy. Divide half of the pecans among the pastry-lined cups. Pour the filling mixture over the nuts and top with the remaining nuts. Bake in a preheated 350-degree F. oven for 20 minutes or until the filling is set. Cool and remove from the pans. Makes 48.

Cheese Strudel

This flavorful cheese-filled strudel, made with a sour cream dough, may be enhanced by sprinkling the rolls of dough with a sugar-cinnamon mixture before baking, or by brushing the rolls with a well-beaten egg, which will provide a glaze.

Dough:

      1 tablespoon sugar
      2 cups sifted cake meal
      ¼ pound butter or margarine
      1 cup sour cream

Filling:

      1 pound cottage cheese
      1 egg, unbeaten
      ¼ cup sugar
      Dash of cinnamon
      ½ cup raisins
      ¼ cup finely chopped nuts
      Grease for the baking sheet

In a medium-sized mixing bowl, sift the sugar with the cake meal. Add the butter or margarine and sour cream. With a pastry blender, work the ingredients together to form a dough. Knead briefly to insure complete blending. Refrigerate the dough while preparing the filling.

Into another medium-sized mixing bowl, press the cottage cheese through a fine sieve or a food mill. Stir in the unbeaten egg, sugar, and a dash of cinnamon. Blend well. Taste and add additional sugar and/or cinnamon if desired.

Divide the dough and filling ingredients in half. Between 2 pieces of wax paper, roll out 1 piece of dough to form a 10 × 12-inch rectangle. Sprinkle a portion of the raisins and nuts on the piece of rolled dough. Cover two-thirds of the surface of the dough with the cheese. Roll up the dough, jelly roll fashion, beginning with the cheese-filled end and ending with the seam on the bottom.

Slide the roll, seam side down, onto a greased 9 × 13-inch baking sheet. Score the top lightly at equal intervals. Repeat with the remaining half of the dough.

Bake in a preheated 350-degree F. oven for 45 minutes or until golden brown. Slice completely through immediately after removing the strudel from the oven. Yields 2 rolls, 10 slices per roll.

Milchig Apple Strudel

Using the sour cream dough of the Cheese Strudel above (an excellent basic dough for many pastries), bake a luscious apple strudel. This will be a welcome change from apple pie.

> **1 recipe Cheese Strudel dough (above)**
> **3 apples**
> **½ cup chopped nuts**
> **¼ cup sugar**
> **¼ cup raisins**
> **1 teaspoon cinnamon**
> **Jelly of your choice**
> **2 tablespoons matzo meal**
> **Grease for the cookie sheet**

Peel, core, and coarsely chop the apples. Place in a medium-sized mixing bowl. Add the chopped nuts, sugar, raisins, and cinnamon. Mix well.

Divide the dough and filling in half. Between 2 pieces of wax paper, roll out 1 piece of the dough to form a 10 × 12-inch rectangle. Spread the jelly of your choice sparingly over ⅔ of the dough surface. Sprinkle a portion of the apple filling over the same surface. Sprinkle with 1 tablespoon of matzo meal. Roll up the dough, jelly roll fashion, beginning with the apple-filled end and ending with the seam on the bottom. Slide the roll, seam side down, onto a greased 9 × 13-inch cookie sheet. Lightly score the top of the roll at equal intervals. Repeat with the remaining half of the dough.

Bake in a preheated 350-degree F. oven for 45 minutes or until golden brown. Slice completely through immediately after removing from the oven. Yields 2 rolls, 10 slices per roll.

Matzo Strudel

> **5 whole matzos**
> **½ cup sweet red wine**
> **2 eggs, separated**
> **2 tablespoons sugar**
> **2 tablespoons matzo meal**
> **⅛ teaspoon salt**
> **½ cup strawberry or cherry preserves**
> **⅛ cup finely chopped (not ground) nuts**
> **1 large apple, peeled, cored, and thinly**
>   **sliced**
> **½ teaspoon cinnamon**
> **1½ tablespoons honey**
> **1½ tablespoons oil**

In a large deep dish, soak the whole matzos in the wine for 5 minutes, being careful not to break them. In a small bowl, beat the egg yolks and sugar until light and lemon-colored. Stir in the matzo meal.

In a clean small bowl, beat the egg whites with the salt until the egg whites are stiff but not dry. Fold the egg whites into the egg yolk mixture.

Combine the preserves and nuts in a small bowl. Mix well. Arrange the sliced apples in a shallow dish; sprinkle with the cinnamon. Heat the honey and oil in an 8 × 8-inch baking pan over low heat. Stir until blended.

Carefully place 1 matzo in the center of the pan and spread with half of the egg mixture. Place the second matzo over the filling and spread with half of the preserves mixture. Place the third matzo on top of this and arrange the sliced apples and cinnamon evenly over the matzo. Cover with the fourth matzo; spread with the remaining preserves mixture. Top with the fifth matzo. Stir any leftover wine into the remaining egg mixture and spread over the top and sides of the strudel.

Bake in a preheated 325-degree F. oven for 30 minutes or until golden brown. Cut into portions while still warm, but leave in the pan to cool thoroughly. Serve cold. Serves 8 to 10.

Matzo Napoleon

    6 apples
    6 tablespoons sugar
 1½ teaspoons cinnamon
    1 teaspoon salt
   ½ to 1 cup apple juice or water
    6 matzos
      Grease for the pan

Meringue:

    2 egg whites
   ¼ teaspoon cream of tartar
    4 tablespoons sugar
    1 teaspoon vanilla sugar (optional)

Peel and slice the apples into a medium-sized bowl. Combine the sugar, cinnamon, and salt in a small dish.

Pour ½ to 1 cup of apple juice or water into a shallow pan (you will need enough liquid for dipping the 6 matzos). Dip each matzo into the apple juice or water. Place a matzo in the bottom of a lightly greased 8 × 8-inch baking dish. Cover with a layer of apples; sprinkle with a portion of the sugar-cinnamon mixture. Repeat, layering matzo and apples, ending with apples.

Set the baking dish into a larger pan containing 1½ to 2 inches of hot water. Bake in a preheated 350-degree F. oven until the apples are tender.

To prepare the meringue, beat the egg whites and cream of tartar in a medium-sized bowl until frothy. Gradually add the sugar, 1 tablespoon at a time, beating well after each addition. Beat until stiff and glossy. Spread the meringue over the baked pudding. Return to the oven and bake until the meringue peaks are golden brown, 10 to 15 minutes. Serves 8.

Lemon Napoleons

Unlike the puff paste napoleons with which we are familiar, these are oblongs of pastry layered with a lemon filling and topped with a meringue. They take a little time to prepare, but they will be immensely enjoyed.

Pastry:

> 1¼ cups matzo meal
> ⅓ cup potato starch
> 3 tablespoons sugar
> ½ teaspoon cinnamon
> ½ teaspoon vanilla flavoring
> ⅔ cup unsalted soft margarine (available in plastic containers)
> 3 tablespoons ice water, approximately

Filling:

> ¼ cup unsalted soft margarine
> 1 cup sugar
> 3 egg yolks

→

⅔ cup lemon juice
Grated rind of 1 lemon

Meringue:

3 egg whites
⅛ teaspoon cream of tartar or a pinch of
   salt
6 tablespoons sugar

To prepare the pastry, combine the matzo meal, potato starch, sugar, cinnamon, and vanilla flavoring in a medium-sized bowl. Add the margarine and cut it in with a pastry blender or 2 knives until the particles are very fine. Add the ice water, 1 tablespoon at a time, until all the particles are moistened. Wrap the dough in plastic wrap and chill in the refrigerator for about 1 hour.

Between 2 sheets of wax paper, roll out the dough into a 12-inch square. Cut the dough into 3 equal pieces, then cut crosswise into 6 equal pieces, making eighteen 2 × 4-inch oblongs. Using a spatula, transfer the pieces of dough to a cookie sheet. Bake in a preheated 350-degree F. oven for about 15 minutes, until lightly browned. Cool.

Prepare the filling by melting the margarine in the top of a double boiler. Add the sugar and mix well. In a small bowl, beat the egg yolks with the lemon juice and rind. Add to the sugar mixture and cook over hot water, stirring constantly for about 20 minutes, until smooth and very thick. Chill for at least 2 hours.

To make the meringue, in a clean small bowl beat the egg whites with the cream of tartar or pinch of salt until stiff. Beat in the sugar, 1 tablespoon at a time. Beat until stiff.

To Assemble: Spread the meringue in peaks on 6 of the pastry oblongs. Place them on a cookie sheet and bake in a preheated 400-degree F. oven for 4 to 5 minutes, until the peaks are lightly browned. Spread lemon filling over the remaining oblongs. Stack 2 of the oblongs topped with filling, 1 on top of the other, and top with an oblong covered with meringue. Repeat until the 6 napoleons have been assembled.

17

Cookies, Squares, and Bars

Here, you will find cookies in variety—from the traditional mandelbreit and teiglach to modern dainty bars, bonbons, cookies, and brownies.

It is prudent to have a variety of cookies stored in your larder during Passover. Cookies have a long shelf life, and with a variety on hand one is never at a loss for goodies to serve to unexpected company.

An attractively arranged tray of delicate diminutive tidbits, served as an accompaniment to tea, coffee, ice cream, or sherbet, will add to everyone's pleasure.

Mock Oatmeal Drop Cookies

If you find the preparation of drop cookies tedious, try making squares or bars. When you tire of squares or bars, cut the baked dough into the shapes of your choice.

When placing drop cookies on the baking sheet, don't forget to allow space for the cookies to spread while baking.

> 1 cup matzo meal
> 1 cup matzo farfel
> ¾ cup sugar

→

> ½ teaspoon cinnamon
> 2 eggs
> ⅓ cup oil
> ½ cup chopped walnuts
> ½ cup raisins
> Grease for the cookie sheet

Combine the matzo meal, farfel, sugar, and cinnamon in a medium-sized bowl. In a separate bowl, beat the eggs and oil until frothy. Pour the mixture over the dry ingredients. Mix well. Fold in the nuts and raisins.

Grease a cookie sheet. Drop the mixture onto the cookie sheet by the teaspoonful; allow 2 inches of space between cookies. Bake in a 350-degree F. oven for 30 to 35 minutes. Yields about 24 cookies.

Honey Cookies

To make these cookies more pleasing to the eye and rewarding to the palate, press a blanched almond half or a few slivers of blanched almonds onto each cookie before baking.

> 3 eggs
> 3 tablespoons shortening
> 1 cup sugar
> 1 cup honey
> Juice and grated rind of ½ orange
> 1 teaspoon cinnamon
> ½ cup chopped nuts
> 2½ cups sifted matzo meal
> Grease and matzo meal for the cookie
> sheet

Beat the eggs, shortening, sugar, and honey in a large mixing bowl until thoroughly blended. Add the remaining ingredients; blend well. Grease a cookie sheet and dust with matzo meal. Drop the batter onto the sheet by the teaspoonful, spacing them 2 inches apart. Bake in a preheated 325-degree F. oven for 12 to 15 minutes. Yields about 48 cookies.

Chocolate Chip (Toll House) Cookies

Crisp, lightly browned cookies with chocolate chips were first made and served at the Toll House Restaurant in Massachusetts. No wonder, then, that they came to be called Toll House cookies.

> 1 cup matzo meal
> ½ cup sugar
> 1 cup matzo farfel
> ½ cup chopped walnuts
> ¾ cup coarsely chopped semisweet chocolate
> 2 eggs, beaten
> ⅓ cup oil
> Grease for the baking sheet

In a mixing bowl, combine the matzo meal, sugar, matzo farfel, chopped nuts, and chopped chocolate. In the small bowl of an electric mixer, beat the eggs with the oil. Beat well. Pour the liquid mixture over the dry ingredients in the mixing bowl. Mix until thoroughly blended.

Drop the dough by the teaspoonful, 2 inches apart, onto a greased baking sheet. Bake in a preheated 350-degree F. oven for 20 to 30 minutes, until golden brown. Yields about 24 cookies.

Chocolate Chip Cookies II

> 3 eggs
> 1 cup sugar
> ½ cup oil
> 3 tablespoons water
> 1 cup chopped semisweet chocolate
> ½ cup chopped pecans
> 2 teaspoons grated orange rind
> ¼ teaspoon salt
> 2 cups matzo meal
> Oil and matzo meal for the cookie sheet

Beat the eggs and sugar in a large mixing bowl until light and fluffy; beat in the oil and water until blended. Stir in the chopped chocolate, chopped pecans, orange rind, and salt. Stir in the 2 cups of matzo meal; stir until thoroughly mixed. Let the batter rest for 10 minutes.

Oil and lightly dust a 10 × 14-inch cookie sheet with matzo meal. Drop the batter by the tablespoonful onto the prepared sheet, forming 4 strips, each about 12 inches long and 1½ inches wide.

Bake in a preheated 375-degree F. oven for about 20 minutes, until a pale golden brown. Remove from the oven. Immediately cut each strip into about fifteen ½-inch wide diagonal slices. With a spatula, remove the slices from the baking sheet onto a wire rack to cool. Yields about 60 cookies.

Coconut-Date Cookies

Here, dates, coconut, and walnuts team up to make a delicious, nourishing cookie. Better double this recipe, these cookies go fast.

> ½ cup sugar
> 3 tablespoons shortening
> 1 egg
> ½ pound dates, cut up
> 1½ cups cut-up walnuts
> 1 cup freshly grated coconut
> Grease for the cookie sheet

In a medium-sized mixing bowl, cream the sugar, shortening, and the egg very well. Add the cut-up dates, walnuts, and coconut; mix well. Drop up the tablespoonful, 2 inches apart, onto a greased cookie sheet. Bake in a preheated 350-degree F. oven for about 15 minutes. Watch the color and remove the cookies from the oven when they are *golden* brown. Do not overbake. Remove the cookies from the cookie sheet when cool. Yields about 36 to 40 cookies.

Almond Macaroons

(Soft and Chewy)

The origin of the macaroon is unknown, but some authorities suggest that it originated in Italy. Whatever, wherever its origin, the small round cookie made of ground almonds, sugar, and egg white has become an extremely popular Passover treat. Its popularity on this holiday may be attributed to the fact that ground almonds make an excellent substitute for matzo cake meal and matzo meal.

Over the years, several kinds of macaroons have evolved, one of the favorites being the coconut macaroon, in which coconut takes the place of the almonds.

It is important to remember that the best way to grind almonds (or any nut) to a very fine powder is with a nut grinder. If a blender is used, care must be taken that the nuts do not become oily or lumpy.

> ½ pound (1½ cups) blanched almonds,
>   ground very fine
> ⅔ cup sugar
> ½ cup egg whites (3 or 4)
> ½ teaspoon almond flavoring
>   Slivered blanched almonds

In a medium-sized bowl, combine the ground almonds with the sugar. Set aside.

In the small bowl of an electric mixer, beat the egg whites, first at low speed then at high speed, until stiff but not dry. Add the almond flavoring near the end of the beating. Fold the stiffly beaten egg whites into the almond-sugar mixture.

Place the nut mixture in a pastry bag. Using a number 8 star tube, press out 1½-inch rosettes 1 inch apart onto a foil-lined cookie sheet. Top each with a few almond slivers. (If you do not have a pastry bag, drop by the teaspoonful.)

Bake in a preheated 350-degree F. oven for about 20 minutes, until the ridges and edges are golden. Do not overbake. Slide the foil with the cookies off the cookie sheet; let stand for about 5 minutes. Peel the foil from the macaroons and transfer them to racks to cool. Yields about 30.

Coconut Macaroons

To "revive" macaroons that are drying out, sprinkle with a few drops of orange juice or sweet wine. Wrap the cookies in aluminum foil and heat in a preheated 300-degree F. oven for 10 minutes.

> **3 egg whites**
> **1 cup sugar**
> **1 cup freshly grated coconut**
> **½ cup chopped walnuts**

In the large bowl of an electric mixer, beat the egg whites until frothy. Gradually add the sugar and beat at high speed until stiff and glossy. Fold in the coconut and walnuts.

Line a baking sheet with wax paper. Drop the dough onto the baking sheet by the teaspoonful, 2 inches apart. Bake in a preheated 300-degree F. oven for 25 to 30 minutes, until set and delicately browned. Remove from the oven. Let rest for a few minutes before removing from the baking sheet. Slip off with a spatula. Makes about 36 macaroons.

Brown-edge Lemon Wafers

A lemon-lover's delight and a good cookie for those allergic to wheat. Easy to prepare and quick to bake.

> **4 eggs, at room temperature**
> **½ cup sugar**
> **1¼ cups potato starch**
> **1½ teaspoons grated lemon rind**
> **¼ teaspoon salt**
> **⅔ cup oil**
> **Oil for the baking sheets**
> **¼ cup cinnamon sugar (see Index for recipe)**
> **½ to 1 teaspoon grated lemon rind for topping**

In the medium-sized bowl of an electric mixer, beat the eggs and sugar at high speed for 3 minutes. Reduce the speed to low; add the potato starch, lemon rind, salt, and oil. Mix just until well blended.

Drop the dough by the teaspoonful onto lightly oiled cookie sheets. Combine the cinnamon sugar with the grated lemon rind in a small dish. Lightly sprinkle the cookies with the lemon-sugar mixture.

Bake in a preheated 350-degree F. oven until the edges are golden brown, about 10 to 15 minutes. Remove from the baking sheets and place on wire racks to cool. Makes about 48 cookies.

Thumbprint Cookies

Nut-rich and especially elegant-looking when a variety of jams is used to fill the indentations made with the thumb.

> ½ cup shortening or oil
> ½ cup sugar
> 2 eggs
> ¾ cup cake meal
> 1 cup chopped nuts
> Grease for the cookie sheet
> Jams of your choice

In a medium-sized mixing bowl, cream the shortening or oil with the sugar until light and fluffy. Add the eggs; beat until well blended. Add the cake meal and chopped nuts; stir until smooth.

Form the dough into 1¼-inch balls. Arrange them on a greased cookie sheet, leaving 2 inches of space between each. With the thumb, make a depression in the center of each cookie. Fill each depression with a small dab of jam. Bake in a preheated 450-degree F. oven for 10 to 12 minutes. Yields approximately 36 cookies.

Coconut Chews

> 1 egg
> ½ cup sugar

⟶

1 envelope (.43 ounces) vanilla sugar or 1
teaspoon vanilla flavoring
1 cup finely chopped pitted dates
1 cup freshly grated coconut
⅓ cup chopped walnuts
Grease for the pan
Grated coconut or chopped nuts for
garnish

In a medium-sized bowl, beat the egg until foamy. Beat in the sugars (or sugar and flavoring) until fluffy-thick. Stir in the pitted dates, coconut, and walnuts. Spoon into a 9 × 9-inch greased baking pan. Bake in a preheated 300-degree F. oven for 30 minutes or until golden and the top springs back when lightly touched. Cool in the pan or on a wire rack just until warm, about 15 minutes.

Cut the dough into 48 rectangles: first cut lengthwise into 8 strips, then cut crosswise into 6. With the palms of the hands, shape each rectangle into a ball. Roll each ball in coconut or finely chopped nuts. Cool completely on wire racks. Yields forty-eight ¾-inch balls.

Ice Box Cookies

¼ pound (1 stick) margarine
1 cup sugar
2 eggs
Pinch of salt
2 tablespoons lemon juice or orange juice
1 cup cake meal
½ cup chopped nuts
¼ cup finely chopped nuts for garnish
(optional)
Grease for the cookie sheet

Cream the margarine and sugar in a medium-sized mixing bowl. Blend in the eggs, salt, and juice. Stir the cake meal into the creamed mixture. Add the chopped nuts.

With the hands, shape the dough on wax paper into 1 or 2 long smooth rolls. (The number of rolls depends upon the cookie diameter desired.) If desired, add a festive touch by rolling the formed rolls in finely chopped nuts. Wrap in a clean piece of wax paper, twisting the ends. Chill in the refrigerator overnight.

Immediately before baking, use a thin sharp knife to slice the cookies to the desired thickness. Bake on a very lightly greased cookie sheet in a preheated 350-degree F. oven for 20 to 25 minutes. With a wide spatula, remove the cookies from the cookie sheet and cool on wire racks. The yield depends on the thickness and diameter of the cookies.

Apple Squares

A light cake with a delicious apple filling. A sprinkling of chopped nuts or raisins adds dimension to the filling. For variety, substitute one cup of sugared blueberries for the apples.

> 3 large apples
> 1 to 2 tablespoons sugar (or more, to taste)
> ½ teaspoon cinnamon
> 3 eggs, separated
> 1 cup sugar
> Juice and grated rind of 1 lemon
> ½ cup oil
> 1 cup matzo meal
> ½ teaspoon salt
> Grease for the baking pan

Peel the apples. Slice the apples into a medium-sized bowl. Sprinkle with the 1 to 2 tablespoons of sugar and ½ teaspoon of cinnamon. Toss the apples to coat well. Taste and sprinkle on more sugar if the apples are tart. Set aside.

In the medium-sized bowl of an electric mixer, beat the egg yolks until light; gradually add the sugar, beating until thick. Add the lemon juice, rind, and oil. Lower the speed of the mixer to low; add the matzo meal and salt. Beat until well blended.

In a mixing bowl, with clean beaters, beat the egg whites until stiff, then gently fold the whites into the yolk mixture. Spread half of the batter in the bottom of a lightly greased 8-inch square pan. Spread the apples in an even layer over the batter.

Cover with the remaining batter. Bake in a preheated 350-degree F. oven for 45 minutes or until browned. Cool and cut into squares. Yields 16 squares.

Date and Chocolate Bit Squares

Here, assembling the ingredients may take a bit of time, but no one lucky enough to taste these irresistible squares will ever forget them. **Note:** These squares freeze very well.

>   1 cup diced pitted dates
> 1½ cups boiling water
> 1½ teaspoons baking soda
>   2 eggs
>   1 cup sugar
>   ¾ cup oil
>   ¾ teaspoon baking soda
>   ½ teaspoon salt
> 1½ cups cake meal
>   ⅛ cup potato starch
>   Grease and cake meal for the pan
>   2 bars (1½ ounces each) semisweet chocolate
>   ¼ cup sugar for topping
>   1 cup finely chopped nuts for topping

Combine the dates, boiling water, and baking soda in a small saucepan. Bring to a slow boil. Remove from the heat. Set aside to cool.

In a medium-sized bowl, cream the eggs with the sugar and oil until well blended; add the cooled date mixture. Sift together the soda, salt, cake meal, and starch into a small bowl. Combine the dry ingredients with the date mixture. Blend thoroughly.

Grease and dust with cake meal a 9 × 13-inch pan. Pour the batter into the pan. Chop the chocolate into bits and sprinkle over the batter. Sprinkle the ¼ cup sugar and 1 cup finely chopped nuts over the chocolate bits. Bake at 350 degrees F. for 40 to 45 minutes. Cool and cut into squares. Yields twenty-four 2-inch squares. The yield is greater if cut into bars: thirty 1½ × 2-inch bars.

Brownies

You can create unusual brownies by substituting grated co-conut, chopped pitted dates, or raisins for all or part of the chopped nuts.

> **3 eggs**
> **1 cup sugar**
> **½ cup oil**
> **2 tablespoons unsweetened cocoa**
> **½ cup potato starch**
> **1 cup chopped nuts**
> **Grease for the pan**

Beat the eggs and sugar in a large mixing bowl until light and fluffy. Gradually add the oil, then add the cocoa and potato starch. Blend together. Stir in the chopped nuts. Pour into a lightly greased 9-inch square pan. Bake at 350 degress F. for 30 minutes. Yields sixteen 2-inch squares.

Fudge Brownies

Not a cookie, not a cake—a fudgy chocolate brownie. About as good as a sweet can be.

A delicious variation on these brownies is made by simply adding a nine-ounce can of drained crushed pineapple to the batter after the eggs and sugar have been beaten smooth with the chocolate and margarine.

> **3½ ounces bittersweet chocolate**
> **¼ cup margarine or oil**
> **2 eggs**

→

⅛ teaspoon salt
⅔ cup sugar
½ cup cake meal
½ cup chopped nuts
  Grease for the pan

Melt the chocolate and margarine in the top of a double boiler over hot water. Cool.

In a medium-sized mixing bowl, beat the eggs and salt until thick and lemon-colored. Gradually add the sugar. Beat in the cooled chocolate mixture. Gradually add the cake meal; beat until well blended. Stir in the nuts.

Spread the batter in a well-greased 8-inch square pan. Bake in a 350-degree F. oven for 35 minutes. Cut while hot. Cool in the pan. Yields sixteen 2-inch squares.

Chocolate-Nut Balls

The easiest of all cookies to make: you don't bake them. The cookies take on a different flavor as you vary the nuts used.

2 egg whites
½ pound ground nuts
1 jigger (1 ounce) brandy
2 teaspoons sifted unsweetened cocoa
2 teaspoons sugar
  Granulated sugar

In a small bowl, combine the egg whites, ground nuts, brandy, cocoa, and sugar. Stir well to bind together. Roll portions of the mixture between the palms of the hands to shape into 2-inch balls. Roll the balls in a dish of granulated sugar. Set each ball into an individual petit four case. Let ripen overnight. Yields about 36 cookies.

Chocolate Farfel Roll

3 cups matzo farfel
5 to 6 tablespoons water

→

4 bars (1½ ounces each) bittersweet
chocolate, divided, or 1 bar (6 ounces)
bittersweet chcolate, divided
¼ cup sugar
3 tablespoons water or wine
1 tablespoon brandy
1 cup margarine
½ cup chopped walnuts
3 tablespoons water
¼ to ½ cup finely chopped nuts or ½ cup
freshly grated coconut (optional)

In a large bowl, lightly moisten the farfel with a few tablespoons of water. Toss the farfel to moisten uniformly.

In the top of a double boiler over hot water, melt 2½ of the small chocolate bars or 4 ounces of the large chocolate bar with the sugar and the water or wine. When thoroughly blended, remove from the heat; stir in the brandy. Set aside to cool slightly.

Cream the margarine in the large bowl of an electric mixer until fluffy. Gradually add the melted chocolate, beating until thoroughly blended. Stir in the matzo farfel and chopped walnuts. Mix well. Pour the mixture onto a piece of wax paper about 12 inches long. Form the mixture into a smooth roll, using the wax paper to help mold the roll. Refrigerate the roll in the wax paper until very firm.

Remove the wax paper and prepare a chocolate glaze by melting the remaining chocolate in the 3 tablespoons of water in the top of a double boiler. Pour the glaze over the top of the roll. Sprinkle the finely chopped nuts or the coconut over the glaze. Chill in the refrigerator for a few hours. Serve cold. Slice crosswise. Serves 12 or more.

Variations:
• For a mocha flavor, substitute 3 tablespoons of strong black coffee for the water or wine when melting the chocolate with the sugar.
• Four matzos, moistened under running water then crumbled into small pieces, may be substituted for the matzo farfel.

Farfel Log

This makes a rich, tasty party slice for adults. Children will love them too, even though they are spiked with wine and brandy.

> 1 to 2 teaspoons brandy
> ¼ cup wine
> 3 cups matzo farfel
> 1 cup (2 sticks) margarine
> 1½ cups sugar
> 2 eggs
> 2 tablespoons unsweetened cocoa
> ½ to ¾ cup chopped nuts or chopped
>   bittersweet chocolate or a combination

In a measuring cup, combine the brandy with the wine. Sprinkle the mixture over the farfel in a medium-sized bowl. Toss the farfel to moisten uniformly.

In a large mixing bowl, cream the margarine, sugar, eggs, and cocoa until very light and creamy. Add the moistened farfel. Stir to mix well.

Sprinkle a sheet of wax paper about 12 inches long with the chopped nuts or bittersweet chocolate bits or a combination. Spread the farfel mixture over the nuts. Roll up into a log, incorporating the nuts and chocolate, removing the wax paper as you roll. Wrap in a clean sheet of wax paper and refrigerate until very firm. Slice crosswise to serve. Freezes very well. Serves 12 or more.

Variation:

Five matzos, crumbled into small pieces, may be substituted for the matzo farfel.

Mocha-Nut Bars

These mocha-nut delights are lavishly flavored with chopped nuts.

> 2 ounces bittersweet chocolate
> ½ cup shortening or margarine

→

   2 eggs
   1 cup sugar
   ¼ teaspoon salt
   1 tablespoon instant coffee
   ½ cup sifted cake meal
      Grease for the pans
   ½ cup chopped nuts

Melt the chocolate and shortening in a small bowl over simmering water. Remove from the heat. Cool.

In a medium-sized bowl, beat the eggs and sugar very well. Blend in the salt and the chocolate and shortening. Gradually stir in the coffee and cake meal.

   Turn the batter into 2 well-greased 9-inch square pans. Sprinkle the top with nuts. Bake in a moderately slow oven, 325 degrees F., for 20 to 25 minutes. Cut into bars while still warm. Serves 18.

Variation:

One-half cup unsweetened cocoa and 1 additional tablespoon of shortening may be substituted for the bittersweet chocolate.

Refrigerator Mocha Bars

You start the preparation but the refrigerator takes over and finishes. If desired, sprinkle with chopped nuts or grated coconut before chilling.

   ¾ cup margarine or oil
   ⅜ cup unsweetened cocoa
   ⅜ cup sugar
   2 tablespoons brandy (optional)
   1 teaspoon instant coffee
   1 envelope (.43 ounces) vanilla sugar
   2 eggs
   4 cups matzo farfel or 6 matzos broken up
      into small pieces

In a medium-sized saucepan, combine the margarine, cocoa, sugar, brandy, coffee, and vanilla sugar. Place over medium heat and stir until the sugar is dissolved and the ingredients are well blended. Cool. Add the eggs and beat until well blended. Put the matzo farfel or broken matzos into a 9 × 13-inch pan and pour the mixture over all. Refrigerate to chill thoroughly. Cut into bars. Serves 12 to 15.

Date Bars

Bars and squares have a built-in no-fuss feature. There is no rolling or dropping from a teaspoon onto a cookie sheet. They are baked in a pan and cut into the desired size and shape.

> 3 eggs, well beaten
> 1 cup sugar
> 1 cup matzo meal
> 1 teaspoon Passover baking powder
> ½ teaspoon salt
> 1 cup pitted dates, finely cut
> 1 cup chopped nuts of your choice
> Grease for the pans
> Superfine sugar

In a large mixing bowl, combine the well-beaten eggs with the sugar; beat until very light and fluffy.

Sift together the matzo meal, baking powder, and salt into a small bowl. Add the dry ingredients to the eggs. Beat together. Fold in the dates and nuts.

Grease two 8-inch square baking pans. Divide the dough and spread in the pans. Bake at 325 degrees F. for 45 minutes. Let cool in the pans for 15 minutes. Cut into bars 4 inches × 1½ inches. Roll in superfine sugar. Each pan yields 12 bars.

Macaroon Jam Slices

Use a little showmanship by filling each "trench" with different color preserves. When served, the slices will add color contrast to the other goodies arranged on the platter. The slices may be topped with a light lemon glaze.

1½ cups finely ground blanched almonds or
  walnuts
⅓ cup sugar
  Dash of cinnamon (optional)
1 to 2 egg whites, unbeaten, at room
  temperature
1½ cups preserves (apricot, raspberry, or
  strawberry)
  Grease for the cookie sheet

In a small bowl, mix together the nuts, sugar, and the cinnamon. Gradually add the egg whites, a little at a time, adding only enough to bind the mixture into a paste firm enough to be shaped.

On a greased cookie sheet, shape the dough into 2 rolls about 1½ inches in diameter, leaving space between the 2 rolls. Using the index finger or the back of a small demitasse spoon dipped into water, make a "trench" down the center of each roll. Bake in a preheated 350-degree F. oven for 15 to 20 minutes, until the rolls are lightly browned.

Meanwhile, heat the preserves in a small saucepan over medium heat until hot. Immediately upon removing the nut rolls from the oven, fill the "trenches" with the hot preserves. Cool slightly before removing from the cookie sheet. When completely cool, cut diagonally into slices. Yields approximately 26 to 28 slices.

Mandelbreit

(Mandelbread)

To blanch the almonds, immerse briefly in hot water, then remove the skins. Make sure the nuts are thoroughly dried before chopping. Dry on an ungreased baking sheet in a very slow, 225-degree F., oven, turning occasionally. Test for dryness. Do not toast.

3 eggs
1 cup sugar
1 cup oil
½ teaspoon salt (optional)

➡

 1 teaspoon almond flavoring or lemon
 juice
1½ cups cake meal
 1 cup chopped blanched almonds
 Sugar and cinnamon
 1 tablespoon unsweetened cocoa (optional)
 Grease for the cookie sheet

In the large bowl of an electric mixer, beat the eggs and sugar at medium speed until light and fluffy. Add the oil, salt, and flavoring or juice; beat until well blended. Add the cake meal; continue beating until well mixed. Stir in the chopped almonds. Let rest for 45 minutes. Divide the dough into 2 lightly greased junior loaf pans (7⅜ × 3⅝ × 2¼ inches). Or with slightly wet hands, shape each half of the dough into a loaf; place the loaves about 3 inches apart on a lightly greased cookie sheet. Sprinkle with sugar and cinnamon. Bake in a preheated 350-degree F. oven for 30 to 45 minutes, until light brown. Remove from the oven and immediately cut each loaf crosswise into diagonal slices.

Arrange the cut mandelbread on a cookie sheet. Set each slice on its side. Return to the oven and bake for 10 to 20 minutes, until lightly browned and toasted. Turn occasionally during the baking to insure even browning. Each loaf pan yields 12 to 14 slices.

Variations:

• Remove a few tablespoons of the batter into a small bowl and mix with 1 tablespoon of unsweetened cocoa. Shape the batter into a small roll. When transferring the remaining batter to the baking pan, encase the small cocoa roll in the center of the batter.
• Instead of toasting the mandelbread, merely set the slices on the baking sheet in the oven. Turn off the heat. Let the baking sheet remain in the oven until the oven cools completely. The mandelbread will be dry but not toasted.

Note: To insure that the mandelbread retains an even loaf shape when placed on the cookie sheet, form the dough into a roll on a long strip of greased aluminum foil. Fold up the sides against the roll, then fold the corners together securely.

Teiglach

Teiglach, pieces of dough (actually a form of knaidel) engulfed in a hot honey syrup, are a crisp and toothsome confection which are served cold.

Syrup:

> 1 pound honey
> 2 cups sugar
> 1 to 2 teaspoons ground ginger
> 1 cup water

Dough:

> 4 large eggs
> 2 tablespoons oil
> 1¼ to 1½ cups cake meal, approximately
> ½ cup boiling water
> Chopped nuts or grated coconut

Combine the honey, sugar, ginger, and cup of water in a large deep pot. Cover and place over very low heat while preparing the teiglach dough.

With a rotary mixer, beat the eggs with the oil very well. Add sufficient sifted cake meal to make a soft, manageable dough. With the palms of the hands, shape the dough, 1 teaspoonful at a time, into balls. Before rolling, lightly dust the hands with cake meal so the dough does not stick.

Uncover the honey syrup, increase the heat, and bring to a rolling boil. Carefully drop in the teiglach, a few at a time, to prevent lowering the temperature of the honey syrup. Lower the heat and cook covered at a slow boil for about 20 minutes. Uncover the pot. Start stirring occasionally and continue to cook for an additional 30 to 45 minutes, until the teiglach are nicely browned and sound hollow when tapped with the back of a spoon. Just before turning off the heat, carefully add the ½ cup of boiling water. Stir. Let stand for 1 minute. With a slotted spoon remove the teiglach from the syrup. Roll them in grated coconut or chopped nuts. Cool thoroughly. Store like cookies. Makes about 36.

Variation:

A raisin or piece of walnut may be enclosed in each teigel formed.

Note: Save the honey syrup used to cook the teiglach. Use it in a tzimmes, as a syrup over pancakes, or in baking.

Sponge Cupcakes

For a lovely dessert, bake these cupcakes in individual Mary-Ann pans. Before serving, fill the center of each cake with sliced strawberries, then garnish with a dollop of whipped cream and top with a whole strawberry.

> **6 eggs, separated**
> **½ cup cake meal**
> **½ cup potato starch**
> **Dash of salt**
> **1⅓ cups sugar, divided**
> **⅓ cup hot water**
> **Juice of 1 lemon**
> **Grease for the cupcake cups**

Separate the eggs into 2 large mixing bowls. Into a third bowl, sift together the cake meal, potato starch, and salt; repeat twice more.

Beat the egg yolks until light and quite thick. Gradually add the sugar, 2 tablespoons at a time, beating very well after each addition, until you have added 1 cup of the sugar. Add the hot water and lemon juice and beat for an additional 3 minutes.

Beat the egg whites until frothy. Add the remaining ⅓ cup of sugar, 2 tablespoons at a time. Beat until stiff.

Fold the sifted cake meal, potato starch, and salt into the yolk mixture. Then fold in the stiffly beaten egg whites. Blend gently until none of the whites can be seen.

Lightly grease only the bottoms of 18 cupcake cups. Fill three-fourths full. Bake in a preheated 350-degree F. oven for 20 to 25 minutes. Remove from the oven. Invert on a cake rack to cool before removing from the pans. Yields about 18 cupcakes.

Caramel Cupcakes

These cupcakes are moist, light, and delightfully frosted, perfect for a dairy lunch or supper. For pareve cupcakes, grease the cups with margarine and omit the cream cheese topping; substitute a sugar glaze of your choice.

>   **3 eggs, separated**
>   **1 cup packed brown sugar**
>   **⅓ cup cake meal**
>   **¼ teaspoon salt**
>   **½ cup finely chopped pecans**
>   **Butter for the cupcake cups**
>   **8 ounces whipped cream cheese**
>   **3 tablespoons granulated sugar**

Separate the eggs into 2 bowls. Beat the yolks until light. Gradually beat in the sugar, 2 tablespoons at a time, beating well after each addition. Stir in the cake meal, salt, and nuts.

Beat the egg whites until stiff but not dry. Gently fold them into the yolk mixture.

Fill lightly buttered cupcake cups three-fourths full with the batter. Bake in a preheated 325-degree F. oven for about 25 minutes, until firm. Cool.

Blend the whipped cream cheese with the sugar. Frost the top of the cupcakes. Yields about 12 cupcakes.

Ladyfingers

These light and airy finger-shaped cakes are good by themselves, but they are also an appropriate accompaniment to fruit, berries, or ice cream. In addition, they are ideal for preparing a trifle, the English dessert traditionally consisting of spongecake soaked in wine, spread with jam, and covered with custard, whipped cream, etc.

For a rich and attractive way to serve ladyfingers, dip one end of each into melted chocolate and sandwich them with a whipped cream mixture or with jelly.

    6 egg yolks
    ¼ cup sugar
    4 egg whites
    ½ cup sugar
    ½ cup sifted cake meal
    ¼ cup sifted potato starch
    Superfine sugar

In a large mixing bowl, beat the egg yolks with the ¼ cup of sugar until light and creamy. In a separate bowl, beat the egg whites until foamy, then gradually add the ½ cup of sugar, beating well after each addition until stiff. Fold the egg whites into the yolk mixture.

    Onto a piece of wax paper, sift the cake meal and potato starch. Sprinkle the sifted cake meal and potato starch over the batter and gently fold in.

Line a large cookie sheet with brown paper. Using a pastry bag fitted with a round tube, pipe the batter onto the paper to form finger shapes approximately 1 inch wide and 4 inches long. Dust with superfine sugar shaken through a small sieve.

Bake for 10 to 12 minutes in a preheated 375-degree F. oven. Using a wide spatula, loosen from the paper immediately. Makes about 24.

Overnight Meringues

Serve plain or with fruit or ice cream.

    ¼ cup finely chopped nuts
    1 ounce semisweet chocolate, grated or
    finely chopped
    ⅔ cup sugar, divided
    2 egg whites
    ⅛ teaspoon salt
    ⅛ teaspoon cream of tarter or ¼ teaspoon
    lemon juice

In a small bowl, combine the chopped nuts and grated or chopped chocolate with 2 tablespoons of the sugar; set aside. In the small bowl of an electric mixer, beat the egg whites and salt until stiff but not dry. Beat in the cream of tartar or lemon juice. Gradually beat in the remainder of the sugar, 1 tablespoon at a time, until the meringue is stiff and smooth. Fold in the chopped nuts and grated chocolate.

Drop by the heaping teaspoonful, 1 inch apart, onto a cookie sheet lined with brown paper. Preheat the oven to 350 degress F. Place the cookie sheet on the center rack of the oven and turn off the heat. Leave the cookies in the oven overnight to dry. Do not open the door. Next morning remove the meringues. Store in an airtight container. Makes about 24.

Variation:

Substitute ½ cup of raisins for the chopped nuts and the chocolate.

18

Bread Substitutes, Rolls, and Muffins

One doesn't realize how important a role bread and its variations play in our daily diet until one begins planning a Passover menu. Of course, matzo is used as a substitute, but there are many superb "breads," rolls, muffins, etc. that can be prepared during Passover as well.

Some of the recipes in this chapter are hand-me-downs. Others, such as those for breadsticks, croutons, and croustades, are originals.

Passover Rolls are excellent make-aheads for the lunch box. Wrapped airtight, they freeze very well. Thaw the rolls to make sandwiches, or drop a frozen roll into the lunchbox and it will have thawed completely by lunchtime.

Passover Rolls

½ cup oil
1 tablespoon sugar
1 teaspoon salt
1 cup boiling water
2 cups matzo meal
4 eggs
Grease for the baking sheet

Add the oil, sugar, and salt to the water in a 1-quart saucepan; bring to a boil. Remove the saucepan from the heat; add the matzo meal all at once. Beat vigorously then place over low heat, beating continuously until the batter leaves the sides of the pan and forms a smooth compact ball.

Remove from the heat and beat in the eggs, 1 at a time, beating vigorously after each addition until each egg is incorporated and the batter is thick and smooth (a portable electric beater would serve you well).

Shape the batter into 8 to 10 balls and place them about 2 inches apart on a well-greased baking sheet. With a moistened kaiser roll or Vienna roll stamp, stamp the top of each ball of dough; or using the tip of a paring knife, cut a roll design on the top of each dough round. Bake in a preheated 375-degree F. oven for 1 hour or until golden brown. Cool on paper towels on a wire rack. Makes 8 to 10 rolls.

Suggestion:

For canapés, make the rolls bite-sized. Fill them with chopped liver or any other savory filling and serve as an appetizer or as hors d'oeuvres. They will be received enthusiastically.

Passover Breadsticks

Prepare the batter as for Passover Rolls, above. With moistened hands, shape portions of the batter into logs about 8 inches long and ¾ inch in diameter. Place the logs on a lightly greased baking sheet. Bake in a 400-degree F. oven for 25 minutes or until puffed and lightly golden. Remove at once to wire racks; let cool completely. To make salt sticks sprinkle the logs lightly with salt before baking.

Passover Bagels I

These ring-shaped rolls are a favorite breakfast treat when served with butter or with cream cheese and preserves. They are not as hard as bagels made with flour, but they are delicious nonetheless.

     ½ cup oil
     1 cup water
     2 cups matzo meal
     1 teaspoon salt
     4 eggs
     Grease for the baking sheet

Bring the oil and water to a boil in a 1-quart saucepan. Turn the heat to low. Mix the matzo meal with the salt; add to the water mixture all at once and beat vigorously until the mixture is thick and comes away easily from the sides of the pan. Remove from the heat.

Add the eggs, 1 at a time, beating thoroughly after each addition until the mixture is smooth and well blended.

Grease the hands and form the dough into 8 or 10 balls. Place 2 inches apart on a greased baking sheet. Wet the forefinger, then press a hole in the center of each ball to form a doughnut shape. Bake in a preheated 350-degree F. oven for 45 minutes. Cool on a wire rack covered with paper towels. Makes 8 to 10.

Variations:

Cinnamon Bagels: Add 2 teaspoons of sugar to the water and oil. Beat in ½ teaspoon of cinnamon along with the last egg.

Onion Bagels: Add 1 to 2 tablespoons of freshly grated onion or 1 teaspoon of onion powder to the batter before baking.

Garlic Bagels: Add 1 clove of fresh garlic put through a garlic press or ⅛ teaspoon of garlic powder to the batter before baking.

Shortcut: Use a moistened ice cream scoop to form balls of dough. Arrange on a greased baking sheet, then make a hole in the center of each ball of dough.

Passover Bagels II

Try the suggested variations. A honey-glazed bagel teams up well with a steaming cup of coffee or cinnamon tea. An onion or garlic bagel is nice with a bowl of hot vegetable soup.

½ cup oil
1½ cups water
1 teaspoon salt
1 teaspoon sugar
2½ cups matzo meal
4 eggs
Grease for the baking sheet

Place the oil, water, salt, and sugar in a 1½-quart saucepan. Bring to a full rolling boil. Remove from the heat. Add the matzo meal all at once; beat until smooth and well blended. Add the eggs, 1 at a time, beating well after each addition. Coat the hands with oil; break off pieces of dough the size of an egg and shape into bagels. Place on a well-greased baking sheet. Bake in a 350-degree F. oven for 50 to 60 minutes. Makes about 14.

Variations:

Plain Glaze: If a plain glaze is desired, brush the bagel with a well-beaten egg before baking.

Honey Glaze:

¼ cup water
¼ cup honey
½ cup sugar
¼ teaspoon cinnamon
2 tablespoons oil or margarine
½ cup finely chopped nuts

Combine the water, honey, sugar, and cinnamon in a small saucepan. Bring to a boil over medium heat. Boil for 2 minutes, stirring constantly. Add the oil or margarine. Cool. Spoon the glaze over each bagel about 15 minutes before the end of the baking time. Remove from the oven when done and sprinkle with the nuts.

Onion Bagels: Add ½ cup finely chopped fried onions to the mixture after the eggs have been added. Or add 1 teaspoon of onion powder to the batter before baking.

Garlic Bagels: Add 1 small clove of garlic, finely minced, or ⅛ teaspoon garlic powder to the batter before baking.

Croutons for Salads and Soups

As a change from farfel, try serving croutons. They add a pleasing crunch not only to soups but to salads as well. If you'd like flavored croutons, sprinkle with onion powder or garlic powder before toasting in the oven.

Passover Rolls (see recipe)
Margarine or butter for the baking
sheet

Cut the rolls into slices, then cubes. Arrange in a single layer on a baking sheet. Brown in a 350-degree F. oven, turning as necessary until crisp and lightly browned. If desired, smear margarine or butter on both sides of the slices before cutting into cubes.

Garlic Croutons:

In a skillet over medium heat, sauté 1 or 2 small cloves of garlic, sliced, in 3 tablespoons of oil. Sauté until golden, about 2 minutes. With a slotted spoon, remove the garlic; add the cubes. Brown quickly in the hot oil, stirring until the cubes are golden. Drain on paper towels.

Croustades

Croustades serve as an excellent substitute for patty shells.

Passover Rolls (see recipe above)

Cut off the top of each roll. Scoop out the center, leaving a shell about ¼ to ½ inch thick. Arrange the shells on a baking sheet and bake in a 350-degree F. oven for 10 to 15 minutes, until golden brown.

Variation:

Brush the inside of each shell very sparingly with melted margarine or butter, then bake. If desired, sprinkle the inside with onion or garlic powder before baking.

Passover Muffins I
("Cake Method")

Depending on the ingredients used and the preparation technique followed, Passover muffins will vary greatly. There are three techniques commonly used: the "cake method," in which the eggs are separated; the "pancake method," in which the liquid is combined with the dry ingredients; and the "pastry method," in which the batter is prepared like a pâte à choux. All methods yield excellent results.

    3 eggs, separated
    ¼ teaspoon salt
    2 tablespoons cold water
    6 tablespoons matzo meal
    Grease for the muffin cups

Separate the eggs into 2 medium-sized bowls. Add the salt to the egg whites. Beat with an electric mixer until stiff peaks form. Add the water to the egg yolks and beat with the same beaters until light. Fold the yolks into the stiffly beaten whites. Fold in the matzo meal. Spoon the batter into greased muffin cups and bake in a preheated 350-degree F. oven for 30 minutes or until golden brown. Makes 6 to 8.

Passover Muffins II
("Pancake Method")

Jam or preserves may be tucked into each muffin before baking.

    2 cups matzo meal
    1 teaspoon salt
    1 tablespoon sugar
    1½ cups boiling water
    ½ cup oil or melted shortening
    4 eggs, well beaten
    Grease for the muffin cups

In a medium-sized bowl, mix the matzo meal with the salt and sugar. Add the boiling water and mix well. Let rest for 5 minutes. Add the oil or melted shortening and eggs. Mix thoroughly. Spoon the batter into greased muffin cups and bake at 400 degrees F. for 30 to 40 minutes, until golden brown. Yields 12 muffins.

Variation:

For jam-filled muffins, spoon the batter into the muffin cups and place ½ teaspoon of preserves or jam in the center of each muffin. The jam will sink in a bit to become a filling.

Passover Muffins III
("Pastry Method")

> ½ cup matzo meal
> 1 cup cake meal
> 1 teaspoon salt
> 1 tablespoon sugar
> ½ cup oil
> 1 cup water
> 5 eggs
> 1 teaspoon onion powder (optional)
> Grease for the muffin cups

Combine the matzo meal, cake meal, salt, and sugar in a small mixing bowl.

Bring the oil and the water to a boil in a 1½-quart saucepan. Add the dry ingredients all at once; turn down the heat. Cook, stirring continuously until the batter pulls away from the sides of the pan. Remove from the heat.

Add the eggs, 1 at a time, beating well after each addition until the egg is absorbed into the batter. The onion powder, if used, is added with the last egg. Beat until the batter is thick and smooth. Set aside to rest for 15 minutes.

Spoon the batter into greased muffins pans. Bake in a preheated

350-degree F. oven for 50 to 60 minutes, until golden brown. Makes 12 to 16.

Potato Starch Muffins

Good for those allergic to wheat.

4 eggs, separated
1 tablespoon sugar
2 tablespoons cold water
Grated rind of ½ lemon
¾ cup potato starch
½ teaspoon salt
Grease for the muffin cups

In a large mixing bowl, beat the yolks until light. Gradually add the sugar. Beat until light and creamy. Add the water and the grated rind. Slowly sift in the potato starch. Blend well.

In another large bowl, beat the egg whites with the salt at low speed until frothy; increase the speed to high and beat until stiff peaks form. Carefully fold the stiffly beaten egg whites into the yolk batter. Fill greased muffin cups half full and bake in a preheated 350-degree F. oven for 12 to 15 minutes. Yields 12 muffins.

Squash Muffins

These muffins may be prepared with unpeeled zucchini. Merely scrub them well before grating.

1½ pounds zucchini squash
4 eggs, separated
1 medium-sized onion, grated
Salt and white pepper to taste
1 cup potato starch
Grease for the muffin cups

Peel the zucchini, then grate on the coarse side of a grater into a large mixing bowl.

Beat the egg yolks. Add the beaten egg yolks and the onion. Season to taste with salt and pepper. Mix to blend.

In a mixing bowl, beat the egg whites until stiff. Gently fold the stiffly beaten egg whites and the potato starch into the yolk mixture. Spoon the batter into greased muffin cups. Bake in a preheated 350-degree F. oven for 50 minutes. Yields 18.

Farfel Muffins

3 cups farfel
2 cups boiling water
2 tablespoons margarine or oil
3 apples, peeled and grated
¼ cup raisins
4 eggs
Dash of white pepper
½ teaspoon cinnamon
3 tablespoons sugar
Grease for the muffin cups
Cinnamon sugar (see Index for recipe)

In a large bowl, combine the farfel, boiling water, and margarine or oil. Mix well. Let cool. Stir in the grated apples and the raisins. In a large mixing bowl, beat the eggs with the pepper, cinnamon, and sugar. Add the beaten egg mixture to the farfel mixture. Blend thoroughly. Spoon the mixture into greased muffin cups. Sprinkle with sugar and cinnamon. Bake in a preheated 375-degree F. oven for 45 minutes to 1 hour, until golden brown. Yields 15 to 20.

Popovers I

(Sweet)

Popovers need complete privacy when put into the oven, so resist the temptation to open the oven door before you turn down the heat. Then, you may peek—if you must.

Popovers are delicious as a "hot bread," but they may also be filled with meat, vegetables, or fish and be served with a sauce as a main course.

> 1½ cups boiling water
> ½ cup oil
> 1 teaspoon salt
> 2 tablespoons sugar
> 1½ cups cake meal
> 7 eggs
> Grease for the muffin cups

Combine the water, oil, salt, and sugar in a 1½-quart saucepan. Boil over high heat for 1 minute. Remove from the heat and vigorously stir in the cake meal all at once. Cool. Add the eggs, 1 at a time, beating well after each addition. Grease and heat the muffin cups. Pour in the batter and bake in a preheated 450-degree F. oven for 20 minutes, then reduce the heat to 350 degrees F. and bake for another 30 minutes. Yields approximately 24.

Popovers II

(Savory)

> ½ cup oil
> ½ teaspoon coarse salt
> 2 cups boiling water
> 2 cups matzo meal
> 6 eggs
> Grease for the muffin cups

Combine the oil, salt, and water in a 2-quart saucepan. Bring to a boil over medium heat; add the matzo meal all at once. Stir constantly until the batter leaves the sides of the pan and forms a smooth compact ball. Remove from the heat. Cool for 5 minutes. Add the eggs, 1 at a time. Mix thoroughly after each addition until the egg is completely absorbed. Bake in heated greased muffin cups in a preheated 375-degree F. oven for 40 minutes. Yields approximately 18 to 20.

French Toast Matzos

4 matzos
1 quart boiling water
2 eggs
¼ cup milk or water
½ teaspoon salt
⅛ teaspoon white pepper
2 tablespoons butter or margarine for
frying

Break the matzos in half. Arrange the matzo halves on a rack or in a colander. Pour boiling water over the matzos; drain immediately; the matzos should be softened slightly.

Beat the eggs with the milk or water and the seasonings in a large mixing bowl. Soak the matzos in the egg mixture, a minute on each side.

Melt the butter or margarine in a skillet. Fry each piece of matzo over medium heat until golden brown on each side. Serve hot with honey, sugar, or applesauce. Serves 2 to 3.

Matzo Toppings

Nowadays, matzos are treated in a wide variety of ways; they are even coated with chocolate. Here are suggestions to help you add a unique touch to the matzo you serve. In general, except for those served at the Seder dinner, matzos benefit by being heated briefly in a slow (300 degrees F.) oven before being served.

Butter Baked:
Brush matzo with melted unsalted butter or margarine, then heat on a baking sheet in a 300-degree F. oven for 5 minutes.

Chicken-Onion Baked:
Add a little grated onion to melted chicken fat. Brush on the matzo and heat in a 300-degree F. oven for 5 minutes.

Zwiebel or Onion Matzo:

Rub matzo with the cut side of an onion. Sprinkle with a little salt and put into a hot oven, to dry, for 3 to 4 minutes. Serve with butter or schmaltz (chicken fat).

Cinnamon-Sugar Coated:

Combine ¼ cup sugar with ½ teaspoon cinnamon. Lightly brush the matzo with butter or margarine. Sprinkle the top with the cinnamon-sugar mixture. Heat for 5 minutes in a 300-degree F. oven, or place under the broiler until the sugar has melted.

Honey-Spiced:

Heat honey to lukewarm; season to taste with cinnamon or ginger. Brush this over the matzos. Heat the matzos on a greased baking sheet in a 300-degree F. oven for 6 to 8 minutes. Serve on a dish to catch any honey that may drip through the matzo perforations.

Orange:

Combine ¼ cup sugar with ½ teaspoon cinnamon, ½ teaspoon grated orange rind, and 1 tablespoon orange juice. Spread 1 tablespoon of the mixture over each matzo. Place in a 350-degree F. oven until the sugar has melted.

Coffee-Cinnamon:

Combine ¼ cup sugar, 1 teaspoon powdered instant coffee, and ¼ teaspoon cinnamon. Serve sprinkled over hot buttered matzo.

Salted Matzo:

Brush the matzo surfaces with chicken fat, butter, or margarine. Sprinkle with coarse salt. Heat in a preheated 400-degree F. oven.

Puffed Matzo:

Quickly dip matzo into a bowl of cold water, then dust lightly with salt and pepper. Heat in a preheated 400-degree F. oven for less than 5 minutes, until puffed up a bit.

19

Salad Dressings, Relishes, and Sauces

There are many commercially-prepared salad dressings available for Passover, but there is no substitute for those made at home with fresh ingredients.

No matter what kind of dressing is being used, to prevent the greens from wilting the dressing should be added to the salad immediately before serving. Or the dressing may be served in a cruet, enabling each individual to toss his or her own salad with the desired amount of dressing.

Relishes add zest to the meal. Often, a dish seems "one" with the relish associated with it, such as gefilte fish and horseradish, or boiled beef and horseradish. Relishes add flavor and/or color to the dishes they accompany.

Sauce is the variable element that can transform an ordinary dish into a work of culinary art. The sauce not only adds to the attractiveness of the preparation but enhances its flavor. However, the sauce served should always complement the dish, not overwhelm it.

Dessert sauces have a delicious function at any time. On Passover these sauces provide a happy foundation on which you can rely. They help dress up or "rejuvenate" desserts of all kinds.

This chapter contains a variety of salad dressings, relishes, and sauces that will delight the most sophisticated palates.

French Dressing

There really is nothing French about this dressing. It contains basic salad dressing ingredients: oil, vinegar, and seasonings.

  1 teaspoon salt
  ½ to 1 teaspoon sugar
  ¼ teaspoon paprika
  Dash of freshly ground black pepper
  ¼ cup cider vinegar or fresh lemon juice
  ¾ cup oil

In a large jar, blend the dry ingredients. Add the cider vinegar or lemon juice. Cover and shake thoroughly. Add the oil; cover and shake again, or stir thoroughly. Always shake or stir before serving.

This dressing can also be made in a blender by placing all the ingredients in the blender jar and blending at high speed for 2 minutes. Yields 1 cup.

Italian Dressing

Adjust the amount of fresh garlic in this dressing to suit your taste. Impale crushed garlic cloves on a toothpick and combine them with the blended ingredients. Remove the garlic before serving the dressing.

  2 tablespoons sugar
  1 teaspoon salt
  ½ teaspoon paprika
  ½ teaspoon garlic powder or 2 cloves
    garlic, crushed
  ¼ cup finely chopped onion
  ½ cup ketchup
  ½ cup wine vinegar
  ½ cup oil

Combine all the ingredients in a blender jar and blend at high speed for 2 minutes; or place all the ingredients in a screw-top jar and shake very well. Yields 1½ cups.

Creamy Italian Dressing

1 cup mayonnaise
1 tablespoon vinegar
1 tablespoon water
1 tablespoon lemon juice
1 tablespoon red wine
1 clove garlic, minced, or ½ teaspoon
  garlic powder
1 teaspoon sugar
1 tablespoon oil
Salt and white pepper to taste

Combine all the ingredients in a blender jar and blend at high speed for 2 minutes or until smooth; or place all the ingredients in a screw-top jar and shake very well. Yields 1¼ cups.

Russian Dressing

1 cup mayonnaise
⅜ cup ketchup
2 teaspoons lemon juice
1½ teaspoons sugar

Combine all the ingredients in a blender jar and blend at high speed for 2 minutes or until smooth. Or place all the ingredients in a large mixing bowl and whip together with a wire whisk until thoroughly blended. Yields 1⅓ cups.

Dairy Dressing for Fish

2 tablespoons ketchup
2 tablespoons mayonnaise
2 tablespoons sour cream

In a small mixing bowl, with a small wire whisk, whip the ingredients until well blended. Coat each piece of fish with dressing before broiling. Yields ⅜ cup.

Fresh Fruit Dressing

Especially recommended as a topping for your favorite fruit or melon salad.

½ cup oil
¼ cup fresh lemon juice
2 tablespoons honey
1 teaspoon salt

In a small mixing bowl, with a wire whisk, blend all the ingredients well. Yields 1 cup.

Sweet-and-Sour Fruit Dressing

¼ cup oil
¼ cup lemon juice
2 tablespoons sugar
¼ teaspoon paprika
3 tablespoons orange juice

Measure all the ingredients into a cruet or jar. Cover tightly and shake well. Yields a generous ½ cup.

Honey Fruit Dressing

An interesting dressing to serve with a dairy fruit salad.

1 cup creamed cottage cheese
½ teaspoon salt
½ teaspoon grated orange rind
1 tablespoon honey
¼ cup orange juice
1 tablespoon lemon juice

Press the cheese through a fine sieve into a medium-sized mixing bowl. Add the salt, orange rind, honey, and juices. Mix to blend thoroughly. Yields 1 cup.

Horseradish—Without Crying

An almost foolproof way to prevent "crying" when preparing horseradish is to do the grating near an open flame.

> ½ pound horseradish root, peeled
> 1 large beet, peeled (optional)
> ½ cup cider vinegar
> ¼ cup water
> ¼ cup sugar
> ½ teaspoon salt

Grate the horseradish root into a medium-sized bowl set near an open flame (at the stove where food is cooking). For red horseradish, grate the beet into the same bowl. Transfer the grated horseradish and grated beet to a jar; cover the jar.

In a small bowl, combine the vinegar, water, sugar, and salt. Taste and adjust the seasoning. Pour the liquid into the jar over the horseradish. Mix, cover, and refrigerate. Yields 1 pint.

Horseradish Mold

An attractive way to garnish individual servings of fish or meat.

> 1 package lemon-flavored gelatin
> 1¼ cups hot water
> 1 jar (6 ounces) red horseradish
> Vinegar, sugar, lemon juice (optional)

In a medium-sized mixing bowl, dissolve the gelatin in the boiling water. Refrigerate until syrupy. Add the horseradish, blending together very well. If necessary, adjust the seasoning by adding vinegar, sugar, and/or lemon juice. Pour the mixture into a 1-quart mold and refrigerate until firm. Unmold and serve a slice or cube of mold as a garnish on each dish. Serves 8.

Beet and Horseradish Aspic

A simple aspic to prepare and gratifying to serve. The beets may be grated instead of diced. Canned beets may be substituted for fresh beets.

> 1 package (3 ounces) lemon-flavored
> gelatin
> 1¾ cups boiling beet juice or strained
> borsht
> 2 cups cooked and diced beets
> 1 jar (4 ounces) white or red horseradish
> Oil

In a large mixing bowl, dissolve the gelatin in the boiling beet juice or borsht. Chill until syrupy. Add the diced beets and horseradish; mix well. Pour the mixture into an oiled 1½-quart mold or 8 individual oiled molds. Cover and refrigerate until set. Serves 8.

Sweet-and-Sour Beet Balls

Beet Balls:

> 2 tablespoons fat
> 1 onion, chopped
> ⅔ cup grated cooked beets
> 2 eggs
> ½ teaspoon salt
> ⅛ teaspoon white pepper
> ½ cup matzo meal

Sweet-and-Sour Sauce

> 1 cup fresh soft tomato pulp
> ½ cup sugar
> ½ teaspoon salt
> ⅛ teaspoon white pepper
> 2 cups boiling water
> 1 onion, chopped
> Lemon juice to taste

To prepare the beet balls, in a small skillet melt the fat and sauté the chopped onion. In a medium-sized mixing bowl, combine the beets with the eggs, salt, pepper, matzo meal, and sautéed onion; mix well. Set aside.

To prepare the sauce, in a small bowl chop the tomato pulp and transfer to a medium-sized saucepan. Add the remaining ingredients and bring to a boil over medium heat. Taste and adjust the seasoning.

Form the beet mixture into meatball-sized balls and add to the sauce. Cook the beet balls in the sauce for 1 hour over low heat. Serves 4.

Pickled Beets

Pickled beets are a colorful complement to many main dishes, meat or dairy.

> 1 to 2 pounds small beets
> Boiling water
> 2 to 3 onions
> 1 cup cider vinegar
> ½ cup sugar
> 1 teaspoon salt
> ¼ cup water

In a large pot, cook the whole beets in boiling water to cover until fork-tender. Cool. Remove the skins and slice the beets into a large mixing bowl. Slice the onions thinly and add to the beets.

In a separate medium-sized mixing bowl, prepare a solution of vinegar, sugar, salt, and water. Taste and adjust the seasonings. Pour the solution over the beets and onions. Mix well. Cover the beet bowl tightly and marinate in the refrigerator for 2 to 3 days. Two pounds of beets will serve 6 or more.

Shalata

(Chopped Eggplant Relish)

Serve this as a condiment with steaks or chops.

    1 medium-sized eggplant
    ½ green pepper, seeded and diced
    1 small onion, grated
    2 cloves garlic
    2 to 3 tablespoons vinegar
    2 tablespoons water
    2 to 3 tablespoons oil
    Sugar, salt, and black pepper to taste

In a foil-lined pan, bake the eggplant in a preheated 450-degree F. oven until soft. Peel the eggplant. Place the eggplant in a chopping bowl and chop it together with the green pepper, onion, and garlic. Add the vinegar, water, oil, sugar, salt, and pepper. Serve cold. Serves 6 to 8.

Zucchini Relish

Zucchini, eggplant, and tomatoes combine here to make a delectable meat relish that may be served warm or cold.

    1 large onion, finely diced
    1 green pepper, seeded and diced
    ½ pound mushrooms, sliced
    2½ tablespoons oil
    1 medium-sized eggplant, peeled and
        diced
    1 pound zucchini, diced or sliced
    2 large or 3 small tomatoes, peeled and
        diced
    1½ teaspoons minced fresh parsley
        (optional)
    1 teaspoon salt
    ¼ teaspoon black pepper
    1 teaspoon sugar
    1 clove garlic, minced (optional)
    ¼ to ½ cup water

In a deep skillet over low heat, sauté the onions, pepper, and mushrooms in the oil for 5 minutes or until the onions are golden. Add the diced eggplant and the zucchini. Cover the skillet and continue to cook over low heat for 10 minutes. Add the tomatoes, parsley, salt, pepper, sugar, and clove of garlic. Simmer uncovered for an additional 30 minutes. If necessary, add ¼ to ½ cup of water to achieve the consistency desired. Taste and adjust the seasonings. Serve warm or cold. Serves 8 to 10.

Carrot Relish

Serve as a relish for meat or as a savory salad.

> 1 pound carrots
> ½ teaspoon salt
> 2 cloves garlic, crushed
> ½ teaspoon pepper
> ¼ cup oil
> 2 tablespoons wine vinegar

Wash and peel the carrots. Thickly slice the carrots into a large saucepan. Boil in salted water until barely tender, 8 to 10 minutes. Put the remaining ingredients in a large mixing bowl and blend together. Add the drained carrots; mix well. Marinate overnight before serving. Serves 6 to 8.

Molded Cole Slaw

A unique combination of shredded cabbage, grated carrot, and minced apple molded with a mayonnaise-sour cream dressing. A dressing made of equal parts mayonnaise and sour cream will complement this salad wonderfully.

> 1 package (3 ounces) lemon-flavored
>   gelatin
> 1 envelope unflavored gelatin
> 1 cup boiling water
> 2 tablespoons cider vinegar
> ½ teaspoon salt
> ½ cup mayonnaise
> ½ cup sour cream

→

2 cups shredded cabbage
½ cup minced apple
½ cup grated carrot
1 teaspoon grated onion

In a large mixing bowl, combine the gelatins. Add the boiling water and stir until dissolved. Stir in the cider vinegar, salt, mayonnaise, and sour cream. Chill until thickened. Fold in the remaining ingredients. Rinse a 1½-quart mold with cold water and pour in the mixture. Chill until firm. Serves 6 to 8.

Molded Vegetable Relish

1 package (3 ounces) lemon-flavored or
  lime-flavored gelatin
1 cup boiling water
¾ cup apple juice
2 tablespoons cider vinegar
2 teaspoons grated onion
¾ teaspoon salt
  Dash of white pepper
½ cup chopped cabbage
½ cup thinly sliced celery
½ cup coarsely grated carrots
¼ cup finely chopped green pepper

In a 1-quart bowl, dissolve the gelatin in the boiling water. Add the apple juice, cider vinegar, grated onion, salt, and white pepper. Chill until thickened. Fold in the vegetables. Pour the vegetable mixture into a 1½-quart mold which has been rinsed with cold water. Chill until firm. Serves 6 to 8.

Variation:

Vary the vegetables used in this salad. Feel free to make substitutions or change proportions. The addition of tiny cubes of avocado transforms this relish into a party salad.

Cucumber Salad

3 cucumbers
2 onions
1 teaspoon salt
⅓ cup vinegar
2 tablespoons water
¼ cup sugar
½ teaspoon salt and ⅛ teaspoon white
pepper
1 tablespoon minced fresh dill (optional)

Peel the cucumbers and onions; slice them wafer thin. Place the vegetables in a large bowl with the 1 teaspoon of salt. Toss the vegetables. Cover and refrigerate for about 1 hour. Rinse off the salt and drain very well.

Arrange the cucumbers and onions in a serving dish. In a separate bowl, make a solution of the vinegar, water, sugar, and salt and pepper. Taste and adjust the seasoning. Pour the mixture over the cucumbers and onions. Refrigerate for at least 1 hour. At serving time, the vinegar solution may be poured off and the cucumbers sprinkled with the minced fresh dill. A nice relish for meat. Serves 6 to 8.

Cranberry Salad

Very good served with poultry or as a dessert topped with whipped cream.

1 package (3 ounces) cherry, lemon, or
lime-flavored gelatin
1 cup hot water
1 cup sugar
1 tablespoon lemon juice
¾ cup pineapple syrup
1 cup ground raw cranberries
1 orange, ground
1 cup drained crushed pineapple

⟶

1 cup chopped celery
½ cup chopped walnuts

In a large bowl, dissolve the gelatin in the hot water. Add the sugar, lemon juice, and pineapple syrup. Stir to mix well. Chill in the refrigerator until partially set.

In a separate bowl, combine the remaining ingredients. Add to the partially-set gelatin. Pour the mixture into a lightly greased 1½-quart shallow pan mold or into individual molds. Chill until firm. Unmold. Serves 8.

Pineapple-Peach Chutney

Pear halves filled with this chutney is a perfect garnish to arrange around a crown roast.

1 cup crushed pineapple, undrained
1 cup sliced cling peaches, chopped
1 tablespoon chopped onions
1 tablespoon cider vinegar
2 tablespoons raisins
1 teaspoon cinnamon
½ teaspoon ground ginger
3 teaspoons brown sugar

Combine the crushed pineapple, peaches, onions, vinegar, raisins, cinnamon, and ginger in a saucepan. Bring to a boil; lower the heat. Simmer for 15 minutes. Remove from the heat. Stir in the sugar. Serve warm or chilled. Yields 1½ cups.

Borsht Sherbet

1 quart borsht
½ cup sugar
¼ teaspoon ground ginger
1 tablespoon grated orange rind
1 tablespoon grated lemon rind
½ cup orange juice

Combine all ingredients except the orange juice in a 1½-quart saucepan. Bring to a boil, stirring constantly. Cool. Add the orange juice. Pour the mixture into a freezer tray and freeze to a mush, that is, until frozen crystals have formed. Remove to a large mixing bowl and beat with rotary beaters. Return to the freezer and freeze. Serve as an appetizer or relish with poultry or meat. Serves 6 to 8.

Wine Sauce for Meats

This sauce is used as a marinade or for basting.

> 2 cloves garlic
> 1 to 2 tablespoons salt
> 1 cup rosé wine
> 1¼ cups oil
> 1 teaspoon freshly ground black pepper
> ¼ cup lemon juice

In a large mixing bowl, finely crush the garlic in the salt. Add the wine, oil, pepper, and lemon juice. Mix well. Yields 2½ cups.

Gourmet Meat Sauce

To stretch one pound of ground meat to serve six, spoon this meat sauce over a generous scoop of mashed potatoes. You might vary the recipe by adding five or six thinly sliced mushrooms ten minutes before the end of the cooking time.

> 2 tablespoons oil
> 1 cup diced onions
> 2 cloves garlic, chopped
> 1 cup diced green pepper
> 1 pound ground beef
> 2 cups peeled tomatoes or 1 can (16
>   ounces) peeled tomatoes
> 6 ounces tomato paste
>   Salt and black pepper to taste
> 1 cup Burgundy wine

In a large skillet over medium heat, heat the oil. Add the onions, chopped garlic, and the diced green pepper. Turn down the heat; sauté the vegetables until transparent. Add the ground meat and continue to cook, stirring frequently until well browned. Add the tomatoes, the tomato paste, and the salt and pepper. Pour in the wine. Allow the mixture to simmer in a covered skillet over low heat for at least 1 hour. Serves 6.

Barbecue Sauce for Chicken

> 1 can (8 ounces) jellied cranberry sauce
> 1 can (10½ ounces) tomato sauce
> 1 tablespoon oil
> 2 tablespoons brown sugar
> ½ teaspoon salt
> 1 tablespoon lemon juice

In a 1-quart saucepan, combine all the ingredients. Heat over medium heat until well blended and smooth, stirring occasionally. Prepare the bird, place it in a roasting pan, and pour the sauce over the bird. Baste frequently during the roasting. Yields approximately 2½ cups.

Chicken or Turkey Glaze

A quick and easy way to glaze a bird and thereby give it a rich and attractive appearance.

> 1 can (16 ounces) jellied cranberry sauce
> ½ cup unsweetened pineapple juice

In a small saucepan over low heat, heat the cranberry sauce until melted. Add the pineapple juice; blend. During the last half hour of roasting, brush the glaze over the bird. Before serving, spoon on the remaining hot glaze. Yields 2¼ cups.

Raisin Sauce

Spoon this sauce over tongue, then savor the flavor.

> 2 tablespoons sugar
> 2 tablespoons potato starch
> 2 tablespoons melted margarine
> ½ teaspoon cinnamon
>   Dash of ginger
> 2 cups apple juice
> 1 cup raisins

In a 1-quart saucepan, mix the sugar, potato starch, melted margarine, cinnamon, and ginger. Gradually stir in the apple juice. Cook over low heat, stirring constantly until thickened and smooth. Add the raisins and cook over low heat 10 minutes longer, stirring occasionally. If the sauce becomes too thick, add more apple juice. Serves 6 to 8.

Carrot Sauce

The grated carrots provide the flavorful base for this lovely sauce. Serve over meat loaf, liver, cutlets, vegetables, or fish. For pareve, use pareve bouillon.

> 2 tablespoons melted margarine
> 1 tablespoon potato starch
> 1 cup bouillon or broth
> 1 cup grated raw carrots
> ½ cup ketchup

In a small saucepan, melt the margarine; remove from the heat. In a small bowl, dissolve the potato starch in the bouillon or broth. Blend the potato starch mixture with the melted margarine and return to low heat, stirring constantly until the mixture is smooth and thick. Add the carrots and the ketchup. Continue to stir over low heat for an additional 5 minutes. The carrots should retain their crispness. For a softer consistency, cook longer. Yields 2 cups.

Variation:

Add ¼ pound thinly sliced mushrooms or a 4-ounce can of mushrooms. drained, when adding the ketchup and carrots.

Pantry Shelf Mushroom Sauce

Made with items found on your pantry shelf.

>   1 can (10½ ounces) mushroom soup
>   1 can (10½ ounces) water
>   1 can (4 ounces) sliced mushrooms,
>   drained
>   1 tablespoon potato starch
>   ½ cup water

In a 1-quart saucepan, combine the can of mushroom soup, can of water, and the can of drained sliced mushrooms; mix well. In a measuring cup, mix the potato starch with the ½ cup water. Add to the saucepan and stir well. Cook over low heat, stirring constantly until thick and heated through. Yields 3½ cups.

Variations:

• For dairy meals, substitute milk for the water.
• One-half pound lightly sautéed fresh mushrooms can be substituted for the canned mushrooms.

Mushroom Sauce

Very nice to serve over meat or vegetable steaks.

>   3 tablespoons oil or margarine
>   1 clove garlic (optional)
>   ½ pound mushrooms, sliced
>   1½ tablespoons potato starch
>   2 cups water
>   ½ teaspoon salt
>   ⅛ teaspoon white pepper

In a large skillet, heat the oil or margarine. Brown the clove of garlic in the skillet and discard. In the same oil or margarine, sauté the mushrooms. With a slotted spoon, remove the mushrooms and set aside.

Dissolve the potato starch in the water in a small mixing bowl;

add the salt and pepper. Pour the potato starch water into the skillet and cook over medium heat, stirring until thickened. Add the mushrooms. Yields 2¼ cups.

Charoses Sauce

This is a sauce based on the *charoses* dish eaten at the Seder. Spoon it over Passover sponge cake that has become somewhat dried out, or serve instead of syrup over pancakes.

> ¾ cup chopped apples
> 1 tablespoon lemon juice
> 1 tablespoon potato starch
> ¼ cup sugar
> ¾ cup water
> ⅓ cup honey
> ½ cup chopped walnuts
> ½ cup Concord grape wine

In a small mixing bowl, mix the chopped apple with the lemon juice; set aside. Combine the potato starch with the sugar in a small saucepan. Gradually add the water, mixing until the potato starch is dissolved. Stir in the honey; mix until smooth. Cook over medium heat, stirring constantly until the mixture thickens and is clear. Remove from the heat and let cool. Add the apples and nuts to the cooled sauce. Chill. Before serving, stir in the wine. Yield 2¼ cups.

Dairy Fish Cocktail Sauce

> 1 cup sour cream
> ½ cup ketchup
> ½ cup finely chopped celery
> 2 tablespoons prepared horseradish
> 1 tablespoon grated onion
> Salt and white pepper to taste

In a medium-sized mixing bowl, with a wire whisk, combine together the sour cream and ketchup. Add the remaining ingredients and continue to whip until well blended. Yields 2 cups.

Pareve Fish Cocktail Sauce

A simple but flavorful recipe to serve as a fish dip.

Prepared horseradish
Ketchup
Lemon juice

Mix equal parts of horseradish and ketchup in a small mixing bowl. Blend in lemon juice to taste.

Tartar Sauce

A wonderful sauce for broiled or fried fish.

1 cup mayonnaise
1 tablespoon finely minced fresh parsley
1 teaspoon minced shallots or green onion
1 to 2 tablespoons chopped pickles
1 hard-cooked egg, finely chopped
1 tablespoon finely chopped green pepper
Salt and white pepper to taste
Lemon juice or wine vinegar

In a medium-sized mixing bowl, with a wire whisk, blend the mayonnaise, parsley, shallots or green onion, chopped pickles, hard-cooked egg, and green pepper. Season with salt and pepper. Add sufficient lemon juice or wine vinegar to thin the sauce slightly and to point up the flavors. Yields 1½ cups.

Puffy Fish Topping

A simple topping that enhances the appearance and taste of broiled fish.

½ cup mayonnaise
½ teaspoon onion powder
½ teaspoon paprika
2 egg whites

In a small mixing bowl, mix the mayonnaise with the onion powder and paprika. In a clean small mixing bowl, beat the egg whites until stiff but not dry. Fold in the mayonnaise mixture. Coat each piece of fish with a little of this topping before broiling. Makes enough topping for 6 pieces of fish.

Quick Fish Sauce

¼ cup ketchup
½ cup mayonnaise
3 to 4 tablespoons prepared horseradish,
    to taste

In a small mixing bowl, with a wire wisk, combine the ketchup with the mayonaise very well. Stir in the prepared horseradish. Yields ¾ cup.

Orange Sauce I

2 cups orange juice
1 cup sugar
2 tablespoons potato starch
2 tablespoons cold water
2 oranges, peeled and sectioned
¼ cup raisins

In a medium-sized saucepan, combine the orange juice and sugar. Bring to a boil over high heat. In a small dish, mix the potato starch with the cold water; add to the hot juice. Continue to cook, reducing the heat to medium and stirring constantly until thickened. Remove from the heat and add the orange sections and raisins. Serve warm. Yields 2½ cups.

Variations:
• The oranges may be diced rather than sectioned, seeds removed.
• Two tablespoons of lemon juice may be added to the sauce.

Note: Oranges and lemons will yield more juice if immersed in warm water for a short time before squeezing.

Orange Sauce II

Unlike Orange Sauce I above, this sauce contains eggs and is cooked in the top of a double boiler. Best served warm.

  1 cup sugar
  Pinch of salt
  1 cup orange juice
  2 eggs, separated
  1 tablespoon potato starch
  2 tablespoons cold water

In the top of a double boiler, combine the sugar, salt, and juice. Place over hot water and bring to the boiling point over medium heat. In a small bowl, beat the egg yolks; stir them into the boiling juice very carefully to prevent curdling.

In a small dish, make a paste of the potato starch and the cold water; add to the yolk mixture. Continue to cook, stirring constantly until thick and clear. Remove from the heat. In a small mixing bowl, with clean beaters, beat the egg whites until stiff peaks form. Carefully fold the beaten egg whites into the orange juice mixture. Use immediately or reheat over boiling water. Yields 1½ cups.

Apple-Lemon Sauce

The perfect sauce to serve, hot or cold, over the Epicurean Carrot Cake (see Index for recipe).

  ½ cup sugar
  2 tablespoons potato starch
  Dash of salt
  2 cups apple juice
  ¼ cup lemon juice
  1 teaspoon grated lemon rind
  2 tablespoons pareve shortening

In a small saucepan, combine the sugar, potato starch, and salt. Gradually stir in the apple juice. Cook over low heat, stirring constantly until thickened and clear. Stir in the lemon juice, lemon rind, and shortening. Continue to cook until the shortening has completely dissolved. Serve hot or cold. Yield 2½ cups.

Lemon Sauce

1 tablespoon potato starch
1 cup sugar
2 cups hot water
Juice and grated rind of 1 lemon
2 tablespoons margarine

In a small saucepan, mix the potato starch with the sugar. Gradually stir in the water. Cook directly over medium heat, stirring until thickened. Add the lemon juice, grated rind, and margarine. Cook until well blended. Remove from the heat. Yields 2¼ cups.

Note: Lemon or orange rind is easier to grate when frozen.

Clear Wine Sauce

To create a dessert with distinction, stir some drained fruit cocktail into this sauce and spoon the sauce generously over a plain cake.

½ cup sugar
1 tablespoon potato starch
⅛ teaspoon salt
½ cup water
1 tablespoon oil
1 tablespoon lemon juice
1 cup Concord grape wine

In a small saucepan, combine the sugar, potato starch, and salt. Add the water and stir until well blended. Cook over low heat, stirring until the mixture thickens and is clear. Add the oil and lemon juice. Continue to cook just until blended. Remove from the heat and stir in the wine. A wonderful dessert sauce. Serve hot or cold. Yields 1½ cups.

Honey Sauce

> **1 cup honey**
> **½ cup boiling water**
> **½ to ¾ teaspoon cinnamon, to taste**
> **¼ teaspoon ground ginger**

In a small saucepan, blend the honey and water. Cook over moderate heat, stirring for 2 minutes. Add the spices and remove from the heat. Before serving the sauce, whip with a rotary beater. Makes 1½ cups.

Appendix

Table of Equivalent Amounts

dash	⅛ teaspoon	2 to 3 drops
1 teaspoon	⅓ tablespoon	⅙ ounce
3 teaspoons	1 tablespoon	½ ounce
1 tablespoon	3 teaspoons	½ ounce
2 tablespoons	⅛ cup	1 ounce
4 tablespoons	¼ cup	2 ounces
5⅓ tablespoons	⅓ cup	2⅔ ounces
6 tablespoons	⅜ cup	3 ounces
8 tablespoons	½ cup	4 ounces
10 tablespoons	⅝ cup	5 ounces
10⅔ tablespoons	⅔ cup	5⅓ ounces
12 tablespoons	¾ cup	6 ounces
14 tablespoons	⅞ cup	7 ounces
16 tablespoons	1 cup	8 ounces
⅛ cup	2 tablespoons	1 ounce
¼ cup	4 tablespoons	2 ounces
⅜ cup	¼ cup plus 2 tablespoons	3 ounces
⅝ cup	½ cup plus 2 tablespoons	5 ounces
⅞ cup	¾ cup plus 2 tablespoons	7 ounces
1 cup	16 tablespoons	8 ounces
1 cup	½ pint	8 ounces
2 cups	1 pint	16 ounces
4 cups	1 quart	32 ounces
16 cups	1 gallon	128 ounces

Approximate Metric Size Equivalents

1 inch = 2.50 centimeters	8 inches = 20 centimeters
2 inches = 5 centimeters	9 inches = 23 centimeters
3 inches = 8 centimeters	10 inches = 25 centimeters
5 inches = 13 centimeters	13 inches = 33 centimeters

Metric Equivalents for Cooking

- Gram (gr.) is the basic unit of weight (mass). There are about 28 grams to the ounce.
- A kilogram equals 1,000 grams.
- A kilogram is just under 2¼ pounds.
- ½ kilogram equals 500 grams, slightly more than 1 pound.
- ¼ kilogram equals 250 grams, marginally more than ½ pound.
- ⅛ kilogram equals 125 grams, slightly more than ¼ pound.
- 1 ounce equals 28 grams.
- ½ ounce equals 14 grams.
- A kilogram is frequently referred to as a kilo.

- Milliliters (ml.) and liter (l.) are the basic units used for measuring liquid volume. There are about 28 milliliters in a fluid ounce.
- 5 milliliters equal 1 teaspoon.
- 15 milliliters equal 1 tablespoon.
- A liter is a little more than 1 quart. Used for milk, wines, or cooking oil.

To Convert a Recipe to Metric Measure

Approximate conversion for weight

When you know	Multiply by	To find
ounces	28	grams (gr.)
pounds	.45	kilograms (kg.)

Approximate conversion for volume

teaspoons	5	milliliters (ml.)
tablespoons	15	milliliters
fluid ounces	30	milliliters
cups	.24	liters (l.)
pints	.47	liters
quarts	.95	liters
gallons	3.8	liters

Approximate conversion for length

inches	2.5	centimeters (cm.)

To Convert a Recipe From Metric Measure

Approximate conversion for weight

When you know	Multiply by	To find
grams	.035	ounces
kilograms	2.2	pounds

Approximate conversion for volume

milliliters	.03	fluid ounces
liters	2.1	pints
liters	1.06	quarts
liters	.26	gallons

Approximate conversion for length

centimeters	0.4	inches

Temperature Conversion

Fahrenheit	subtract 32 and multiply by 5/9 to find Celsius temperature
Celsius	multiply by 9/5, then add 32 to find Fahrenheit temperature

Oven Temperatures

Degrees Fahrenheit		Degrees Celsius
200	extremely low	100
225	very low	110
250	very low	120
275	low	135
300	low	150
325	moderately low	165
350	moderate	175
375	moderately hot	190
400	hot	205
425	hot	220
450	very hot	230
475	very hot	245
500	extremely hot	260
525	extremely hot	275

Boiling Point: 212 degrees Fahrenheit
100 degrees Celsius

Adapting Recipes for Passover Use

To adapt a year-'round recipe *(chometz)* for Passover use, follow these guidelines:

For	Substitute
Bread crumbs	Matzo meal
Graham cracker crumbs for pie shells	Passover cookie or cake crumbs; ground nuts or ground soup nuts; matzo meal
Flour for thickening gravy	Use half the amount of potato starch or egg yolk, 1 yolk being equal to 1 tablespoon flour

For	Substitute
Cornstarch	Potato starch
1 cup all-purpose flour	⅝ cup of potato starch; matzo cake meal; or a combination of cake meal and potato starch
1 teaspoon baking powder	¼ teaspoon baking soda plus ½ teaspoon cream of tartar; Passover baking powder
1-ounce square of baking chocolate	3 tablespoons cocoa plus 1 tablespoon shortening; Passover chocolate (melted, shaved, or chopped)
Flavoring extracts	Lemon juice or zest from lemon peel; orange juice or zest from orange peel; Passover brandy; vanilla sugar or crushed vanilla bean; Passover flavorings
1 cup confectioner's sugar	1 cup granulated sugar less ½ tablespoon, pulverized in a blender and sifted together with 1½ teaspoons potato starch
1 cup sour milk for baking	1 tablespoon lemon juice plus enough milk to make 1 cup. Let stand for 5 minutes.
1 cup light cream	⅞ cup milk plus 2 tablespoons melted butter—for cooking only
1 cup heavy cream	¾ cup milk plus ⅓ cup melted butter—for cooking only, not whipping
Alcoholic beverages in cooking	If comparable Passover ingredient is not available, substitute apple, orange, wine, or grape juice in the same

→

For
Alcoholic beverages
(*cont.*)

Substitute
amount, or bouillon in the
same amount, depending on
the nature of the recipe.

Recipe Conversion

To convert a recipe from one category—*milchig* (dairy), *fleishig*
(meat), or pareve (neutral)—to another category, substitute
ingredients as follows.

For	Adapted for	Substitute
Butter	Fleishig	Pareve margarine Solid white shortening Chicken fat Oil or a combination of oil plus one of the above
	Pareve	Pareve margarine Solid white shortening Oil Combination of oil plus margarine or shortening
Milk	Pareve or fleishig	1 cup water plus 2 tablespoons

→

For	Substitute	
Milk (*cont.*)		pareve shortening for pareve baking Potato water— in baking Water Fruit juice Black coffee Water from cooked vegetables
Chicken or meat stock	Pareve	For each cup of stock, one pareve bouillon cube dissolved in 8 ounces of hot water; or an equal quantity of water flavored with a pareve soup mix powder.
Cream	Fleishig or pareve	Prepare "cream" sauce (potato starch, pareve fat, and liquid) to the desired consistency

→

For
Cream (*cont.*)

Substitute
before
adding to
the mixture.
Use the basic
proportions
of potato
starch, fat,
and liquid.

Temporarily Out

For best results, use the ingredient called for in a recipe, but in an emergency:

Instead of:	**You may use:**
1 cup whole milk	4 tablespoons nonfat dry milk plus 2 teaspoons fat (butter or margarine) blended in 1 cup water 1 cup fruit juice or 1 cup potato water in baking
1 cup light cream	⅞ cup milk and 3 tablespoons melted butter—for cooking only
1 cup heavy cream	¾ cup milk plus ⅓ cup melted butter—for cooking only, not whipping
1 cup buttermilk for baking	1 cup sweet milk mixed with 1 tablespoon lemon juice. Let stand for 5 minutes.
1 cup butter	1 cup margarine or ⅞ cup oil
1 whole egg for thickening	2 egg yolks
1 cup honey	1¼ cups sugar plus ¼ cup liquid

→

Instead of:	You may use:
1 cup tomato juice	½ cup tomato sauce plus ½ cup water
1 cup canned tomatoes	1½ cups chopped fresh tomatoes simmered for 10 minutes, or ½ cup tomato sauce plus ½ cup water
1 cup ketchup	1 cup tomato sauce plus ¼ cup sugar and 2 tablespoons vinegar—for cooking only
½ pound mushrooms	4-ounce can of mushrooms
½ cup seedless raisins	½ cup dried prunes
1 small clove garlic	⅛ teaspoon garlic powder
1 medium-sized onion	1 teaspoon onion powder or 1 tablespoon instant minced onion, rehydrated

---

What Makes What

When your recipe calls for:	You will need:
Crumbs	
1 cup potato chip crumbs	2 cups firmly packed potato chips
1½ cups matzo farfel	2½ matzos, finely broken
Dairy	
½ cup butter or margarine	¼ pound or 1 stick
2 cups butter or margarine	1 pound
1 cup freshly grated cheese	¼ pound
1 cup cottage cheese	8-ounce container or ½ pound
1 cup whipped cream	½ cup cream for whipping
1 cup sour cream	8-ounce container or ½ pint

→

When your recipe calls for: **You will need:**

Eggs

1 cup whole eggs	4 to 6 eggs
1 cup egg whites	8 to 10 whites
1 cup egg yolks	12 to 14 yolks

Meats

2 cups ground raw meat	1 pound raw meat
2 cups cooked meat	1 pound cooked meat
3 cups diced cooked meat	1 pound cooked meat
4 cups diced cooked chicken	1 5-pound cooked chicken

Nuts

1 cup blanched whole almonds	5 ounces shelled almonds
1 cup toasted slivered almonds	5 ounces shelled almonds
1 cup chopped walnuts	¼ pound shelled walnuts
1 cup pecans	3 ounces shelled pecans
1 cup cashew nuts	¼ pound shelled cashew nuts
1 cup grated coconut	¼ pound fresh coconut

Fruits, juices, peels

1 cup cut-up dates	½ pound dates
2 cups cooked prunes	½ pound prunes
4 cups sliced apples	4 medium-sized apples
2 cups sliced strawberries	1 pint strawberries
2 cups pitted cherries	4 cups unpitted cherries
2 cups sliced fresh peaches	2 pounds or 8 medium-sized peaches
4 cups cranberries	1 pound cranberries
1 teaspoon grated orange rind	½ orange
1 cup orange juice	3 medium-sized oranges
1½ teaspoons grated lemon rind	1 lemon
3 tablespoons lemon juice	1 lemon
1 cup lemon juice	4 to 6 lemons
1 cup mashed bananas	3 medium-sized bananas
3 cups seedless raisins	1 pound raisins

Cake Pan Conversions

If cake calls for:	It will also bake in:
1 8-inch layer	1 11 × 4½ × 2¾-inch rectangle
	9 to 12 2½-inch cupcake pans
2 8-inch layers	2 thin 8 × 8 × 2-inch squares
	18 to 24 2½-inch cupcake pans
	1 13 × 9 × 2-inch rectangle
3 8-inch layers	2 9 × 9 × 2-inch squares
1 9-inch layer	1 8-inch square
	15 2½-inch cupcake pans
2 9-inch layers	2 8 × 8 × 2-inch squares
	3 thin 8-inch layers
	1 15 × 10 × 1-inch rectangle
	30 2½-inch cupcake pans
1 8-inch square	1 9-inch layer
2 8-inch squares	2 9-inch layers
	1 13 × 9 × 2-inch rectangle (with leftover batter)
1 9-inch square	2 thin 8-inch layers
2 9-inch squares	3 8-inch layers (with leftover batter)
	1 15 × 10½ × 1-inch rectangle
1 12 × 8 × 2-inch rectangle	2 8-inch layers
1 13 × 9 × 2-inch rectangle	2 thin 9-inch layers
	2 8 × 8 × 2-inch squares
	2 8-inch rounds
1 8 × 4 × 3-inch loaf	1 8 × 8 × 2-inch square
1 9 × 5 × 3-inch loaf	1 8-inch round
	1 9 × 9 × 2-inch square
	1 11 × 4½ × 2¾-inch rectangle
	24 to 30 2½-inch cupcake pans
1 9 × 3 ½-inch tube pan	2 9-inch layers
	24 to 30 2½-inch cupcake pans
1 10 × 4-inch tube pan	2 9 × 5 × 3-inch loaves
	1 13 × 9 × 2-inch rectangle
	2 15 × 10 × 1-inch rectangles

Index